The

GRIM REAPER'S
Book of Days

A Cautionary Record of Famous,
Infamous, and Unconventional Exits

Ed Morrow

A Citadel Press Book
Published by Carol Publishing Group

A Citadel Press Book
Published by Carol Publishing Group
Citadel Press is a registered trademark of Carol Communications, Inc.
Editorial offices: 600 Madison Avenue, New York, N.Y. 10022

Sales and Distribution Offices: 120 Enterprise Avenue, Secaucus, N.J. 07094
In Canada: Canadian Manda Group, P.O. Box 920, Station U, Toronto, Ontario M8Z 5P9
Queries regarding rights and permissions should be addressed to Carol Publishing Group,
600 Madison Avenue, New York, N.Y. 10022

Carol Publishing Group books are available at special discounts for bulk purchases, for
sales promotions, fund raising, or educational purposes. Special editions can be created
to specifications. For details, contact Special Sales Department, Carol Publishing Group,
120 Enterprise Avenue, Secaucus, N.J. 07094

Manufactured in the United States of America
10   9   8   7   6   5   4   3   2   1

Library of Congress Cataloging-in-Publication Data

Morrow, Ed.   The Grim Reaper's book of days : a cautionary record of famous,
    infamous, and unconventional facts / Ed Morrow.
        p.   cm.
    "A Citadel Press book."
    ISBN 0–8065–1364–0 (pbk)
    1. Curiosities and wonders—Chronology.   2. Death—Chronology.
    3. Accidents—Chronology.   I. Title.
    AG2443.M677 1992
    031.02—dc20

                                                                92-26997
                                                                CIP

A critical priest: "Remember, all your beauty will turn to dust and ashes."
To which Marie de Sévigné (1626–96), a court lady, replied: "Yes, but I am not *yet* dust and ashes!"

———

"It's not that I'm afraid to die. I just don't want to be there when it happens."
—Woody Allen

———

"Strange, isn't it? Each man's life touches so many other lives, and when he isn't around he leaves an awful hole, doesn't he?"

—Clarence, the angel, in
It's a Wonderful Life (1946)

Introduction

My mother told cautionary tales. Perhaps your mother did too. A trip to the toaster would bring "The True Story of the Boy Who Fished for Toast With a Fork and Was Spectacularly Electrocuted." Dawdling on the way home from school brought "The Cruel Boy Who Worried His Mother to Death and How He Found Her on the Kitchen Table Slumped Over His Cold Supper." Changing a light bulb evoked "The Tale of the Careless Thumb That Went Amiss." As I was raised on a farm in rural Vermont, there were also many occasions for tales related to that environment—"The Farm Boy Who Bent Over Behind a Sinister Cow and Had His Head Kicked In," "Why You Don't Kiss a Metal Flagpole When It's Thirty Below," "How Fast to Run When a Black Bear Says Hello to You in the Raspberry Bushes," "Why I Shouldn't Fill My Pockets With Firecrackers and Wooden Matches if I Ever Intend to Like Girls in the Future," and my personal favorite, "What Will Happen If My Father's Hay Scythe With the Three-Foot Razor-Sharp Blade Fell From Its Place on the Barn Wall While I Thoughtlessly Loiter Beneath It." Lightning was a particular villain of these stories, as in "The Case of the Lightning Bolt That Followed the Waterpipes Into the House and Leapt Up Through the Floor Into the Young Bigelow Girl's Feet Which Were Bare and Therefore Uninsulated and How She Was Instantaneously Killed," or "The Grim Result of Sheltering Beneath a Crab Apple Tree During a Thunderstorm, With the Illustrative Incident of the Sudden Demise of Twelve of Grampa Sivegny's Cows and the Permanent Confusion of One Heifer," or the shorter, "Standing by Window on Stormy Day."

My sisters, brother and I grew up unamended by accident, so the stories must have worked. But they also had the unintended effect of making such accounts very interesting to me. This is generalized in this volume into an account of how various and sundry notables met their final moment. I've organized it around a calendar, as propinquity and odd congruence make the events more immediate. I've striven to make my subjects come alive by describing both positive and negative aspects of their lives. Where conjecture enters, I've tried to be scrupulous in identifying it as such.

Perhaps these are my cautionary tales, but I find it hard to tag a moral to them. They are as varied as the individuals they describe. Some passed bravely with wise or witty observations. Some died in oddball ways that define black humor. Some were victims of evil, and some were doers of evil called to task. I've reflected as I put them together, and the only unifying ideas I find are these: Every death has its own irony, and we will all have our very own tête-à-tête with the Grim Reaper.

References

In compiling this work, I have consulted thousands of documents and hundreds of books. I have attempted to be as accurate as possible, but it is amazing how often the details of an individual's death are obscure or cloaked in legend. Often, the medical arts were unable to identify the cause of death. Relatives hid unflattering details. Newspaper reporters and others invented details. Even locations and dates vary. In compiling these accounts, I've attempted to be judicious and identify points that are controversial. I would appreciate documented corrections and am eager to hear your favorite "deadly" stories. Please provide all details.

Some of the more valuable sources used in compiling this book were the Associated Press, the *New York Times*, *Panati's Extraordinary Endings of Practically Everything and Everybody* by Charles Panati, Kenneth Anger's *Hollywood Babylon I* and *II*, *The Intimate Sex Lives of Famous People* by the Wallaces and D. Wallechinsky, Dr. Thomas Noguchi's two books, Paul Harvey's numerous books, *Final Placement* by Robert Dickerson, *Proust's Last Beer* by Bob Arnebeck, *Time* magazine, *Newsweek* magazine, the *International Film Necrology* by William Stewart et al., Malcolm Forbes's *They Went That-a-way...*, Oxford University Press's *Dictionary of National Biography*, and *The New York Public Library Desk Reference* (Paul Fargis and Sheree Bykofsky, editorial directors).

Acknowledgments

I am very grateful for the generous assistance of my wife, Laura Morrow, in writing this book. Not only did she make valuable editorial suggestions and help run down facts, she also made what could have been a very dark enterprise bright and fun. I could never have completed it without her cheerful support. I fully intend to make her do it all over again for my next book.

I also want to thank my agent, Sheree Bykofsky, whose acute advice, editorial comments, and encouragement were invaluable. A writer couldn't hope for a better, more professional literary agent.

I owe particular thanks to my editor, Bruce Shostak, for his expertise and resourcefulness in converting the manuscript into its final form.

– January 1 –

1953   Puroil Gas Station, Oak Ridge, West Virginia. Singer Hank Williams, 29, was found dead in his limo by his driver. Williams had been using whiskey and chloral hydrate. Earlier, a policeman had stopped the driver for speeding and, after peering into the backseat, remarked that Williams looked dead. The driver thought the hard-drinking Williams was just unconscious and kept driving. Williams's last song was "I'll Never Get Out of This World Alive."

1972   Paris. Entertainer Maurice Chevalier, 83, died of a heart attack following kidney surgery. Drafted into the French Army during World War I, he was wounded and spent two years in a POW camp. During World War II, while France was occupied, Chevalier continued to make his living as an entertainer. After the war, when many Frenchmen were forgetting their own commerce with Germans, Chevalier was much attacked. He survived this and remained one of France's most beloved entertainers. He once said, "Many a man has fallen in love with a girl in a light so dim he would not have chosen a suit by it."

– January 2 –

1937   Hollywood. Actor Ross Alexander, 29, had appeared as a West Point cadet in *Flirtation Walk* (1934), as Demetrius in *A Midsummer Night's Dream* (1935), and as Jeremy Pitt in *Captain Blood* (1935) with Errol Flynn. Nevertheless, his career began to fail, he was deep in debt, and his wife shot herself on December 6, 1935. Alexander climbed into the hayloft of a barn behind his ranch home and copied her example. His parents received $3,500 from Alexander's insurance. If he had waited one more month for his policy's suicide clause to lapse, they would have received $35,000. It is said that Alexander's studio, Warner Brothers, hired Ronald Reagan as his replacement. This was Reagan's first Hollywood job.

– January 3 –

1967   Parkland Memorial Hospital, Dallas. Jack Ruby, 55, who had killed Lee Harvey Oswald on live TV, died of a blood clot in his lungs following a battle with lung cancer.

Ruby, a small-time hood and stripclub owner, was friendly with the police. Because of this, newsmen hired him to get inside information. The police, aware of this job, had no reason to suspect that Ruby would shoot Oswald. Ruby's rabbi (before and after the killing) says Ruby loved the Kennedys and wanted to spare Jackie the ordeal of Oswald's trial. He also says that when Ruby saw the sneering face of the man who killed his president, he couldn't stop himself from using the pistol he often carried. Ruby related the same story to his brother the day he died.

Ruby was shocked that he was treated as a criminal and that some thought he was part of a conspiracy. He wanted to go to Washington to explain his patriotic motives. The authorities, satisfied with Ruby's trial and guilty verdict, saw no purpose in such an open-ended trip. Conspiracy theorists have used this refusal to conjecture that mysterious forces wanted to prevent Ruby's confessing some grand secret.

In December of 1991, the gun Ruby had used to kill Oswald was auctioned off for $220,000.

– January 4 –

1931 Chihuahua, Mexico. Cowboy star Art Acord, half Ute Indian and a real cowboy from Oklahoma, performed in Wild West shows with Buffalo Bill. He began making films in 1909 and starred in a series of Westerns based on his own life. Acord enlisted during World War I and won a Croix de Guerre in fierce hand-to-hand combat. When he returned to Hollywood, he and Hoot Gibson made a custom out of beating each other up and then drinking themselves sick.

Most Western stars made the transition to talkies, but Acord couldn't. His voice didn't record well. He lost his money, went to prison for smuggling booze during Prohibition, and later worked as a miner. He staged a phony kidnapping of himself by Mexican bandits for publicity, but it failed to revive his acting career. He had once been given up for dead after a stunt accident. At 41, he gave up on himself and took cyanide.

– January 5 –

1724 Kofrosch, Austria. Czartan Petrarch died. He claimed to be 185 years old. An observer described him as spry but as having traces of green in his beard that caused it to resemble "moldy bread."

1933 Northampton, Massachusetts. Calvin Coolidge, 60, thirtieth U.S. president, died of coronary thrombosis. Days before, his doctors had pronounced him healthy. His wife, Grace Anna Goodhue Coolidge (she died July 8, 1957), found his body on their bedroom floor after returning home from shopping. His last words were to a carpenter working on his home: "Good morning, Robert."

Coolidge directed that his grave in Notch Cemetery in his hometown, Plymouth, Vermont, be kept simple so as not to diminish the appearance of his neighbors' graves. Indeed, his father, John Coolidge, has a larger gravestone. Plymouth residents reportedly feel this is appropriate, since John was important locally, serving as deputy sheriff, justice of the peace, state representative, and notary public, whereas Calvin made his mark elsewhere.

Calvin Coolidge was famous for his sparse Vermontish conversation, a trait no doubt enhanced by his stoic American Indian ancestry on one side of his family tree (the only president so related). On one occasion, the First Couple were said to be touring a poultry farm. Mrs. Coolidge was ahead of Mr. Coolidge in progressing through the facility. A guide showed her their best rooster, announcing that the bird performed the sexual act twelve times a day. Mrs. Coolidge reflected and said, "Tell Mr. Coolidge." When it came Mr. Coolidge's turn to view the rooster, the guide did as Mrs. Coolidge asked. Mr. Coolidge regarded the bird, then asked the guide, "Same hen every time?" "Oh, no. Twelve different hens." The president said, "Tell Mrs. Coolidge." In psychology, the effect of novelty upon the libido is sometimes called the "Coolidge effect."

When I was a schoolboy in Vermont, one of my teachers told me about a motor trip she took as a girl in the 1920s with assorted relatives to see Washington, D.C. On the way, they passed a field where an old farmer was racing to get in his hay before a gathering rainstorm. It wasn't an uncommon custom in those days for passersby to stop and help in such a situation. All literally pitched in, and the grateful farmer just beat the rain. The travelers told the old farmer of their travel plans. He said his boy worked down in Washington and would be happy to give them a meal when they got to town. The travelers asked the address. "1600 Pennsylvania Avenue," Calvin Coolidge's father replied. My teacher said the White House meal was very nice.

– January 6 –

1919 Oyster Bay, New York. Theodore Roosevelt, 60, twenty-sixth U.S. president, died. At various times, he'd been wounded in battle, cast forty feet in a carriage/trolley wreck, shot while giving a speech in 1912 (he finished despite broken ribs and a bullet near his lung), afflicted by a leg abscess during a jungle trip, plagued by rheumatism, and deafened by mastoiditis, but the exact cause of death is unknown. He went to bed, telling his servant, "Please put out the lights." Later, the servant noticed Roosevelt wasn't breathing regularly. By the time help arrived, the former president was dead. A coronary embolism was blamed, but there was no autopsy. He was buried at Young's Memorial Cemetery in Oyster Bay. As part of the honors, a flight of biplanes flew over. Some believe that depression over the death of one of his sons in an air crash in 1918 was the cause of the president's death.

A relative of Roosevelt's once said, "When Theodore attends a wedding, he wants to be the bride, and when he attends a funeral, he wants to be the corpse."

– January 7 –

1967   Orbit Inn, Las Vegas, Nevada. Richard James Paris, who had twice deserted from the army, was on his honeymoon. Once in his room with his new bride, he presented her with a package containing fourteen sticks of dynamite. Her reaction is unknown, as he detonated it with a handgun, killing her, himself, and five other honeymooners.

1972   Minneapolis. Poet John Berryman, 57, removed his glasses, waved, then jumped from a bridge into the Mississippi River. He had long battled alcoholism. Berryman missed the river and hit the riverbank 100 feet below. The ultimate effect was the same. Berryman, a Pulitzer Prize winner, left no suicide note. His father had killed himself when Berryman was twelve.

– January 8 –

1642   Arcetri, Italy. The astronomer Galileo Galilei, 77, died of a "slow fever." His disciple, Vincenzio Viviani, said: "On the night of January 8, 1642, with philosophical and Christian firmness, he rendered up his soul to its Creator, sending it, as he liked to believe, to enjoy and to watch from a closer vantage point those eternal and immutable marvels which he, by means of a fragile device, had brought closer to our mortal eyes with such eagerness and impatience."

The Inquisition had condemned Galileo's view that the earth revolved around the sun. It forced him to recant, keeping him under house arrest. His last words were "Yet it still moves." The Church originally refused him burial in consecrated ground, but in 1737, Galileo's body was moved to a tomb in the Church of Santa Croce in Florence. During the move, a souvenir hunter cut off three of Galileo's fingers. An Italian doctor currently owns two of these, but the third, one of Galileo's middle fingers, is now on exhibit in Florence's Museum of the History of Science. It is in an upright position.

– January 9 –

1936   Beverly Hills. Actor John Gilbert, 38, died of a heart attack in his home following years of alcohol abuse. Gilbert is reputed to have lost his career when a talking picture revealed that the handsome leading man had a squeaky, effeminate voice. It is suspected that his studio boss, L. B. Mayer, used this false rumor to ruin Gilbert. Gilbert's daughter traces this to Gilbert's romance with Greta Garbo. Gilbert proposed several times, and eventually she accepted but failed to show up at the church. Mayer, a guest, made a crack about Gilbert's not needing to marry Garbo, since Gilbert had the use of her body anyway. When Gilbert knocked Mayer down, Mayer screamed that he would destroy Gilbert if it cost him a million dollars.

   Gilbert married another actress, but reportedly the un-wifely comparisons she made between their careers didn't help him deal with his troubles. She was rising fast, while he was washed up. The story of his fall, Hollywoodized to make the wife a heroine, is a partial source of the film *A Star Is Born* (1937). Although they were divorced at the time of his death, she received the bulk of his $500,000 estate.

– January 10 –

1917   Denver. Frontiersman and showman William "Buffalo Bill" Cody, 70, died of uremic poisoning. His last words, when told of his impending death, were, "Let's forget about it and play high five," and of his son, who was hurrying to see him, "I wish Johnny would come."

Cody had been a Pony Express rider, an Indian scout, a Civil War soldier, a professional hunter, and a world-renowned showman with his Wild West show. Although Cody received his nickname for killing buffalo to feed railroad workers, his show spread the news of the creature's dwindling numbers and helped save it from extinction. According to sharpshooter Annie Oakley, who starred in his show, Cody was an easy mark for con men, beggars, or anyone with a sad tale. He lost nearly all of the millions his show earned.

Cody's funeral was a grand show. Twenty-five thousand spectactors filed past his coffin, while a silk-hatted master of ceremonies urged them to move quickly. The Colorado National Guard marched in the funeral procession, complete with regimental band; Cody's white charger was led, riderless, behind the hearse. Cody had asked to be buried atop Lookout Mountain overlooking Denver; he lies there beneath a monument built with pennies donated by schoolchildren.

1951   Düsseldorf, Germany. A carpenter working on his roof died when a six-foot icicle fell and speared him.

– January 11 –

1841   London. American daredevil Samuel Gilbert Scott had leapt from a precipice at Niagara Falls, and, during a tour of England, he dove 240 feet into 8 feet of water. In pre-dive performances, Scott held his breath for long periods and did acrobatic stunts while suspended by the neck from a hangman's noose. During one performance, the noose slipped and Scott was nearly strangled while his audience, thinking it part of the show, cheered. An observant sailor saw Scott's face turn black and saved him. Scott hoarsely proclaimed, "The hemp that's to hang me is not grown yet."

On this date, Scott announced that he would run from Drury Lane to Waterloo Bridge, leap forty feet into the river, and run back, all in a single hour. At the bridge he went through his noose routine, and again the rope slipped. Again the audience cheered, but this time, when a bystander finally cut the rope, it was too late. Scott was dead.

1985   Manzanillo, Mexico. Actress Carol Wayne, 42, the silly bombshell Matinee Lady in Johnny Carson's "Tonight Show" skits, drowned. Although the silliness was an act, her bomb-shellness was real. She had appeared nude in *Playboy* magazine to demonstrate that women in their forties were sexy. Wayne was unable to swim and hated the water. This led to speculation of suicide or foul play.

Comic Pat McCormick, a friend of Wayne's, had once joked with Wayne on a television show that because of her buxom figure, "This woman will never drown."

– January 12 –

1928   Sing Sing Prison, New York. Henry Judd Gray, 35, and Ruth May Snyder, 32, were electrocuted for the murder of Snyder's husband, Albert. Ruth had talked Gray into killing her husband after insuring him for $96,000. Gray struck the sleeping Albert with a sash weight, but when this failed to do the trick and Albert called to Ruth for help, Ruth hit him with the weight herself. This still proved ineffectual, so Ruth and Gray resorted to chloroform and a picture-wire noose. Gray then tied up Ruth so that police would believe her story of a murderous burglar. The police thought the ropes had been rather gently secured, and after finding Gray's name in Ruth's address book, they tried an old police stratagem. They told her that Gray had confessed, implicating her. She confessed, implicating Gray. With her confession, they easily got Gray to admit his part.

Photographers were barred from the executions, but an enterprising reporter strapped a camera to his ankle. When the switch was thrown on Ruth, he raised his pant leg and snapped what would become one of the most grotesque front pages in history.

This murder served as the inspiration for a number of movies, most notably *Double Indemnity* (1944) and *The Postman Always Rings Twice* (1946).

1976   Wallingford, Oxfordshire, England. Mystery writer Dame Agatha Christie, 85, died of natural causes. Foul play wasn't suspected.

Originally, Christie planned to become an opera singer, but marriage and World War I changed her plans. While Christie was working as a volunteer pharmacist, her sister dared her to write a mystery. After many rejections, Christie got her novel,

The Mysterious Affair at Styles, into print in 1920. Christie went on to write over 100 mysteries, creating the eggheaded Hercule Poirot and the ever-observant Miss Marple. She called herself the "sausage machine" because of her ability to grind out book after book. Christie is the all-time best-selling novelist, having sold over a billion volumes.

Some think Christie may have tried to murder her philandering first husband. On a cold night in 1926, she pushed her car into a quarry, leaving the ignition switch off and her fur coat inside. This suggested that she hadn't been driven there by accident, and the presence of her fur would indicate that she hadn't left voluntarily. Allegedly, she registered at a hotel under the name of her husband's lover and waited for the police to arrest him for her murder, planning to feign amnesia after he was hanged. The police suspected him, but before they took action, a fan recognized Christie, so she was forced to reappear. Whether Christie wished just to make trouble for her husband or intended to let the courts kill him isn't known. Perhaps she experienced a nervous breakdown. She was later happily married to an archaeologist.

Christie said, "Every murderer is probably somebody's old friend."

– January 13 –

1864   New York City. Stephen Foster, 37, composer of Southern favorites, died in a hospital. Among his works were "Oh! Susanna," "Jeannie With the Light Brown Hair," "Camptown Races," and "My Old Kentucky Home."

Foster had become a drunkard. A chambermaid found him naked, lying in a pool of blood in his Bowery apartment. He had fallen against his washbowl, smashing it into sharp pieces and cutting his neck badly. Before dying, Foster told a friend, "I'm done for," then asked for a drink. Foster's last written words were found on a slip of paper: "Dear friends and gentle hearts."

Foster was a Yankee born in Pennsylvania. He visited the South only once, when he traveled to New Orleans in 1852.

1929   Los Angeles. Lawman Wyatt Earp died of natural causes. He was nearly 81. After the shoot-out at the O.K. Corral in Tombstone, Arizona, Earp had traveled on to Colorado,

Alaska, and, finally, California, where he spent his later years living on investment income. Earp had been bedridden but had gone out to send a get-well telegram to a friend. The exertion proved too much.

1941   Switzerland. Irish writer James Joyce, 58, died following surgery for a duodenal ulcer. His last words: "Does anybody understand?"

Joyce's works include *A Portrait of the Artist as a Young Man*, *Dubliners*, *Finnegans Wake*, and *Ulysses*. While rejecting Catholicism, Irish politics, and his middle-class origins, and even placing himself in voluntary exile, Joyce and his works remained tightly tied to his Dublin home.

Joyce's life was hard. After running off with a chambermaid, he traveled about Europe with her and his two children, supporting them with poorly paying jobs as a translator and clerk. He didn't earn a living with his writing until late in his life. By then, he was nearly blind. His works were pirated, banned, and mocked. His daughter was confined to an asylum. Perhaps because of these difficulties, Joyce spent years polishing his fiction. *Ulysses*, for example, took seven years to finish, and he spent seventeen years on *Finnegans Wake*.

Virginia Woolf didn't appreciate Joyce's prose. She described it as "the work of a queasy undergraduate scratching his pimples." Joyce's wife, Nora, once said, "Why don't you write books people can read?"

– January 14 –

1898   Guilford, Surrey, Britain. The Reverend Charles L. Dodgson, known as Lewis Carroll, the author of *Alice in Wonderland*, died of influenza two weeks short of his 66th birthday. His last words: "Take away those pillows—I shall need them no more."

1957   Los Angeles. Actor Humphrey Bogart died in his sleep after a two-year battle with cancer of the esophagus. He was nine days short of 58. His last words were to his wife, actress Lauren Bacall: "Goodbye, kid, hurry back." He was cremated. Buried with his ashes at Forest Lawn Cemetery was a gold whistle inscribed with the words, "If you need anything, just whistle." It was a line Bacall had spoken to him in *To Have and Have Not* (1944), the movie that introduced them to each other.

Bogart could be cantankerous. William Holden said he was "an actor of consummate skill, with an ego to match." Dave Chasen said, "Bogart's a helluva nice guy till 11:30 P.M. After that, he thinks he's Bogart." Reportedly, Bogart was seldom the first choice for the roles that made him famous. The studio planners wanted Edward G. Robinson for *The Petrified Forest* (1936), George Raft for *The Maltese Falcon* (1941), Gregory Peck for *The African Queen* (1951), and, for Bogart's most famous film, *Casablanca* (1942), the studio wanted Ronald Reagan.

– January 15 –

1919   Boston. A large tank holding 2 million gallons of molasses burst. A thirty-foot wall of goo smashed buildings, killing 21.

1947   South Norton Avenue and Thirty-ninth Street, Los Angeles. A girl on her way to school with her mother discovered the mutilated body of Elizabeth Short, 22, in a vacant lot. Elizabeth had come to Hollywood to get into the movies but wound up a prostitute with the nickname "Black Dahlia" because of her fondness for slinky black evening wear. Her body was completely bisected, and the initials "B.D." had been cut into her thigh. The coroner estimated that she had been tortured to death over a three-day period.

The hideous crime has never been solved. Hundreds have confessed, but all have been disproved by police. One woman, Janice Knowton of Anaheim, has recently claimed that her father was the killer. She says that he courted Short, then trapped her in his garage where Knowton, then a child of ten, witnessed him murder Short. Knowton says she suppressed the memory until surgery caused her to recall the killing.

– January 16 –

1794   London. English historian Edward Gibbon, 56, best known for *The History of the Decline and Fall of the Roman Empire*, died. He was obese, feeble, and plagued by gout, but he was killed by the treatment for hydrocele, which causes water to collect in the scrotum. In Gibbon's case, his scrotum swelled over the years till it reached the size of "a small child." A surgeon tapped the swelling, releasing four quarts of fluid, but Gibbon swelled up again and in days died of infection.

1935   Lake Weir, Florida. Ma Barker, 63, and her boys were killed in a gun battle with police and FBI agents. Ma's last words were orders to her sons to open fire: "All right! Go ahead!" She was found with a warm machine gun in her lap. Present owners of the house where the shoot-out occurred report that it is haunted by the sounds of raucous card playing.

J. Edgar Hoover said, "[The Barkers were] the most vicious and cold-blooded crew of murderers and kidnappers we've known in our time. In the case of the Barker gang, you can say that the major criminal factors were home and mother." He also said, "In her sixty or so years, this woman became a monument to the evils of parental influence."

It has been suggested that Ma Barker's relationship with her boys was unnatural. After Mr. Barker left the scene, she had only one gentleman friend, and her boys killed him. She didn't seem to mind.

1942   Table Rock Mountains, Nevada. Actress Carole Lombard and twenty-one others, including her mother, were killed in an air crash. Lombard was 32. She was buried at Forest Lawn Cemetery in Los Angeles. Lombard had been traveling to sell war bonds and wanted to fly back to California to rejoin her husband, Clark Gable, quickly. Her mother was reluctant to fly, as a fortune teller had told her it was an unlucky day. They flipped a coin, and Lombard won.

Gable felt guilty about the crash. He thought Lombard wouldn't have been killed if he had gone with her. Saying he didn't give a damn whether he came home or not, he enlisted in the Army Air Corps, became a major, and flew on several bombing missions.

Lombard took her stage name from the Carrol, Lombardi Pharmacy on Lexington Avenue and Sixty-fifth Street in New York City. The glamorous Lombard and Gable referred to each other as "Ma" and "Pa."

– January 17 –

1874   Mount Airy, North Carolina. The Siamese twins Chang and Eng, who were joined by a band of flesh at their chests, died at 62. Chang, who had suffered a stroke four months earlier, died three hours before Eng. They believed they would die together but had agreed to be separated if either died. Eng died, apparently of fear, before a doctor could arrive to separate them.

The brothers toured the world and made a fortune being exhibited but sought to be separated in 1840, when they met a pair of sisters they wished to marry. Because doctors said at least one would probably die, they didn't try the operation. They went ahead and married. The twins spent three days with one wife on one farm, then the next three days with the other wife on another farm. Between them they had twenty-two children. Today, they have over a thousand descendants.

Reportedly, the twins often argued and spent days without speaking to each other.

1893   Fremont, Ohio. Rutherford B. Hayes, 70, nineteenth U.S. president, died of heart disease. He had suffered a heart attack at the Cleveland railroad station. He refused medical help, insisting he be brought by train to his home, Spiegel Grove. He said, "I would rather die at Spiegel Grove, than live anywhere else." He died that night in his own bed. His last words concerned his wife, who had predeceased him: "I know that I am going where Lucy is." He was buried in Oakwood Cemetery in Fremont.

1910   London. Thomas Crapper, 73, the inventor of the modern flush toilet, died. A similar device was patented in 1778 by Joseph Brahma, but Crapper perfected a working model. Crapper also invented many plumbing valves and vents, which eliminated the problem of sewer odors following drainpipes back into homes. Crapper's work shouldn't be belittled—disease accompanies poor sanitation, and his inventions saved uncounted lives.

– January 18 –

1862   Richmond, Virginia. John Tyler, 71, tenth U.S. president, died of a "bilious fever" and respiratory problems. Tyler's final words were "Doctor, I'm going. Perhaps it is best." His will requested that he be buried at his plantation in Virginia, but since the Civil War was in full swing, his body was buried in

Richmond's Hollywood Cemetery beside the grave of President James Monroe. After the war, Congress refused to move his body, deeming it a useless expense. It did, however, erect a monument over the unmarked grave and give his impoverished wife a pension.

Tyler was vice president and had become president following the death of William Henry Harrison (see 4/4/1841)—the first such elevation in U.S. history. Perhaps this is why Tyler was sometimes called "His Accidency." Tyler married twice and had fifteen children, more than any other president.

1990   De Ridder, Louisiana. Rusty Hamer, 42, shot himself in the head with a .357 Magnum. He had been a child star on the TV series "Make Room for Daddy." Danny Thomas said, "He was the most brilliant young comedy actor I ever met in my life. Great memory, marvelous timing. He had it all."

Hamer's career disappeared as he grew up. He left Hollywood to live as a handyman in a trailer in rural Louisiana. Shortly before his death, he was interviewed by a TV tabloid show. He seemed optimistic, but he was actually depressed. Hamer's older brother, John, said, "Some people know how to be happy, and some don't, like my brother." He also observed of Hamer, "At eighteen, he was a has-been with a star on Hollywood Boulevard."

– January 19 –

1729   London. British playwright William Congreve, 58, died of internal injuries received in a carriage accident. He was buried in Westminster Abbey. Congreve left his estate to his mistress, Henrietta, duchess of Marlborough.

Henrietta had a death mask made of Congreve's face, which she then had attached to a life-size dummy. She treated this dummy as if it were alive and insisted that visitors do so, too. Henrietta dressed the dummy each morning and undressed it each night. She slept with it and spent hours talking with it. Her servants waited upon the dummy, and when Henrietta thought it was ill, she had doctors treat it. Eventually, she was buried with the dummy.

– January 20 –

1936   The royal country house at Sandringham, Norfolk. King
       George V of England died at 70. He was terminally ill, but the
       cause of death wasn't natural. It was recently revealed that two
       days earlier, Lord Dawson, the royal physician, had been
       visited by the Prince of Wales (later Edward VIII). The prince
       told Lord Dawson that he and the queen didn't want the king
       to undergo a lingering death. Lord Dawson agreed. When he
       felt that George had suffered enough, he administered a lethal
       dose of morphine and cocaine directly into the king's jugular
       vein. Lord Dawson timed the death so that the news would be
       carried in the morning papers rather than in what he felt were
       the more sensational evening papers. Euthanasia was illegal;
       technically, the doctor murdered the king.
           The newspapers gave the king's last words as, "How is the
       Empire?" Dawson's notes, however, recorded that his last
       words were far different. Before receiving the fatal shot,
       George received another injection to help him sleep, and,
       perhaps dissatisfied with the skill with which it was admin-
       istered, he remarked to Dawson, "Goddamn you."
           George has been quoted as saying, "My father was fright-
       ened of his father, I was frightened of my father, and I am
       damned well going to see to it that my children are frightened
       of me."

1965   Palm Springs, Florida. Disc Jockey Alan Freed, 43, died of
       uremia. He is credited with introducing the term "rock and
       roll" and was instrumental in the advent of rock music. He
       made a fortune but was convicted of involvement with payola
       and died in poverty. His friends had to pass the hat to pay for
       his funeral.

1984   Acapulco. Johnny Weissmuller, who played Tarzan in nine-
       teen films, died at 79. He had been an invalid since 1979,
       suffering from heart disease and a series of strokes.
           Weissmuller got his Tarzan job by accident. He was a well-
       known swimmer and was invited by sports fan Clark Gable to
       visit Gable's film studio. When Weissmuller arrived, the
       guard wouldn't let him inside, as studio policy barred casual
       visitors. Someone mentioned that the studio was testing actors
       to play Tarzan. The guard amiably suggested Weissmuller use

this as a pretext to get inside, adding, "You'll get a free lunch, whether you get the part or not." Weissmuller got in, got the lunch, and beat out seventy-five actors for the role.

When an aspiring actor asked his advice on how to succeed as an actor, Weissmuller replied, "Don't let go of the vine."

1989   Henley-on-Thames, Oxfordshire, England. Canadian-born actress Beatrice Lillie, 94, died of natural causes. She was famous for her double entendres and her trademark extra-long cigarette holder. As a hobby, she collected humorous newspaper clippings. She said her favorite was from the conservative London *Times*. It reported the marriage of a man in his eighties to a woman in her thirties, and noted, "The bridegroom's gift to the bride was an antique pendant."

– January 21 –

1793   Paris. King Louis XVI of France was guillotined in his 39th year. Upon the scaffold, he addressed the crowd: "I die innocent of all the crimes of which I am charged. I forgive those who are guilty of my death, and I pray God that the blood which you are about to shed may never be required of France." Revolutionary authorities had assembled a large body of drummers whose drumming obliterated the rest of the king's comments lest he sway the crowd to rescue him. Louis was shoved into position under the knife. Some heard him cry, "May my blood cement the happiness of France!" Then the blade fell.

Louis and his queen, Marie Antoinette, had nearly escaped the revolutionaries two years earlier, but when Louis stuck his head out of his carriage window, a postmaster recognized the king by comparing his face to the king's profile on a coin. Just then, the wheel of the carriage struck the side of a bridge; the frightened horses reared and broke their harnesses. Before repairs could be completed, a mob captured the king.

Louis and Marie's marriage had remained unconsummated for seven years. Louis had an anatomical defect (phimosis), which, until it was corrected by surgery, made him impotent.

1924   Nizhny Novgorod, near Moscow. Vladimir Ilyich Lenin, 53, died of respiratory failure following a cerebral hemorrhage. Lenin was at his country estate (confiscated from a millionaire after the Revolution) and had spent the day sitting in a sleigh watching his companions hunt. After eating a large meal, he went to bed, where he fell into a coma and died. His last intelligible words were about a hound that had been used in the hunt: "She is all right. If you give her time and do not hustle her too much. She is young and stupid still and overeager, but she will learn if you give her time."

Britain's *Morning Post* observed, "The death of Lenin removes one of the most sinister and somber figures that ever darkened the human stage. At the time when his wretched country needed a physician, the cruel fates foisted on it a fanatic." Bertrand Russell said of Lenin, "I think he was the most evil man—and certainly one of the most imperturbable—I ever met."

Lenin was embalmed and put on display in a glass case in a monument in Red Square—sort of a Commie Sleeping Beauty. Millions of Russians have filed by the cadaver. Unbeknownst to these tourists, Lenin's skull is empty. In 1991, Artyom Borovik, a Russian reporter for CBS, revealed that Lenin's brain had been removed as part of a secret scientific project to determine the characteristics of the "perfect, Socialist brain."

The KGB, under the direction of Joseph Stalin, established the Brain Institute in Moscow, which, for sixty-seven years, gathered the brains of famous Soviets for study. Some were pickled, but the more important brains, after molds were taken, were encased in wax, then cut into thousands of wafer-thin slices, mounted on slides, and stored in "Room 19." Lenin's and Stalin's brains are there. The institute also has the brains of film director Sergei Eisenstein, writer Maxim Gorky, poet Vladimir Mayakovsky, and physicist Andrei Sakharov. Borovik was shown the most secret corners of the institute, but he wasn't allowed to view the entirety of the wax copy made from the mold of Lenin's brain. The technician insisted on showing only the left side of it. The right side was spotted with pockmarks that the institute believes were caused by syphilis.

1959　North Hollywood. *Our Gang* child star Carl "Alfalfa" Switzer, 32, was less than amiable. His father, a proud German, convinced Alfalfa he was one of the "master race." According to an interview with Darla Hood, the "leading lady" of the series, by film historian Walter Wagner, Switzer

sometimes pinched Darla till she bled. Once, he persuaded her
to reach into his pocket, where he had an open jackknife that
sliced her fingers. On another occasion, when they were to
play a scene in a pool, Switzer talked the director into filling
it with fish. Switzer knew Darla was terrified of fish, and
when she was dumped into the water, she became hysterical.

As Switzer grew up, he hoped to become a serious actor.
One of his later performances can be seen in the Frank Capra
classic *It's a Wonderful Life* (1946), wherein his character causes
Jimmy Stewart and Donna Reed to tumble into a swimming
pool. But Switzer had little success developing his career, and
he became a heavy drinker.

In 1959, Switzer borrowed Bud Stills's dog to go hunting.
Stills and Switzer were partners in a bear-hunting business.
When Switzer lost the animal, he placed an ad offering a $50
reward. The dog was found. Switzer paid the reward,
returned the dog to Stills, then asked his friend to give him
the $50 he'd spent for the reward. His friend refused, insisting
Switzer should pay because he had lost the dog. On this date,
Switzer drank himself into a rage, then, with his friend Jack
Piott, went to Stills's house. Switzer and Stills scuffled. Stills
got a gun. Switzer drew a jackknife. While Piott later said
Stills was not in danger, Stills claimed Switzer charged him.
The killing was ruled self-defense. Switzer's last words were:
"I want that 50 bucks you owe me, and I want it now."

– January 22 –

1901   Osborne, Isle of Wight. Queen Victoria, 81, following a short
illness, died in the arms of her grandson, Kaiser Wilhelm of
Germany, after a 61-year reign. Her last word was "Bertie."
Her husband Albert had died many years before. The
bedroom where she died has been preserved unchanged.

Following her death, her son Edward discovered that
Victoria had a hobby. In a room only she was allowed to visit,
she had assembled hundreds of photographs of dead friends
and relatives. Every photograph had been taken at the
subject's funeral, with the subject laid out in his coffin.

1973   San Antonio International Airport, Texas. Lyndon B. Johnson,

64, thirty-sixth U.S. president, died of a heart attack while being flown to a hospital. His last words were spoken over the phone at his ranch, when he summoned a Secret Service agent for help: "Send Mike immediately!" He was buried at the LBJ Ranch, which he left to the National Park Service. Some think that Johnson, disappointed with his retirement from power, deliberately courted death by drinking and smoking excessively.

Johnson launched the "War on Poverty," which had dubious success, but his own battle with poverty turned out differently. He began public life a poor man and finished a millionaire. As President, he bullied those around him, forcing those he thought of as overrefined to take orders from him while he was using the bathroom. He once kicked his Vice President, Hubert Humphrey, in the shins to hurry him off on an errand and, on another occasion, said to Humphrey, "When I want your advice, I'll give it to you." He was also fond of saying, "I don't trust a man unless I've got his pecker in my pocket."

– January 23 –

1943 New York City. Critic Alexander Woollcott, 56, suffered a heart attack while participating in a debate on Hitlerism on the CBS radio program "People's Platform." He was rushed to a hospital but died soon thereafter. His last words were to a cast member: "Go back in there. Never mind me. Go back in there." Woollcott was known for his acidic reviews, such as: "The scenery in the play was beautiful, but the actors got in front of it." In his will, Woollcott directed that his ashes be buried at his alma mater, Hamilton College. His friends mailed them. They arrived with sixty-seven cents postage due.

1978 Woodland Hills, California. Terry Kath, 32, lead singer and guitarist of the rock group *Chicago*, was playing with a pistol following a party at the home of roadie Don Johnson. Johnson asked Kath to stop but Kath pointed the gun at his head, saying, "Don't worry, it's not loaded, see?" and pulled the trigger. It was.

– January 24 –

A.D.　Rome. The Roman emperor Caligula, 29, was stabbed to death by his guards as he left a theater where he had participated in a human sacrifice. His last words were, "I am still alive!" Some say the killer was Chaerea, whom Caligula had forced into his bed. Chaerea resented Caligula for later embarrassing him in front of his fellow guards.

Caligula, a renowned sadist, killed any who troubled him. He ordered his father-in-law to cut his own throat and closed the granaries, as he enjoyed starving his citizens.

1948　Tokyo. Sadamichi Hirasawa, 56, entered a bank and told the clerks he was the company physician, there to inoculate them against dysentery. Obediently, the clerks lined up to drink his "medicine." Ten died on the spot, two more in the hospital. Hirasawa had given them cyanide. He robbed the bank while they writhed on the floor. The take was about $700.

Hirasawa was sentenced to death by hanging. His lawyers claimed that the sentence violated Japan's new constitution, which banned suicide. They said that he had committed the crime knowing the penalty was death, so therefore he was attempting suicide. Their logic prevailed, and Hirasawa was resentenced to life in prison. When Hirasawa was 88, in 1980, the emperor granted Hirasawa's thirteenth clemency plea and paroled him. Hirasawa died seven years later.

1965　London. Winston Churchill, 90, died of cerebral thrombosis. His last words were, "Oh, I am so bored with it all." His funeral was elaborate, involving all branches of the British military. At one point, the coffin was carried down Westminster Abbey's steps by pallbearers from each service. The representative of the Royal Navy misstepped and broke his ankle. This wasn't apparent, as the stalwart sailor carried on without treatment. Later he said, "I would have carried him all over London."

On his 75th birthday, Churchill had said, "I am ready to meet my Maker. Whether my Maker is prepared for the ordeal of meeting me is another matter." As if in confirmation of this, David Lloyd George once said, of how Churchill would behave in Heaven, "Winston would go up to his Creator and say he would very much like to meet His son, about Whom he has heard a great deal."

– January 25 –

1947   Palm Island, Florida. Alphonse "Scarface" Capone, 48, died of
       syphilis. He had suffered a brain hemorrhage on the nine-
       teenth and newspapers reported his death six days before he
       actually died.
           Capone had spent seven years in prison for tax evasion. He
       began his sentence in 1932 in an Illinois prison, but when the
       luxuries he enjoyed through bribery became public, Capone
       was transferred to the stricter Alcatraz. Doctors there told
       him he had syphilis, but he refused to believe them and bribed
       other prisoners to take his medicine. Soon he started to exhibit
       syphilitic insanity. He talked gibberish, slurred his words, and
       put his clothes on backward. In 1939, when it was clear that
       his case was hopeless, he was released. He spent his last years
       in his Florida mansion in increasing madness.
           At Alcatraz, Capone was paid seven cents an hour to run a
       clothes press. As the gangland boss of Chicago, he had earned
       more than $100,000 a week and had half of the police force on
       his payroll. The high point of his power came in 1929 when he
       successfully executed the St. Valentine's Day Massacre while
       vacationing in Florida. Once, when Capone was accused of
       smuggling booze in from Canada, he scornfully replied, "I
       don't even know what street Canada is on."
           Capone's tombstone in Chicago's Mount Olivet Cemetery
       reads: "My Jesus Mercy." Capone isn't buried there, however.
       His family, fearing souvenir hunters, planted the gangster in
       Mount Carmel Cemetery on the other side of Chicago.

1989   Rochester, New York. Police discovered the corpse of Robert
       Hamm, 73, on his front porch. Hamm had become stuck in a
       trash can up to his armpits. His predicament hadn't gone
       unnoticed. An 11-year-old newsgirl saw him and told her
       mother, but the mother thought the girl was exaggerating or
       mistaken, so she did nothing.
           The postman also saw Hamm. Hamm waved his arms,
       gesturing for help, but the postman thought Hamm was only
       being friendly. He just acknowledged the wave and walked
       on.
           Hamm spent three days in the trash can dressed in a thin
       nightshirt as temperatures plunged into the twenties. He died
       of exposure.

– January 26 –

1973   Hollywood. Actor Edward G. Robinson (Emmanuel Golden-
        berg), 79, died of cancer. Robinson received a posthumous
        special Academy Award for lifetime contributions to the film
        industry. Robinson is remembered for his gangster roles. He
        observed, "Some people have youth, some have beauty. I have
        menace."

– January 27 –

1967   Cape Kennedy. Astronauts Virgil "Gus" Grissom, 40, Edward
        White, 36, and Roger Chaffee, 31, died in a fire during a drill
        in the *Apollo I* spacecraft. Grissom once said, "If we die, we
        want people to accept it...We are in a risky business and we
        hope that if anything happens to us, it will not delay the
        program. The conquest of space is worth the risk of life."

1975   Brattleboro, Vermont. Ida Fuller, 100, died of natural causes in
        a nursing home. She received the first social security check on
        January 31, 1940. She had paid $22 into the fund and received
        over $20,000 in total payments. As a child, Fuller had to walk
        a mile to school (a classmate was Calvin Coolidge). She said
        that the highlight of her life was the appearance in Vermont of
        school buses.

1989   Oklahoma City, Oklahoma. A meter maid discovered the
        body of Leonard Hobson, 67, slumped in his van. An autopsy
        labeled the death as natural but placed the date of death four
        days before its discovery. There was other evidence of the date
        of death. Less observant meter maids had been placing
        parking ticket after parking ticket on the van's windshield for
        three days. Local police said the tickets would be canceled.

        Lest this incident be thought unusual, in 1984, in San
        Diego, California, another meter maid ticketed a car parked
        illegally with what she thought was a peacefully sleeping
        couple inside. It turned out they were the product of a
        murder-suicide.

– January 28 –

1829   Edinburgh. In the nineteenth century, dissection of human
corpses was tangled in illegality, so medical researchers had to
deal with body snatchers. Following a funeral, the snatchers
would unearth the head end of the coffin, smash it open, and
haul the corpse out by the ears or hair. Digging up the whole
coffin took too long, and if the body was pulled out by the
feet, then the arms could get jammed in the coffin and cause a
grisly tug-of-war with the grave.

Innkeeper William Burke and his pal William Hare didn't
wait for natural deaths. They smothered Burke's lodgers, then
peddled the bodies, which were prized by surgeons because of
their freshness (the surgeons deliberately ignored this suspicious freshness). The murderous pair killed thirty-one,
becoming very prosperous. Burke was spending some of his
money on a pretty whore when he was discovered by his wife.
To convince her that the encounter wasn't romantic, Burke
smothered the prostitute and sold her body to a medical
school. The body wasn't dissected, however. It was pickled in
whiskey and displayed in medical classes. Artists also came to
view the lovely body, which became a great curiosity. The
police became interested. Fearful of arrest, Hare informed on
Burke and was pardoned. On this date, Burke was hanged
before a crowd of over 20,000.

Burke's body was given to Edinburgh's College of Surgeons
for dissection. His skin was tanned and cut into souvenirs.
Charles Dickens is said to have used one strip for a book-
marker. Burke's skeleton still decorates an anatomy museum.
The notoriety of the killings helped bring about reforms that
allowed surgeons to practice their skills without resort to
criminals.

– January 29 –

1933   Finland. The skeleton of a child missing for two years was
found in an eagle's nest.

1956   Baltimore. Journalist Henry Louis Mencken died at 75. He
       had suffered a stroke in 1948, which greatly reduced his power
       to use and understand language. He had proposed as his own
       epitaph: "If, after I depart this vale, you remember me and
       have some thought to please my ghost, forgive some sinner
       and wink your eye at some homely girl."

1977   Los Angeles. Comedian and TV star Freddie Prinze, 23, blew
       his brains out. Prinze's family claimed it wasn't suicide (a
       large insurance policy was in question), and the court backed
       them up. His family said that Prinze was under the influence
       of Quaaludes and that he was just goofing around with the
       gun. They cited an incident earlier the same day wherein
       Prinze put the gun to his head in front of his secretary, then
       faked shooting himself as a joke. The fatal shot was fired in
       front of Prinze's business manager. His family believes he was
       joking again, unaware the safety was off. If this is true, the
       joke had an incredibly bad punch line.

1980   Santa Monica, California. Comedian Jimmy Durante died at
       nearly 87 of pneumonia. Once Durante was asked to play
       Hamlet. He replied, "To hell with them small towns. I'll take
       New York."

1992   Ketchum, Idaho. Clinton Richard Doan, 35, enjoyed beer. He
       enjoyed it so much that he kept a keg in a refrigerator in his
       garage. On this date, Doan went to the refrigerator to put his
       next day's lunch away. According to Chief Sheriff's Deputy
       Gene Ramsey, the beer keg ruptured when it was jostled and
       the pressurized beer launched the keg "like a missile." It hit
       Doan in the head, killing him. A faulty regulator on the keg
       was blamed for the accident.

– January 30 –

1649   London. Charles I of England, 48, was beheaded. He wore
       two shirts to his execution lest the cold make him shiver and
       the crowd think him afraid. He also wore a suit of black satin,
       a velvet coat, and pearl earrings, and carried a gold cane.
       Charles had brought on his death by his unwillingness to deal
       squarely with Parliament following his defeat in the English
       Civil War. But Charles died well. His last words were, "I lay
       not my blood on you, or on my people, and demand no other

compensation for any punishment than the return of peace and a revival of the fidelity which the kingdom owes to my children. My friend, I go from a corruptible crown to an incorruptible," and then, to his friend Bishop Juxon, "Remember."

1948   New Delhi. Indian politician Mahatma Gandhi, 78, was passing through a garden on his way to deliver his daily prayer meeting message when a young Hindu man knelt before him. Gandhi blessed the youth, who in turn, produced a pistol and shot Gandhi. Gandi's last words, as he fell mortally wounded were, "Oh, God."

Gandhi's nonviolent leadership brought India self-rule. He subscribed to many habits of Eastern mystics, including celibacy (he was married) and drinking his own urine.

1948   Dayton, Ohio. Airplane coinventor Orville Wright, 76, died of lung congestion and coronary arteriosclerosis. On the same day, three air crashes killed fifty. When Wright was buried in Dayton's Woodland Cemetery by his brother's grave, four P-80s flew overhead in the "missing man" formation. In his eulogy, the attending minister remarked on Orville's horror at the bombing of World War II and quoted Orville as saying, "Obviously, Wilbur and I couldn't foresee what awful use would be made of the airplane, but it is, and will be, of tremendous importance in peace."

On December 17, 1903, Orville had become the first man to fly in a heavier-than-air machine. The distance he covered was 120 feet, less than the wingspan of a modern 747.

Orville's brother, Wilbur died, on May 5, 1912, at age 45 of typhoid fever.

– January 31 –

1956   Hartfield, Sussex, England. Writer Alan Alexander Milne, best known for *Winnie-the-Pooh*, died at 74. He had suffered a stroke in 1952 and spent four years as an invalid.

Milne's son, Christopher Robin Milne, upon whom Milne based his famous character, said of his father, "Some people are good with children. Others are not...it was precisely because he was *not* able to play with his small son...that he wrote about him instead." Christopher also wrote that when,

as a demobilized, World War II soldier, he sought employment and experienced difficulty because of his fictional self,
"it seemed to me, almost, that my father had got to where he
was by climbing upon my infant shoulders, that he had filched
from me my good name and had left me with nothing but the
empty fame of being his son." Recent biographies depict A. A.
Milne more favorably and blame his wife, Daphne, for the
commercial exploitation of their son.

  After his marriage, Christopher saw his father only twice,
and, after the memorial service, Christopher never saw his
mother again, despite her living another fifteen years. He
spurned his inheritance till he decided that the money could
help his disabled daughter. Part of the estate went to the Royal
Literary Fund, which aids impoverished writers.

  Christopher had a stammer, which, when his father died,
disappeared.

– February 1 –

1954   New York City. Inventor Edwin Howard Armstrong, 63, loved music and disliked the static that clouded AM radio, so in the early 1930s, he devised stereo FM radio. The broadcasting networks, knowing this would render their stations obsolete, used their money and influence to attack Armstrong, who was sidetracked by World War II defense research (he allowed the military free use of his patents). NBC's parent company, RCA, tied Armstrong up in litigation over his patents. He battled all the way to the Supreme Court, where the justices sided with the network. The Institute of Radio Engineers (the professional organization for electronic engineers) backed Armstrong, but it was too late.

     His work stolen, his health and fortune ruined, his marriage in trouble, Armstrong dressed to go out this cold February night high in his Manhattan apartment. He put on coat, gloves, scarf, and hat, then left by means other than the elevator or the stairs—he used the window.

1966   Hollywood. Gossip columnist Hedda Hopper, 75, died of pneumonia. An unsuccessful silent movie actress, she became the most feared columnist in Hollywood, where she made and broke careers with a couple of sentences. She once said, "Nobody's interested in sweetness and light."

In *Hedda and Louella*, George Eells wrote how, when Hopper's 83-year-old mother once visited, Hopper gathered important actresses for a tea party. Hopper's mother was deaf, but she enjoyed the party, marveling at the lovely stars. Hopper was sorry that her mother couldn't hear the conversation, so when she visited again, Hopper purchased her a hearing aid and restaged the tea party. Afterward, Hopper asked her mother whether she had had more fun this time. Hopper's mother held out the hearing aid, saying, "I want you to take this back. They had such sweet, smiling faces at the first party, but this time I could hear all the ugly things they said about other people..."

– February 2 –

1969   Midhurst, Sussex, England. British actor Boris Karloff (William Henry Pratt), 81, died of a respiratory ailment. His family wanted him to enter the diplomatic service, but when he showed no aptitude for it, they sent him to Canada in 1909 to make his fortune. He struggled along as a farmhand and ditchdigger before joining a traveling theatrical company. He wound up in Hollywood in 1917, where he stacked flour sacks and drove a truck till he got a role as a Mexican soldier in a Douglas Fairbanks film. He played bit parts until a role as a killer got him the monster's part in *Frankenstein*.

Frankenstein was Hollywood's first big monster film, and studio officials were concerned that it might shock audiences. Dr. Frankenstein (Colin Clive) was emphasized in the publicity, and Karloff wasn't even invited to the premiere, but the monster won the public's interest. Karloff went on to make more horror films and had a long stage career. Of the creature, Karloff said, "The monster was inarticulate, helpless, and tragic, but I owe everything to him. He's my best friend."

1979   New York City. Punk rocker John Simon Ritchie, 21, better known as Sid Vicious of the rock group Sex Pistols, was found nude and dead of a heroin overdose in his Greenwich Village apartment. His girlfriend Michele Robinson was found with him. Ritchie had just been released from jail on $50,000 bail after being charged with stabbing to death his longtime girlfriend Nancy Spungeon on October 12, 1978. He was reportedly celebrating his release with drug.

Attempts were made to sentimentalize his death, but not everyone went along. "Sid Vicious died for what? So that we might rock? I mean, it's garbage, you know," observed John Lennon.

– February 3 –

1889   Eufaula, Oklahoma. Outlaw Myra Belle Shirley, known as Belle Starr, got involved with crime through her brother, a Confederate guerrilla and later a bandit with the James and Younger boys. Belle befriended them and moved to Dallas, Texas, where she befriended more men as a prostitute. She had two children—Pearl, by Cole Younger, and Ed, by James gang member Jim Reed. To supplement her earnings, Belle masterminded a horse- and cattle-rustling racket. She married a Cherokee named Sam Starr (there are no wedding records, but there are records of a joint jail stay). Dime novel writers seized upon this aptly named female outlaw for their fiction. She became famous. For a time, she actually performed as an outlaw in a Wild West show.

On this date, Belle's career ended two days before her 41st birthday, when she was shot in the back with buckshot and in the face with finer shot. Her daughter, Pearl, said Starr blamed her 18-year-old son, Ed. It is rumored that Starr was incestuously romanced by him and that when she refused to let him ride her favorite horse, he murdered her. He had threatened Belle, but Pearl thought her mother was mistaken. Ed was never prosecuted. The children placed a marker on Belle's grave at Youngers Bend in Eufaula reading:

> Shed not for her the bitter tear,
> Nor give the heart in vain regret,
> 'Tis but the casket that lives here,
> The gem that fills it sparkles yet.

Belle once said, "I regard myself as a woman who has seen much of life."

1924   Washington, D.C. Following an exhausting tour unsuccessfully promoting the League of Nations, Woodrow Wilson, twenty-eighth U.S. president, suffered a stroke that paralyzed his left side and brought personality changes. For seventeen months, Wilson's wife, acting as intermediary, was virtually president. Wilson remained an invalid for three years after leaving office, suffering additional strokes. He died in his sleep on this date at 67. He was buried at the National Cathedral in Washington, D.C.

Following Wilson's death, the German Embassy in Washington refused to lower its flag to half-mast. On the day of the funeral, angry American World War I vets demonstrated in front of the German embassy, nailing an American flag to the embassy's door. The German ambassador hastily lowered the embassy's flag, then resigned and fled to Germany.

1933   Cleveland, Ohio. When a mental institution caught fire, the patients were evacuated, but nine female patients found the cold night air uncomfortable. They went back inside to get warm and were killed.

1959   Mason City, Iowa. Rock pioneers Ritchie Valens, 17, J. P. "The Big Bopper" Richardson, 28, and Buddy Holly, 22, were killed in an air crash. This was "the day the music died." They were on tour, and Holly chartered the plane so he could reach Fargo, North Dakota, in time to get his shirts cleaned before show time.

Valens sang "Donna" and "La Bamba." Richardson was known for "Chantilly Lace." Holly is remembered for "Peggy Sue," "That'll Be the Day," "It's So Easy," and other rock classics.

Holly made little money while alive, but since his death, his recordings have earned a fortune. Recently, an auction of Holly memorabilia brought in $700,000 for his widow. Gary Busey, who played Holly in a 1978 film, paid $242,000 for one of Holly's guitars. A pair of Holly's trademark horn-rimmed glasses sold for $45,100.

– February 4 –

1982   The desert, outside Phoenix, Arizona. David M. Grundman blasted a rare giant saguaro cactus twice with his sixteen-gauge shotgun. According to the *Arizona Republic*, Grundman went on to blast another twenty-six-foot cactus. A companion said Grundman had just started to playfully yell "Timber!"

when a limb of the cactus, severed by his fire, fell upon him, crushing Grundman to death.

– February 5 –

1881   Edinburgh. British historian Thomas Carlyle, 85, died of natural causes. He had been in feeble health for years. His last words: "So this is death...well..." Upon completing his great work on the French Revolution, Carlyle asked John Stuart Mill to proofread the only copy. Mill's housemaid mistakenly kindled a fire with it. Carlyle had destroyed his notes but managed to reconstruct the entire work from memory.

In the 1980s, after thirteen years of effort, Swedish writer Ulf af Trolle finished a 250-page book. He had only one copy, so he went to a copy shop to have an extra made. The clerk took the book, carefully set it into a machine, and pushed a button. Instead of copies, the clerk got thousands of strips of paper. The clerk had mistaken a document shredder for a copier.

1987   Palm Springs, California. Entertainer Liberace (Wladziu Valentino Liberace), 67, died at his home of AIDS. The tabloids went wild with fictional stories about him, but the most far-out story was headlined LIBERACE'S DOG HAS AIDS.

According to Jessica Mitford, "[Liberace] once visited a funeral parlor and evidently felt at home there; he said the make-up and wardrobe departments were 'just like a studio.'"

– February 6 –

1685   London. Charles II of England died at 54. On February 2, he suffered what was probably a stroke. His doctors treated this by bleeding (they bled sixteen ounces from him the day before he died), by inducing vomiting through caustic medicines, by applying a mustard plaster containing Spanish fly to his shaved head to induce urination, by blowing a poisonous substance up his nose to induce sneezing, and by a strong purgative. They believed that these treatments would expel unhealthy humours from his body.

Charles was a merry king who loved the ladies, whom he treated with kindness and respect. This included his wife, who, despite his weaknesses, never left him. The duke of Buckingham said that a king was supposed to be the father of his people, and that Charles was indeed father to many. Charles's last words referred to his mistress Nell Gwyne: "Let not poor Nelly starve."

– February 7 –

1968   Beverly Hills. Nick Adams, 36, TV star of "The Rebel" (1959–61), was found by a friend sitting against his bedroom wall, dead. The cause was a combination of sedatives used to treat alcoholics. Curiously, Adams wasn't an alcoholic. Police couldn't find any drugs in the house—not even empty bottles or syringes—and Adams was fully dressed, with a telephone within arm's reach. His career had been in the doldrums, but he had just gotten a new film contract. There were no signs of a struggle, so authorities decided the death was suicide.

1979   Brazil. Dr. Josef Mengele, 67, Nazi monster, drowned during a beach outing. He had been in hiding for thirty-four years. His death remained secret for years.

– February 8 –

1587   Fotheringay Castle, Northamptonshire, England. After blind-folding herself, placing her head upon the block, and saying, "In te, Domine, confido spiritum meum," Mary Stuart, Queen of Scots, was beheaded at 44. She had spent eighteen years in prison and was crippled by rheumatoid arthritis.

It was the custom for the condemned to tip the executioner to encourage a speedy execution. But if Mary tipped her executioner, then her money was wasted because the first blow only opened the back of her skull, causing her to scream "Sweet Jesus!" It took fifteen blows to sever her head.

The executioner lifted her head by the hair to display it to the crowd. But Mary was wearing a red wig, and her head slipped free and rolled around messily. Her real hair, which was short and gray, was exposed to the surprised crowd. As a further embarrassment, Mary had been accompanied to the block by her terrier lapdog, which hid under her petticoat. The dog refused to leave Mary's body till she was carried off. Every item associated with the execution was burned, and Mary's body was placed in a lead coffin that was hidden behind a castle wall till a later, less hostile time. It was then transferred to Westminster Abbey. The terrier reportedly died of grief.

1933   Tomahawk, Kentucky. During a religious ceremony in her home, Mrs. Lucinda Mills, 67, was strangled to death by her family.

– February 9 –

1881   St. Petersburg. Russian writer Fyodor Dostoyevski, 59, author of *Crime and Punishment* and *The Idiot*, died of a hemorrhage. As a young man in czarist Russia, Dostoyevski became involved in politics, was arrested, and faced a firing squad. He was reprieved at the last moment. Later, he wrote a very authentic account of a condemned man's thoughts.

Dostoyevski said, "Shower upon him every blessing, drown him in a sea of happiness, give him economic prosperity, such that he should have nothing else to do but sleep, eat cakes, and busy himself with the continuation of his species, and even then, out of sheer ingratitude, sheer spite, man would play you some nasty trick."

1988   Yellowstone National Park. Visitor John Mark Williams, 24, was viewing the park's natural wonders. Unfortunately, he got too close to one wonder. He fell into a thermal pool and was boiled to death.

– February 10 –

1837   Moscow. Poet Aleksandr Pushkin, 37, died of wounds received in a duel defending his wife's honor. She had become involved with an army officer. Perhaps this is why his last words were addressed to his books: "Farewell, my friends."

1989　St. Clairsville, Ohio. Former Congressman Wayne L. Hays, 77, died of a heart attack. Hays began as a small-town mayor, but became a powerful member of Congress as chair of the House Ways and Means Committee, which dispenses Congressional perks ranging from parking spaces to staffing. Hays spent nearly thirty years in Congress but was forced from office when, in 1976, clerk Elizabeth Ray, 33, claimed he'd paid her $14,000 annually in federal money for sexual services. She said, "I can't type, I can't file, I can't even answer the phone."

– February 11 –

1933　Island of Oshima, Japan. Schoolgirl Kiyoko Matsumoto, 19, committed suicide by jumping into the 1,000-foot-deep crater of Mihara-Yama Volcano. It started a bizarre fad that led over three hundred other Japanese children to jump in. A fence, and making it a crime to buy a one-way ticket to the island, helped police stop the craze. The fad had entertained thousands of tourists who visited the island, ate lunch, and watched the suicides. A camel ride to the top of the volcano was available.

1963　London. American writer Sylvia Plath, 30, had literary but not personal success. Her marriage over, she was ill and on the edge of a nervous breakdown; she was living in a small flat with her two young children during one of England's coldest winters. Plath laid out a plate of bread and butter with two mugs of milk for her children, then committed suicide by placing her head in a turned-on, unlit gas oven.

　　　Most of Plath's work was published posthumously, but the one novel she wrote, *The Bell Jar*, was published under a pseudonym before her death. It dealt with a young woman's compulsion to kill herself.

– February 12 –

1789　Burlington, Vermont. Ethan Allen died at 51. His last words, upon being told that the angels in heaven were waiting for him, were, "Waiting are they, waiting are they? Well, goddamn 'em, let 'em wait!"

Purportedly, Allen's fatal illness began when he was returning to Vermont from a drinking party in New York. He was crossing frozen Lake Champlain in a sleigh loaded with hay. Overfilled with cheer, he fell off, and his injuries, compounded by the chill, caused his death.

Allen led the Green Mountain Boys, a militia formed to combat New Yorkers. Although the settlers of Vermont had purchased their land from New Hampshire, New York claimed the area and insisted that the settlers pay again. When the Revolution came, Vermonters switched to fighting the British. The Continental Congress sent an officer, Benedict Arnold, to take charge, but Allen resisted the usurpation, and Arnold shared command with Allen when eighty Green Mountain Boys captured Fort Ticonderoga. The fort had withstood thousands in the French and Indian Wars, and the capture shocked the British. The fort's guns became the core of the Continental Army's artillery.

Despite his fame, no authenticated portrait of Allen exists.

1804   Konigsberg, Prussia. Philosopher Immanuel Kant died at 83. His last words: "It is enough." Kant once said, "From such crooked wood as that which man is made of, nothing straight can be fashioned." One critic said, "You could read Kant by yourself, if you wanted to; but you must share a joke with someone else."

– February 13 –

1883   Venice. German composer Richard Wagner, 69, died of a heart attack. His last words: "I am fond of them, of the inferior beings of the abyss, of those who are full of longing."

Kurt Vonnegut observed of the bombastic composer, who enjoyed wearing historical costumes while composing, "I am quick to agree with the feeling of Nietzsche that the thundering, melodious balderdash of Wagner was the most addling experience imaginable for the German intellect." Oscar Wilde said, "I like Wagner's music better than any other music. It is so loud that one can talk the whole time without people hearing what one says." Leo Tolstoy wrote of *Siegfried*, "Siegfried seized some bits of a sword and sang: 'Heaho, heaho, hoho! Hoho, hoho, hoho! Heaho, haho, hahoo, hoho!' And that was the end of the first act. It was all so artificial and stupid...I fled out of the theater with a feeling of disgust that I have not yet forgotten." Mark Twain said it more simply, "Wagner's music is better than it sounds."

1976   Hollywood. Actor Sal Mineo, 37, remembered for his role in *Rebel Without a Cause* (1955), was stabbed to death in the carport of his West Hollywood apartment building. In 1979, Lionel Ray Williams was convicted of the killing. A mugger, he killed Mineo while trying to rob him. That night, Williams told his wife about the murder, and she informed the authorities a year later. They didn't believe her, but using her description of the murder weapon, they purchased a similar knife. It matched the fatal wounds. Williams, who had been jailed in Michigan for forgery, bragged to fellow inmates of the killing. He even had a tattoo of the murder weapon on his arm. For the murder and ten robberies, Williams was sentenced to fifty-one years in prison.

– February 14 –

1779   Hawaii. Captain James Cook, 50, was killed by natives. He was attempting to take the chief of a tribe hostage to prevent the tribe's continuing thieving from his men. The natives threatened to overwhelm his party, so Cook ordered a retreat to his ship. Cook was captured, stabbed, then drowned. The natives mutilated the body, but politely returned the scalp, hands, and skeleton to Cook's crew, who buried them at sea. Cook's remains weighed nine pounds.

1891   New York City. Civil War general William Tecumseh Sherman died three days before his 71st birthday.

Sherman fought at Bull Run, Shiloh, and Vicksburg and led the "march to the sea" immortalized in "As We Were Marching Through Georgia" and, from a Southern viewpoint, in *Gone With the Wind*. He is credited with having said "War is hell." The march across Georgia was certainly hellish for the South. Sherman destroyed railroads, plantations, mills, bridges, and every economic target he could find. It is said that the path he took can still be seen from the air. The march was daring, as until he reached the sea, Sherman had no supply line to Union forces. No other army has ever matched the feat.

After the war, Sherman continued in the army, retiring in 1884. In 1890 he said, "I feel it coming sometimes when I get home from an entertainment or banquet, especially these winter nights. I feel death reaching out for me, as it were. I suppose I'll take cold some night, and go to bed never to get up again." On February 5, he caught cold, which developed into fatal pneumonia. A train carried his body to St. Louis for burial. All along its route, Union veterans turned out to fire old rifles in salute and to wave bullet-torn battle flags.

1929   2122 North Clark Street, Chicago. During the gangland era, over 5,000 died in mob killings in Chicago. On this date, seven members of Bugs Moran's North Side Gang joined that total when they were lined up against a wall in an auto garage that served as Moran's headquarters and machine-gunned by hoods dressed as cops in the St. Valentine's Day Massacre. The killers were part of Al Capone's Gang and were hoping to find Moran in the garage, but Moran was late. He saw the black sedans the "cops" arrived in and, thinking it was a police raid, went discreetly home. Later, when the press asked who was responsible, Moran said, "Only Capone kills like that." One of the victims, Frank Gusenberg, lived long enough to be questioned by the police. They asked him who shot him. He said, "No one. Nobody shot me." Then he died.

Most of the killers soon died in gangland misadventures. Two were said to have had their brains bashed out by Capone with a baseball bat. When Capone learned they were plotting to kill him, he staged a testimonial dinner for them and, after an effusive toast, produced the bat. Moran outlived Capone, dying in his 64th year in Leavenworth Prison of lung cancer.

– February 15 –

1949   New York City. Radio actress Patricia Ryan, 27, was cast as a girl with a headache. During the performance, she got head pains and afterward died.

1973   Bel Air, California TV comic actor Wally Cox, 48, known for playing timid characters, died of a heart attack. Cox was a regular on "The Hollywood Squares," which was filmed ahead of its broadcast. Consequently, Cox appeared on TV months after his death.

Cox was great friends with Marlon Brando. Following the cremation of Cox's body, Brando was given his ashes. According to Hollywood private investigator Don Crutchfield, Brando often takes the urn in hand and talks to his departed friend.

– February 16 –

1925   Cave City, Kentucky. Floyd Collins was exploring a cave when a boulder shifted, pinning his leg. Rescue workers spent eighteen days trying to free Collins while the entire nation followed their efforts through newspapers and radio. The rescue failed, and Collins died on this date of exposure. His body remains in the cave.

– February 17 –

1673   Paris. Playwright Molière (Jean Baptiste Poquelin), 51, died after going into convulsions while playing the lead in his play *The Imaginary Invalid*. Two nuns attended him at his death, but the Church refused his request for a priest because it considered his works irreligious. It denied him burial in sacred ground, then relented, but insisted that the interment be nocturnal to avoid scandal. The result was a beautiful torchlight procession.

1856   Paris. German poet Heinrich Heine, 58, died of syphilis. He had been paralyzed and in pain from the disease for eight years, after collapsing in front of the Venus de Milo. He complained that "the goddess did not stretch an arm to help me!" His will left his money to his wife only if she remarried, so that "one man [will] ...regret my death." His last words: "God will forgive me—that's his job." This was followed by, "Write...write...paper!...pencil!"

1909   Fort Sill, Oklahoma. Chiricahua Apache chief Geronimo died at 78. Under house arrest for fifteen years, he had prospered by selling souvenirs of himself and had become a well-to-do farmer. The aged chief fell in a creek while tipsy and couldn't extricate himself. His neighbors found him, but although he developed pneumonia, he refused to be taken to a hospital. The Apaches called them "death houses," as people often died there. Geronimo died in his own bed.

The Mexicans gave him the name "Geronimo." His tribe earlier called him "Goyathlay," which means "one who yawns."

1977   Florida. Tina Christopherson, 29, had an IQ of 189 but was terrified that she would die of stomach cancer like her mother. To ward off this fate, she went on long fasts during which she ate nothing and drank great quantities of water. Sometimes she drank as much as four gallons a day. On this date, her kidneys failed. Water migrated into her lungs, and she drowned while on dry land.

– February 18 –

1564   Rome. Artist Michelangelo died at nearly 89. He had suffered from chronic kidney stones and arthritis, but a stroke was the probable cause of death. A friend, learning that Michelangelo was ill, visited and discovered the artist wandering in the rain, pale and incoherent. He persuaded Michelangelo to go inside, but Michelangelo restlessly went from his bed to an armchair by his hearth and back again, over and over. He died in a few days.

The citizens of Rome wanted to bury Michelangelo in their city, but he had often stated his desire to be buried in his native city, Florence. His nephew arranged to have the body stolen and shipped to Florence disguised as ordinary freight. There, local artists wanted to stage the funeral. They stole the body and carried it in a torchlight procession to a church. A crowd crammed the edifice, and the artists were compelled to open the coffin to prove that Michelangelo's body was indeed present. Fortunately, it was well preserved.

While he was primarily a sculptor, Michelangelo is best remembered for painting his fresco upon the Sistine Chapel ceiling, which depicts Creation and Judgment Day. Because many figures were nude, prudish folks objected. The writer Aretino, who was a secret pornographer, wrote "such things may be suitable in a bathroom, but not in the holiest chapel." Suitable camouflage was added.

1857 South Africa. Nongqawuse was a surprised 14-year-old girl. A member of the Gcaleka Xhosa tribe, she had gazed into the Gxara River in 1856 and had a vision of her dead ancestors. They told her that they would return to the physical world to lead her tribe against the white man, but that first the tribe must destroy all their property. On February 18, 1857, the spirits would reverse the course of the sun and lead the tribe to glory. If the tribe didn't do as they were told, they would all be turned into bugs or reptiles and killed by a tempest to boot. Nongqawuse told the tribal elders of her vision, and the whole tribe set to work destroying their worldly goods. This took nearly a year. On this, the appointed date, the tribe assembled for their reward. It didn't arrive. Hence Nongqawuse's surprise and the subsequent death by starvation of 25,000 members of her tribe. Nongqawuse didn't die in the famine, but she spent the rest of her life in exile.

1992 Wilmington, Delaware. An unidentified man of about 60 was run down and killed by a truck when he tried to cross a six-lane highway. The truck was carrying 102 caskets.

– February 19 –

1405 Plains of Utrar, beyond Sir-Darya. The oriental conqueror Timur (Tamerlane) died at 69. On his deathbed, he said, "Never yet has death been frightened away by screaming." He had been leading an army into China when they were stalled by cold weather. Timur couldn't warm himself and resorted to wine, spices, spirits, and drugs. He took no food. His stomach and bowels became inflamed, and he died of a fever. His body was anointed with camphor, musk, and rose-water, then entombed, with his face toward Mecca. He was later moved to Samarkand.

Timur, who nearly destroyed Western civilization, played polo with the skulls of his enemies and memorialized his victories with thirty-foot pyramids of severed heads.

1951 Paris. Nobel-Prize winner André Gide, 81, died in his home of pneumonia. He had refused to be taken to a hospital. His last words were, "It is well." Earlier, he had said, "Before you quote me, be sure I'm conscious." Another account gives his last words as "I am afraid my sentences are becoming grammatically incorrect." He once said, "Know thyself! A maxim as pernicious as it is ugly. Whoever observes himself arrests his own development. A caterpillar who wanted to know itself well would never become a butterfly."

− February 20 −

1895   Washington, D.C. Antislavery leader Frederick Douglass died at about 78 (no record of his slave birthdate was kept). His last words referred to the sudden stroke that killed him: "Why, what does this mean?"

Douglass was the son of a Maryland planter and Harriet Bailey, a slave. He was taken from his mother after a few months so that she could go back to work in the fields. Harriet had to walk twelve miles each night to see him and faced a whipping if she wasn't in the fields at sunrise. She died when he was seven. Douglass couldn't remember ever seeing her in daylight.

Douglass escaped slavery in 1838 and became a spokesman for the antislavery movement. Although he was harassed by mobs, his renown grew. He published a book and toured Great Britain, earning enough money to purchase his freedom. He founded a newspaper, promoted the use of black troops during the Civil War, and battled for black rights following the war.

1972   Los Angeles. Radio personality and columnist Walter Winchell, 74, died of prostate cancer. A vaudeville song-and-dance man turned newsman, his rapid-fire news reading could hit 227 words a minute. Winchell was an associate of Franklin Roosevelt, J. Edgar Hoover, Damon Runyon, and other 1930s notables, including gangsters such as Dutch Schultz. But not everyone liked him. He feuded for years with rival columnist Ed Sullivan. Ethel Barrymore said: "I don't see why Walter Winchell is allowed to live." Writer Dorothy Parker observed, "Poor Walter. He's afraid he'll wake up some day and discover he's not Walter Winchell." Her words came true. Winchell offended too many people. He lost his readership and his radio program, and left the business in

1963. His retirement was made more painful by the suicide of his son in 1970. Winchell was buried in Phoenix, Arizona. Winchell's daughter, Walda, allowed no graveside attendents other than herself and the officiating rabbi.

Among other accomplishments, Winchell coined the phrase "making whoopee." At his prime, Winchell said, "Other columnists print it—I make it public." He later observed, "Nothing recedes like success."

– February 21 –

1965   New York City. Black Muslim leader Malcolm X, 39, was assassinated while addressing a contentious meeting of that organization. His last words were, "Let's cool it, brothers—" A rival faction within the Black Muslims was responsible for his assassination. Malcolm had broken with his mentor Elijah Muhammed and was taking a more moderate approach to racial relations.

1986   Manassas, Virginia. CIA employee Larry Wu-tai Chin, 63, had passed secrets to Red China for decades before being caught. On this date, he suffocated himself in his jail cell with a plastic bag.

– February 22 –

1976   Detroit. Singer Florence Ballard, 31, died of a heart attack. As a member of the Motown group the Supremes (the group was her idea), she had earned as much as $250,000 annually. In 1967, she left the group, and her fortunes turned bad. She wound up living in public housing with her three children on a welfare payment of $95 a week.

1987   New York City. Andy Warhol, 58, died following routine gallstone and hernia surgery. His private nurse was charged with negligence, as she took forty-five minutes to respond to his heart attack. The estate sued for malpractice, saying death resulted from overhydration. Warhol's representatives claimed that intravenous fluids were improperly administered and that Warhol "drowned" after too much fluid was put into his body. In 1991, the estate settled for a "substantial," but unrevealed, sum.

Warhol's memorial service was held at New York's St. Patrick's Cathedral. Some of Warhol's own musings about death were read. Warhol, who called himself "a deeply superficial person," wrote:

> "When I die, I don't want to leave any leftovers. I'd like to disappear. People wouldn't say he died today, they'd say he disappeared. But I do like the idea of people turning into dust or sand. And it would be very glamorous to be reincarnated as a big ring on Elizabeth Taylor's finger."

Of a more lively subject, Warhol once pronounced: "Sex is the biggest nothing of all time."

– February 23 –

1821   Piazza di Spagna, Rome. Romantic poet John Keats, 25, died of tuberculosis. His last words were: "Thank God it has come." During his illness, he had said: "I feel daisies growing over me."

Keats, the son of a stable groom, studied medicine following his mother's painful death by tuberculosis. One of his first patients was his brother, who also had tuberculosis. When his brother died in agony, Keats left medicine. In 1818, while holidaying in Scotland, Keats caught a cold, which persisted. Keats fearfully diagnosed his own illness as tuberculosis. His condition grew worse despite his traveling to the warmer climate of Italy. His lungs bled daily, and even with the devoted care of his painter friend Joseph Severn, who kept Keats from killing himself, the poet couldn't recover. Keats was buried in Rome's Protestant Cemetery. He had directed that a nameless marker be placed on his grave bearing the self-deprecating epitaph: "Here lies one whose name was writ in water."

Because literati of Keats's era despised writers who didn't share their own aristocratic backgrounds, Keats's work was denigrated till after his death. Lord Byron wrote, "Here are Jonny Keats' p-ss a bed poetry...No more Keats, I entreat: flay him alive; if some of you don't, I must skin him myself: there is no bearing the drivelling idiotism..." Carlyle called a collection of his poems "fricassee of dead dog." Byron and

Shelley rose to Keats's defense after his death, guiltily convinced he had been killed by bad reviews. In his tubercular deliriums, Keats had been certain that his critics or his mistress, who had abandoned him to avoid tuberculosis, were poisoning him.

1848   Washington, D.C. John Quincy Adams, 80, sixth U.S. President, died following a stroke. Unlike other presidents, he returned to the legislative branch after being chief executive. While debating in the House of Representatives, he suffered a stroke. The issue was a resolution calling for the presentation of ceremonial swords to officers who were veterans of the Mexican-American War. Adams had condemned the war as a device for extending the domain of slavery, so when the voice vote was called, he shouted "No!" Suddenly, he collapsed. He was carried to the Rotunda, where he roused, thanked his bearers, then fell into a coma. His doctors tried to revive him with mustard plasters, leeches, and "cupping"—a technique whereby a wine glass is made to suck upon the flesh by lighting a fire in the glass and pressing it against the skin. Perhaps these ministrations, or the pain they caused, were effective. Adams revived for a few moments that night and mumbled, "This is the last of earth. I am content." He fell back into the coma and died two days later on this date.

Author Alfred Steinberg observed, "John Quincy Adams was a short, stout, bald, brilliant and puritanical twig off a short, stout, bald, brilliant, and puritanical tree." Ralph Waldo Emerson said, "He is an old roué, who cannot live on slops, but must have sulfuric acid in his tea." Adams said, "I am a man of reserved, cold and forbidding manners." Adams is the only president to be a son of a former president. His father was John Adams.

1965   Santa Monica, California. Stan Laurel, 74, of the Laurel and Hardy comic duo, died of heart disease. His grave is in Forest Lawn Cemetery in Los Angeles. Born Arthur Stanley Jefferson in England, the son of actors, he came to the United States in 1910 to understudy Charlie Chaplin in a stage revue. He spent a decade in vaudeville before becoming first a writer, then a director, and, finally, an actor for Hal Roach. In 1926, he was teamed with Oliver Hardy. They became a legend as bumbling, but persistent, losers. The Laurel and Hardy fan club is called the "Sons of the Desert," after the lodge they belonged to in their films. Laurel suggested their motto, "Two Minds Without a Single Thought." He rarely made public appearances after Hardy's death (see 8/7/1957).

Laurel knew how serious his condition was. He said to his nurse, "I'd rather be skiing than doing this." She asked him if he skied. "No," he answered, "but I'd rather be doing that than this."

1990   Henniker, New Hampshire. In 1989, Michael Doucette, 17, of Concord, was named America's safest teenage driver in a contest sponsored by the Dodge Motor Company and AMVETS, a veterans' organization. Doucette received a $5,000 scholarship, a trophy, and the use of a new automobile for one year. Doucette was driving that car just after 5:00 P.M. on this date when he apparently fell asleep. His car drifted over the center line, head-on into a car driven by Sharon Ann Link, 19, of Lebanon, New Hampshire. Both Doucette and Link were killed. A passenger of Link's was seriously injured.

– February 24 –

1946   Topeka, Kansas. Writer and Prohibition promoter Charles M. Sheldon, 88, died of a cerebral hemorrhage. He wrote *In His Steps*, which sold 23 million copies. Sadly for Sheldon, a faulty copyright prevented his receiving any royalties. He was more fortunate as the publisher of the *Topeka Daily Capital*, greatly increasing circulation after turning it into a religious newspaper. Among other changes, he forbade patent medicine and hose-and-garter ads.

– February 25 –

1922   Versailles prison, France. Henri Landru, known as "Blue-beard," was guillotined in his 53rd year for the murder of ten women and a boy. His count was probably much higher. He ran ads in lonely hearts columns and married the women who replied. He then took them on a one-way honeymoon to his villa outside Paris. There, he murdered them and chopped up and burned their bodies in a cast-iron stove. He supported himself by selling their furniture and possessions. He was uncontrite and at his trial jeered at the prosecution. The judge once said, "You are a habitual liar, are you not, Landru?" Landru replied, "I am not a lawyer, Monsieur!"

1983   New York City. American playwright Tennessee Williams died at 71. He had tilted his head back to use some nose spray but had forgotten that he had left the cap sitting loosely on the spray bottle. When the cap fell into his mouth, he half-swallowed it and suffocated.

Williams once remarked, "We all live in a house on fire, no fire department to call; no way out, just the upstairs window to look out of while the fire burns the house down with us trapped, locked in it." And he warned, "Don't look forward to the day when you stop suffering. Because when it comes you'll know that you're dead."

– February 26 –

1903   New York City. Despite having heart disease, Richard Gatling, 84, insisted on keeping a business appointment while suffering from a bad cold. He returned exhausted and died of a heart attack in his daughter's arms. His Gatling gun, the first practical machine gun, was available during the Civil War. Northern officials preferred muzzle-loading rifles and spurned it, while Southerners didn't have the industrial capability to copy it. At the time of his death, Gatling was working on a more peaceful invention—a motorized plow.

1990   Las Vegas. Singer Cornell Gunter, 53, was shot to death in his car at an intersection. Police couldn't find a motive or suspect. Gunter was the lead singer of the 1950s do-wop group The Coasters. Their hits included "Yakety Yak" and "Charlie Brown."

– February 27 –

1859   Washington, D.C. Congressman Daniel Sickles shot to death Philip Key, son of Francis Scott Key, on a public street. Sickles suspected Key of adultery with his wife. He was acquitted after the first use in the United States of temporary insanity as a defense and went on to become a Civil War general.

1958 Phoenix, Arizona. Movie mogul Harry Cohn, 66, died of coronary occlusion. He was extremely abrasive. He said, "I don't get ulcers, I give them." Few liked him. Elia Kazan said, "He liked to be the biggest bug in the manure pile." Hedda Hopper commented, "You had to stand in line to hate him." Frank Sinatra said, "He had a sense of humor like an open grave." Red Skelton observed of Cohn's funeral, "It proves what they always say: Give the people what they want to see, and they'll come out for it."

In 1949, as an executive for Columbia Pictures, Cohn let the contract of a young actress lapse because she didn't have "star quality." Her name was Marilyn Monroe.

1987 Paris Metro. A drunken vagrant shouted insults at passersby. One, a well-dressed man in his thirties, reached into his briefcase, pulled out a machete, and hacked the drunk to death.

– February 28 –

1916 London. Boston-born American expatriate writer Henry James, 62, died of a stroke and pneumonia. His last words were, "So here it is at last, the distinguished thing."

William Faulkner said, "Henry James was one of the nicest old ladies I ever met." H. L. Mencken considered James "an idiot, and a Boston idiot to boot, than which there is nothing lower in the world."

James once remarked, "Life is a predicament which precedes death." He was involved in a predicament after death. He was cremated in London, and his sister was forced to smuggle his ashes through strict customs inspections—it was the middle of World War I—to bury them in the James' family plot in Cambridge, Massachusetts.

– February 29 –

1960 Florence, South Carolina. FBI agent Melvin Purvis, 56, committed suicide in his home by shooting himself. Head of the Chicago branch of the FBI, he figured prominently in the disposal of many famous gangsters. He is credited with shooting Public Enemy Number One, John Dillinger (see 7/22/1934). He used the same gun in his suicide. His family blamed J. Edgar Hoover for the death. They said that Hoover, envious of Purvis's fame from killing Dillinger, hounded Purvis out of the FBI.

Purvis is credited with being the first person to belch on radio. In 1935, while appearing on a radio talk show, Purvis inadvertently belched loudly in the middle of a Fleischmann's Yeast commercial. That product was known as "Purvis's Folly" for years thereafter.

– March 1 –

1932   Hopewell, New Jersey. Charles A. Lindbergh, Jr., the 20-month-old son of aviator Charles A. Lindbergh and Anne Morrow Lindbergh, was kidnapped from his crib. Minutes later, the child's skull was fractured by a heavy blow. His body was hidden under leaves five miles from the Lindbergh home. The kidnapper pretended the child was alive, and Lindbergh paid $50,000 ransom. No word of the child was heard till the body was discovered on May 12.

On September 15, 1934, Bruno Hauptmann bought gas in the Bronx with some of the ransom. The attendant had made a ritual of checking serial numbers against a list of the ransom bills and notified the authorities. When Hauptmann was arrested, $14,000 of the ransom was found in his garage. Witnesses recognized him as the receiver of the money and as being in the area at the time of the crime. The ladder used to enter the child's room matched lumber in Hauptmann's attic. Hauptmann, a carpenter, claimed he would never have made such a crude ladder, but it was suggested that he concealed his skills when he made it. Hauptmann's service in the German army during World War I and his criminal record increased suspicion. He was convicted and electrocuted. To this day, his

wife, citing problems with the identifications, maintains his
innocence and has attempted to reopen the case.

— March 2 —

1930   Vence, France. Writer D. H. (David Herbert) Lawrence, 46,
        known for *Lady Chatterley's Lover*, died from pleurisy. His
        last words, after receiving a morphine injection to calm him,
        were, "I am better now; if I could only sweat I would be
        better." He then fell asleep and died.
            Katherine Anne Porter said of Lawrence's writing, "The
        ineptitudes of these awful little love-scenes seem heart-
        breaking—that a man of such gifts should have lived so long
        and learned no more about love than that!" Joseph Conrad
        said, "Filth. Nothing but obscenities."

1987   Los Angeles. Western actor Randolph Scott, 85, died in his
        sleep at his California home from a brain tumor. "He made
        ninety-six films after getting his start when he met producer
        Howard Hughes on a golf course in 1929.

— March 3 —

1991   Honolulu. Ballroom dance teacher Arthur Murray, 95, died of
        pneumonia. Raised in a New York City ghetto, Murray had
        been so shy that he dropped out of high school and quit ten
        jobs in the following six months. He conquered his shyness by
        going to a dance in a settlement house. His first partner told
        him he danced like a truck driver, but Murray persisted. He
        returned to high school, where a patient classmate taught him
        more steps. His self-respect grew with his skill. He set up a
        mail-order dance school. He eventually had 400 schools in 50
        countries and a television show that ran 11 years.
            Murray didn't like rock and roll, saying, "I don't like
        dancing alone, and I feel silly flailing my arms around."

— March 4 —

1859   New York City. Around midnight. Commodore Matthew
        Perry, 63, died of a heart attack related to rheumatic gout

while sitting in an armchair in his library. Five years earlier, Perry, under orders of President Millard Fillmore, had sailed into Tokyo Bay and, at cannon point, insisted the Japanese sign a treaty establishing diplomatic relations. His action set the Japanese on the course of Westernization and modernization.

1943   London. One hundred seventy-eight died when overcrowding in an air-raid shelter caused a panic. It isn't widely known, but if someone faints in a crowd and can't lower his head, his brain can die from lack of blood.

– March 5 –

1770   Boston. The "Boston Massacre" occurred after a snowball fight grew into an anti-British riot. British soldiers guarding the customhouse opened fire on the mob, killing seven. Crispus Attucks, a black, became the first casualty of the American Revolution.

1953   Russia. Soviet premier Joseph Stalin, 73, responsible for more deaths than any other man in history, died. According to Nikita Khrushchev, "We never knew, when called to his office, if we'd ever see our families again. You know, people don't do their best work in that atmosphere."

   According to one of Stalin's bodyguards, on March 1, Stalin was found sprawled on the floor of his country mansion, unable to talk. It was thought he had lain there three or four hours. Guards placed him in bed and called Lavrenti Beria, head of the secret police. He arrived with Georgi M. Malenkov, who would succeed Stalin. Beria announced over Stalin's comatose form that the guards had panicked and that Stalin was asleep. Hours passed. Khrushchev arrived and insisted doctors be summoned. The doctors diagnosed a brain hemorrhage, but when Beria demanded they guarantee Stalin's life, they were too fearful to operate. Stalin's daughter, who was present, claims that her father was aware of his surroundings. She says he started to point a finger at someone in the assembly, then died. The death was recorded as occurring on the fifth. An autopsy showed that he had suffered a series of strokes over the last years of his life. Beria was later shot as a traitor.

It took six months to embalm Stalin's body so that it could be displayed beside the body of Lenin in his tomb in Moscow's Red Square (Stalin's brain was preserved by the KGB). It remained there till later dictators decided to reduce the cult that had grown up around his memory. Stalin's body was removed at night and buried.

Stalin once said, "Gaiety is the most outstanding feature of the Soviet Union."

1982 Bungalow 3, Chateau-Marmont Hotel, Los Angeles. Comedian John Belushi, 33, of "Saturday Night Live" and *The Blues Brothers* (1980), died of a drug overdose. Because he didn't like needles, a "friend" obligingly injected him.

Dan Aykroyd said of Belushi, "A good man, but a bad boy." A card on Belushi's grave read, "He could have given us years of laughter—but noooooooo!" Reportedly, the grave has become sort of a junkie shrine. Drug users often shoot up near it and leave their used syringes behind.

1984 Palm Springs, California. Actor William Powell, 91, died of natural causes with his wife of forty-four years, Diana Lewis Powell, at his bedside. He made many films but is remembered as debonair Nick Charles in the *Thin Man* movies he made with Myrna Loy in the 1930s and 1940s. This series was recently ranked at the top in a survey of the films TV viewers requested. Myrna Loy said, "I never enjoyed my work more than when I worked with William Powell. He was a brilliant actor, a great friend and, above all, a true gentleman."

Powell is thought of as the Thin Man. Actually, the Thin Man was the victim in the first film. He was "thin" because his corpse had been reduced by quicklime to just a skeleton.

– March 6 –

1836 San Antonio. The Battle of the Alamo began. One hundred and eighty-five Texans held off 4,000 Mexicans for twelve days at an old mission, killing 1,500. By some accounts, seven Texans were captured, reputedly including Davy Crockett. Santa Anna ordered them tortured and executed. The Mexicans stripped and burned the corpses as a final insult.

Popularly, it is believed that there were no survivors of the battle. In fact, some of the dependents of the defenders were spared by the Mexicans, and there was also a surviving soldier, Louis "Moses" Rose, a Frenchman in his early forties. The night before the final fight, the Alamo's commander, 27-year-old Colonel William Barrett Travis, drew a line in the dirt with his sword and said, "We have no hope for help, for no force that we could have reasonably expected could cut its way through the strong ranks of these Mexicans. Then let us band together as brothers and vow to die together. Let us resolve to withstand our adversaries to the last ... I now want every man who is determined to stay here and die with me to come across this line." Every member of the garrison—except Rose—stepped across the line and into history. Rose slipped out of the Alamo and made it through the Mexican lines to safety.

Rose's war ended with his escape. He made his way to Grimes County, Texas, where he was taken in by the W. P. Zuber family, exhausted and suffering from infected leg wounds caused by cactus thorns. The thorns were embedded deep in his flesh, unremovable by the medical care available. Rose recovered enough to work on a plantation in Nacogdoches, Texas. He lived there for fourteen years, dying in 1850. The cause of death was believed to be the unremoved thorns. Descendants of Rose still live in the Corpus Christi area.

Rose is a curious figure. Illiterate, he had a near-photographic memory. He freely told of his experiences at the Alamo, including the speech given by Travis. Without him, it would have gone unrecorded. Rose could have claimed to have been sent out from the Alamo as a messenger or scout, but he didn't. He simply gave the facts, apparently unconcerned that he might be thought a coward. Perhaps he reasoned that the fight hadn't really been his, or perhaps he thought he had nothing to prove, since the Texas War of Independence hadn't been his first war. Rose had earlier been decorated for service in the French Army under Napoleon Bonaparte. He had fought in many campaigns, including the horrible retreat from Moscow and the grand disaster of Waterloo.

Rose was buried in the Ferguson Cemetery near Funston, Louisiana. The grave is unmarked by anything but briars and yucca plants. Rose is mistakenly listed on some monuments as having died with his compatriots at the Alamo.

1888   Boston. Louisa May Alcott, 56, author of *Little Women*, died. She had nursed her dying father and, exhausted after his death, caught a cold that led to spinal meningitis or apoplexy; her death was so sudden that the doctor had no time to determine which. She died the day of her father's funeral. At her father's bedside she had asked, "What are you thinking of as you lie here so happily?" He replied, "I am going up. Come with me." She had said, "Oh, I wish I could."

– March 7 –

322   Chalcis. The philosopher Aristotle died, reputedly of indiges-
B.C.   tion, in his 62d year. The tutor of Alexander the Great, his writings were the basis of Western science for over a thousand years, despite many errors. For example, he believed that the brain had nothing to do with thought, that it was merely a radiator for cooling the blood. Reportedly, Aristotle stuttered and bit his fingernails. He once pronounced, "Mothers are fonder than fathers of their children because they are more certain they are their own."

1988   Regency Plaza Hotel, Hollywood. Three-hundred-pound female impersonator Harris Glenn Milstead, 42, known by his stage name Divine, was found dead of asphyxiation (some accounts suggest heart failure) related to his obesity. Known for his cult classics *Pink Flamingos* (1972) and *Lust in the Dust* (1985), Divine had broadened his career (still in drag) to mainstream movies with the well-received *Hairspray* (1988). Divine's friend, director John Walters, called Divine "the girl next door—almost."

– March 8 –

1874   Buffalo, New York. Millard Fillmore, 74, thirteenth U.S. president, was particular about his diet and fitness. In January 1874, he said, "My health is perfect. I eat, drink and sleep as well as ever." In February, while he was shaving, his left hand became paralyzed. The numbness spread to his face. After two weeks of paralysis, he died on this date. His last words were, after he was offered food, "The nourishment is palatable."

1930   Washington D.C. William Howard Taft, 72, twenty-seventh U.S. president and later Chief Justice of the Supreme Court, died on this date of a heart attack in his sleep. Taft was the first president to be buried in Arlington National Cemetery.

Taft was the heaviest U.S. president at 352 pounds and kept getting stuck in his White House bathtub till he had an oversized one installed. His administration was noted for its honesty. Theodore Roosevelt chose Taft as his political heir but later became a rival of Taft's, which perhaps explains a comment Teddy once made: "Taft meant well, but he meant well feebly."

1941   Colon, Panama. Writer Sherwood Anderson, 64, remembered for *Tea and Sympathy*, died from peritonitis. He had swallowed a toothpick while eating an hors d'oeuvre at a cocktail party. The Centers for Disease Control reports that over 8,000 people a year in the United States are injured by toothpicks.

– March 9 –

1274   On the road to the Council of Lyons, St. Thomas Aquinas, 49, died several days after being knocked from his donkey when it trotted under a low tree limb. Legend says the donkey died of regret. What happened to the tree is unknown.

– March 10 –

1948   Czechoslovakia. Soviet agents "defenestrated" Czech nationalist leader Jan Masaryk—that is, they threw him out a window. The Soviets claimed he fell while relaxing on the window sill in a yoga position.

1948   Asheville, North Carolina. A fire in an asylum killed nine women, including Zelda Fitzgerald. She was 48 and had spent most of the previous twenty years in mental institutions.

– March 11 –

1888   A great blizzard struck the northeastern United States. Six hundred died as up to four feet of snow covered 40,000 square miles over three days. Two hundred died in New York City alone, and rail transport was halted for days. A worker at the Elizabeth, New Jersey, Singer factory froze to death while walking a quarter of a mile to the railroad station. So many telegraph lines fell under the weight of the snow that communication between New York City and Boston had to be routed through Great Britain by transatlantic cable. An observant fellow in Danbury, Connecticut, spotting a figure buried in a snowdrift, frantically dug it free. The stiff figure turned out to be a toppled cigar-store Indian.

– March 12 –

1507   Near Viana, Spain. When Pope Alexander VI died, his son Cesare Borgia tried to inherit that office (he had made it to archbishop at 16), but was pushed aside by rivals. He became a general for Navarre, and on this date, when raiders attacked his lines, he led a charge against them. Unfortunately, no one followed. He faced the enemy alone and was killed by a blow to the armpit at age 31 (see 8/18/1503).

1957   New York City. Actress Josephine Hull, 71, died of a cerebral hemorrhage. She won the 1951 Best Supporting Actress Academy Award for the film *Harvey* (1950). She played the put-upon sister of the visionary drinker played by Jimmy Stewart, whose boon companion was an invisible six-foot rabbit. Stewart had also performed in the play on Broadway. He swore that not a single matinee performance passed without some child in the audience loudly demanding, "Where's the bunny?"

1992   New Orleans. Frankie Thomas, 40, wanted her son Darrell, 14, to clean his messy room. He refused. They argued heatedly. The argument ended when Thomas shot to death her son. She told police that she had thought the gun was unloaded and that she had intended merely to frighten Darrell with the weapon.

– March 13 –

1619   London. Actor Richard Burbage, 52, one of Shakespeare's company, died, probably of a stroke. He is credited with painting the Felton portrait of Shakespeare. His epitaph reads: EXIT BURBAGE.

1901   Indianapolis. Benjamin Harrison, 67, twenty-third U.S. president, died following a chill that became pneumonia. He was buried at Crown Hill Cemetery in Indianapolis. The White House was wired for electric lights during his tenure. However, he and his wife were so fearful of electrocution that they barely dared touch a switch, and the lights, even in their bedroom, often burned all night because they were afraid to turn them off. Teddy Roosevelt called Harrison "a cold-blooded, narrow-minded, prejudiced, obstinate, timid old psalm-singing Indianapolis politician."

1938   Chicago. Clarence S. Darrow, 80, died of heart disease after two months in bed. The famous lawyer was a law school dropout, finishing his legal education on his own. He enjoyed cigars and used them to disrupt his opposition's summing up. He simply sat and let the ash grow longer and longer. To assure a long ash, Darrow would insert a wire in the cigar. The suspense of this simple act would distract the jury from the other lawyer's words.

     Darrow once said, "History repeats itself; that's one of the things that's wrong with history.

1964   Queens, New York. Kitty Genovese, 28, was stabbed to death over several hours during which her murderer left and returned. There were thirty-seven witnesses, but none called the police. No one wanted to get involved.

– March 14 –

1883   London. Karl Marx, 64, inventor of a theory of history that inspired more tyranny than any other human idea, died of natural causes in poverty. He refused to be a "moneymaking machine," subsisting on handouts and meager fees for his writing, much of which was done by his friend Friedrich Engels, the son of a wealthy textile manufacturer.

Marx disliked bathing and suffered all his life from severe boils and hemorrhoids. Of a Jewish family boasting a long line of rabbis, he rejected religion and was an anti-Semite. Marx grew his beard so he would resemble a bust of Zeus in his study. Only three of his seven children reached adulthood. Two of these killed themselves.

Reportedly, Marx's last words were, "Get out of here and leave me alone. Last words are for fools who haven't said enough already."

1915   Panama Pacific Exposition, San Francisco. Barnstormer Lincoln Beachey, called "the greatest aviator" by Orville Wright, performed daring stunts but showed signs of strain. For example, when the California governor tried to congratulate him after a flight, Beachey took off in his plane and, while circling the field, removed his clothes. He also took more elaborate safety precautions. On this date, he had straps wrapped around his waist, legs, and ankles so that he wouldn't fall while looping. He made a steep dive he called the "Death Dive" and was about to pull up when his airplane's wings ripped off. He plummeted into San Francisco Bay while 50,000 watched. The crash didn't kill him. He drowned while trying to free himself from the safety straps. Beachey once said, "They call me the Master Birdman, but they pay to see me die."

1932   Rochester, New York. Inventor-industrialist George Eastman, 76, after suffering from a long illness, shot himself through the heart. His suicide note read: "To my friends: My work is done. Why wait? E. G." Eastman had introduced the Kodak camera in 1888, launching the snapshot recording of everyday life. Originally, the film wasn't removable. The entire camera was sent back to the factory, where the film was developed.

– March 15 –

44 B.C.   Rome. Roman senators, seeking to preserve the Republic, attacked Julius Caesar, 56, with daggers. An autopsy revealed that only one of his many wounds was fatal. Plutarch thought Brutus, who was a member of the assassination conspiracy, was Caesar's illegitimate son. He was, at any rate, a friend, and his dagger blow hurt Caesar more than just physically. Caesar's famed last words were, "Et tu, Brute?" During the civil wars that followed, the Republic disappeared.

It was the Roman custom to make a death mask of the deceased. This mask, with the death masks of other family members, was carried in the funeral procession. Because of this custom, we have a good idea of Julius Caesar's appearance, for his death mask still ·exists.

1991 Philadelphia. Postal carrier Arnie Zebekow died of a heart attack. Shortly afterward, a woman calling herself "Betty" visited each of the patrons on Zebekow's mail route, collecting money to give to Zebekow's family. Betty kept the money and has since worked the same scam on seven other mail routes, whose carriers are quite alive.

– March 16 –

1898 Menton, France. Aubrey Beardsley, 25, died of tuberculosis. Having undergone a religious conversion, he wanted his erotic artwork burned, saying, "Destroy all obscene drawings; all bad drawings, too." The words reveal a sad, yet interesting view of the artist—even in extremis, a bit of vanity remains. Beardsley's last wishes weren't followed.

1971 Bal Harbour, Florida. Three-time New York governor and two-time Republican candidate for president Thomas E. Dewey, 68, was found dead in his room at the Seaview Hotel of a heart attack. He was vacationing and had finished eighteen holes of golf a few hours earlier. Dewey was to have been a guest at a St. Patrick's Day party at the Nixon White House. It was Dewey who had persuaded Eisenhower to choose Nixon as vice president.

When Dewey was running against Franklin Roosevelt in 1944, he discovered that the U.S. government had broken the Japanese diplomatic code before Pearl Harbor. Dewey suspected that Roosevelt had let the Japanese attack in order to get America into the war. Had Dewey told the American people of his suspicions, FDR could have been driven from office, but General George Marshall asked Dewey not to, saying the news might help the Japanese. Dewey kept quiet and lost the election.

– March 17 –

461? Saul-on-Strangford Lough in Downpatrick. St. Patrick died at about 71. This was the location of the first church he built in Ireland. He was buried in its churchyard. His death was brought about by years of hardship and labor. Just before he died, he spent forty days and nights upon Mount Aigli, fasting and praying for Ireland. Legend says he was much troubled by great multitudes of birds, which were so thick he couldn't see the sky, the sea, or even the land below. It was then revealed to him that they were the disguised forms of Ireland's saints— both past and future—sent by God in response to St. Patrick's prayers to bless all the tribes of Ireland.

St. Patrick wasn't Irish. He was a French missionary named Succat sent to Christianize Ireland. The shamrock became a symbol for Christian Ireland after he used it to explain the Holy Trinity.

1990 Lausanne, Switzerland. French film actress Germaine Lefebvre, 57, who used the stage name Capucine, committed suicide by jumping from her eighth-floor attic apartment. After working as a model, she went to Hollywood in the 1950s but soon returned to Europe. Her most prominent leading roles were with John Wayne in *North to Alaska* (1960), as Wayne's shady-lady girlfriend, and with Peter Sellers in *The Pink Panther* (1964), as Mrs. Inspector Clouseau. Capucine suffered from the enduring rumor that she was a transsexual. This untrue story stemmed from the fact that a well-known female impersonator also went by the name Capucine.

– March 18 –

1584 Moscow. Ivan the Terrible, 53, czar of Russia, died while playing chess. The illness that killed him is unknown, but it caused him "grievously to swell in the cods." As was the custom at that time, Ivan was made a monk on his deathbed (his hair was cut in a tonsure, and he was put in monk's robes) in the hope that this would assure his entry into heaven. This may not have been enough, as Ivan had killed and tortured thousands. He fed his pet fish and bears with his enemies.

One servant who had displeased him was hanged by his heels and hacked to bits. In a fit of anger, he had struck his own son with his cane, killing him. A rumor that the Russian city of Novgorod was thinking of becoming part of Lithuania prompted Ivan to torture its citizens for five weeks, then kill all 60,000 of them.

1845   Fort Wayne, Indiana. John Chapman, 70, known as "Johnny Appleseed," died. He had made a trip to an orchard to repair damages and caught a chill, which led to fatal pneumonia. For fifty years, Chapman had traveled the American frontier, planting apple orchards by the thousands.

1937   New London, Texas. A school explosion killed 413. The school was hooked to a "waste" gas line from a nearby refinery. The gas was odorless, and unnoticed leaks filled the basement. An errant spark blew the building off its foundation; then the roof collapsed. A blackboard in a classroom read: "Oil and gas are East Texas' greatest mineral blessings. Without them, this school would not be here, and none of us would be learning our lessons."

1965   Rome. Three-hundred-pound Farouk I, 45, the last monarch of Egypt, died after overindulging in food. He had eaten a dozen oysters, a leg of lamb, two oranges, beans, fried potatoes, two bottles of Coke, one bottle of ginger soda, and a glass of mineral water. He topped this with a Havana cigar.

Farouk was a compulsive thief. After he was deposed, the Egyptian government discovered Winston Churchill's gold watch and the shah of Iran's sword and medals in his collection. The latter were stolen from the shah's casket as it passed in state through Egypt.

Errol Flynn observed of one of Farouk's appearances, "He came to be entertained, to be fed, to look on, and to belch."

– March 19 –

1943   Chicago. Frank Nitti, Al Capone's enforcer, 47, shot himself to death while walking along the Illinois Railroad tracks. He was about to be sent to jail for extorting money from the film industry through his control of film unions. The measure of his reluctance to go to jail is that when his first shot failed to kill him, he shot himself again.

1957   Richmond, Virginia. For thirty years, she gave psychic advice to the rich and powerful in Washington. She said Franklin Roosevelt would become president before he was nominated. She predicted the depression, picked Truman over Dewey, and thought the Maginot Line would fail. She helped despairing parents find the body of their missing child, and even informed a doctor that his dog, whom a kennel claimed had died, had actually been sold. In 1944, army officers quizzed her on where the Allies should invade France. Who was this miracle? She was "Lady Wonder," a horse with a white streak down her nose.

Lady Wonder answered questions using a sort of horse typewriter. She stumped thousands, but probably operated in the same fashion as previous "wonder" animals. The owner, Claudia Fonda, trained the animal to react to tiny signals. Human confederates would secretly watch as customers wrote down the answers to personal questions (writing was supposed to help them concentrate on the telepathic transmission). Then, the humans would pass the information to Claudia, who would guide the horse. As is the case with many human prognosticators, positive results based on vague guesses were trumpeted, while errors were ignored.

Lady Wonder died on this date of a heart attack at 33. She was typing out EISENHOWER at the time. Her bones lie in the ritzy Pet Memorial Cemetery in Henrico County, Virginia.

1980   Betterton, Maryland. City Mayor Monica Myers, 70, took her duties seriously. On this date, she was inspecting the waste treatment plant by herself. She was testing for chlorine and sediment when she slipped from a catwalk, falling into a huge tank of human waste. No one heard her cries, and she drowned.

– March 20 –

1899   Sing Sing. Martha M. Place became the first woman to be executed by electrocution. She had murdered her step-daughter.

1964   Dublin, Ireland. Irish playwright Brendan Frances Behan died of a combination of ailments that were aggravated by alcohol abuse. He was 41. He once said, "Critics are like eunuchs in a harem: they know how it's done, they've seen it done every day, but they're unable to do it themselves."

1974   Bozeman, Montana. TV newsman Chet Huntley died at 62 of lung cancer.

1974   Santa Monica, California. Actor Ed Platt, best known for his role as Chief on TV's *Get Smart*, died at 58 of a heart attack.

– March 21 –

1617   Gravesend, Kent, England. Although the Indian princess Pocahontas, daughter of Powhatan, saved Captain John Smith from beheading, she married another English colonist, John Rolfe. They traveled to England, where they were received by King James I and Queen Anne. The Rolfes were about to return to Virginia when Pocahontas contracted smallpox and died at 22. She was buried at Gravesend. Rolfe returned to the New World and was killed in 1622 in an Indian attack led by his uncle-in-law.

Pocahontas's only child, Thomas Rolfe, was educated in England but lived in Virginia, where he left many descendants. The princess's name was actually Matoaka. "Pocahontas" was a nickname meaning "playful."

– March 22 –

1687   Paris. Conductor Jean-Baptiste Lully, 54, was conducting a work he had written to celebrate the recovery of Louis XIV from a painful surgery. While using a large staff to beat time, he accidentally stabbed his toe with it. The toe became gangrenous, but he refused to have it amputated. The infection spread to his leg and after he refused to allow it to be amputated, he died.

– March 23 –

1989   Daytona Beach, Florida. Every year, thousands of college students converge on this city to spend their spring breaks partying. A grim part of this tradition is balcony falls. In 1989, four died and seven were injured in this way. On this date, a 22-year-old Illinois student was using his balcony to play a game of Frisbee. He lunged after an errant throw and plummeted to his death.

– March 24 –

1603 Richmond, Surrey, England. Elizabeth I, 69, died of a gum infection. She had been certain she would die and had refused food and medicine. Her last words: "All my possessions for a moment of time." She was the last Tudor monarch.

Elizabeth created a vogue that lasted centuries for wearing wigs. She wore them because when she contracted smallpox at 29, she lost all her hair. It never grew back.

Elizabeth was known as the "Virgin Queen" because she never married (hence the naming of Virginia). She said, "I would rather be a beggar and single, than a Queen and married ... I should call the wedding ring the yoke ring."

1882 Cambridge, Massachusetts. Poet Henry Wadsworth Longfellow died at 75. He had been in delicate health for a long time. He was buried in Cambridge's Mount Auburn Cemetery. Longfellow was the first American to have a bust placed in the Poet's Corner of Westminster Abbey. Among his poems are "The Song of Hiawatha" and "Paul Revere's Ride." His poem "The Courtship of Miles Standish" was about two of his relatives, John and Priscilla Alden. His friend the essayist Ralph Waldo Emerson (see 4/27/1882) attended Longfellow's funeral. Emerson had become senile, and said, "I cannot recall the name of my friend, but he was a good man."

Longfellow is always pictured wearing a beard. On July 9, 1861, he was napping while his wife was sealing locks of their daughters' hair in wax packets as keepsakes. When burning wax spilled on her dress, it caught fire. Longfellow tried to extinguish the flames with a rug but failed. The flames were finally smothered by his embrace, but his wife died the next day. Longfellow's hands and face were badly burned, and he grew the beard to hide the scars.

– March 25 –

1911 New York City. A fire in the Triangle Shirtwaist Factory killed 145 people, mostly young girls. The doors had been locked, and fifty of the girls jumped to their deaths from high windows rather than burn.

1990 New York City. Cuban immigrant Julio Gonzalez, 36, argued with his girlfriend, a ticket seller for the Happy Land social club, an unlicensed bar. Bouncers threw him out, but Gonzalez secretly returned with a jug of gasoline, which he splashed around the club and ignited. The blaze killed 87. Most died of smoke inhalation. Some expired so fast that they were found holding drinks at the bar. Others perished in the horrible stampede to escape. Some tried to smash through the walls. Only three got out. Gonzalez's girlfriend survived. Arrested with his sneakers still damp with gasoline, Gonzalez received a sentence of only twenty-five years. It was the worst fire in New York City since the Triangle Shirtwaist Factory fire on this same date in 1911.

– March 26 –

1827 Vienna. Ludwig van Beethoven, fifty-six, died of cirrhosis of the liver and pneumonia. His last words: "Friends, applaud, the Comedy is over." Another version says his doctor prescribed wine, but the vintage that Beethoven wanted was slow arriving. He satisfied himself with lesser wines. When the prescribed wine arrived, Beethoven said, "Pity, pity, too late," and died. Still another version has the deaf musician saying, "I shall hear in Heaven." He was buried in Vienna's Central Cemetery.

Beethoven had been in poor health for years—plagued with irritable bowels, an autoimmune disease, migraine, and the deafness that almost drove him to suicide. It was, however, another's depression that led to Beethoven's death. Beethoven had assumed the guardianship of an orphaned nephew. When the nephew tried to kill himself the night before a university exam, Beethoven, not stopping to dress warmly, took his charge to his brother, whom he felt could dispel the boy's suicidal mood. Following the long, cold trip home, Beethoven fell ill. After two months of suffering, he died.

1881 Madison, Wisconsin. Old Abe the Eagle died. He was the regimental mascot of the Eighth Wisconsin of the Union Army during the Civil War and was in thirty-six battles, during which he soared over the battlefield squawking disapproval of the Rebels. He lost a few feathers but survived the war and spent years touring. He earned $80,000 at Philadelphia's Centennial Fair. A cold spell forced his keeper to keep Old Abe indoors for several days, and the eagle stopped eating and weakened. The bird died while his keeper rocked him in his arms.

1892 Camden, New Jersey. Poet Walt Whitman, 72, died of a cerebral hemorrhage aggravated by tuberculosis and cerebral arteriosclerosis. One of his lungs was so infected that it had collapsed. Whitman had suffered many strokes since the publication of *Leaves of Grass* in 1855. In 1888, a stroke confined the poet to his bed and confused his mind and speech. He partially recovered, but by 1891, he was coughing up infected mucus and blood. He lingered in a stupor for nearly three months before dying. He was buried in Camden's Harleigh Cemetery.

Whitman was a homosexual, and contemporary poet Allen Ginsberg claims to be able to trace a chain of male lovers back to Whitman.

Whitman once said, "I no doubt deserved my enemies, but I don't believe I deserved my friends."

– March 27 –

1931 London. Writer Arnold Bennett, 63, died of typhoid. He had sought to demonstrate to some friends that the water in a Paris hotel was safe by drinking it. It wasn't.

Bennett started out as a clerk, but his editorship of a women's magazine led to a literary career and enough success so that he could afford a yacht and an actress mistress. Bennett once said, "It is well, when judging a friend, to remember that he is judging you with the same godlike and superior impartiality."

1968   Near Moscow. Russian cosmonaut Yuri Gagarin, 34, the first
        man to orbit the Earth, died in an air crash. It was recently
        revealed that the crash was the result of an air traffic
        controller's error.

– March 28 –

1941   River Ouse near Rodmell, Sussex, England. British writer
        Virginia Woolf, 59, who had suffered severe breakdowns,
        filled her pockets with stones and went wading in deep water.
        In her diary, she once compared death to Niagara Falls and as
        "active, positive, like all the rest [of life's experiences], exciting;
        & of great importance—as an experience. 'The one experience
        I shall never describe' I said to Vita [Sackville-West]
        yesterday."
           Virginia's sister, Vanessa Bell, wasn't an intellectual. At a
        dinner party she couldn't think of a thing to say to her dining
        partner, so she asked him if he was interested in politics. He
        replied that he was, explaining that he was the prime minister
        of England.

1969   Walter Reed Hospital, Washington, D.C. Dwight D.
        Eisenhower, 78, thirty-fourth U.S. president, died of heart
        disease. He had suffered from heart problems, gallstones, and
        inflammation of the intestines since the 1950s. In February
        1969, he underwent intestinal surgery from which he never
        completely recovered. After a month of desperate treatment,
        he died with his wife, Mamie, at his side. His last words, "I've
        always loved my wife. I've always loved my children. I've
        always loved my grandchildren. I've always loved my coun-
        try." He lay in state in the Rotunda of the Capitol in
        Washington, dressed in full uniform, which included the
        short jacket christened the "Eisenhower jacket" during World
        War II. His military-issue coffin cost $80.
           Eisenhower, one of America's most successful commanders,
        was the son of pacifist parents and never directly led troops
        under fire. During World War II, he became involved with
        his driver, Kay Summersby. According to Harry Truman,
        Eisenhower wrote General George Marshall, his superior,
        after the war, asking to be released from duty. He wanted to
        divorce Mamie and marry Kay. Marshall refused, and Truman

said he destroyed the correspondence to protect Eisenhower's reputation.

Of the presidency, Eisenhower said, "You know, once in a while I get to the point, with everybody staring at me, where I want to go back indoors and pull down the curtains."

– March 29 –

1848   New York City. Millionaire John Jacob Astor, 85, died of natural causes. He had been in feeble health for years, unable to take any food other than breast milk. Even his friends remarked upon his great love of money. The richest landlord in the United States, with a $20–$30 million estate, he was cajoling his assistants to squeeze the rent out of a widow just days before his death. One friend related how, in his eighties, Astor had chartered a boat for a sail. The friend teasingly told the parsimonious Astor that the boat was costing Astor twenty-five cents a minute even as they were walking to the docks. Astor broke into a trot.

– March 30 –

1840   The Asylum of the Bon Sauveur, Caen. British fashion trendsetter Beau Brummel, 61, died in madness, poverty, and rags. Brummel showed signs of imbecility in 1837, imagining that he was holding receptions for beautiful women and important people. The former dandy lost his habits of personal hygiene, becoming so "loathsome that an attendant could hardly be found for him." In happier days, Brummel had made red the color of hunting rigs and popularized trousers.

1968   The Lower East Side, New York City. Two children found the corpse of a speed freak. Officials blamed heart disease related to drug abuse for the death. The dead man was buried in New York's Potter's Field as a John Doe because no one recognized him. A year and a half later, when his father was dying and wished to see his son, a search matched the corpse's fingerprints to those of Bobby Driscoll, 31. Bobby had been a child star for the Disney Studio, appearing in *Song of the South* (1946) and later as the model and voice of Peter Pan. His career fell apart when he began using drugs at 17.

— March 31 —

1631   London. Poet John Donne died at about 59. The cause of his death isn't certain, but was probably chronic tonsillitis, which had troubled him most of his life. Donne, a well-known Anglican priest and dean of St. Paul's Cathedral, prepared for death by having his portrait painted while he posed in his shroud, so that after Donne's death, the stone carver would have a model for Donne's tomb effigy at St. Paul's. Donne's last words were, "I were miserable if I might not die. Thy Kingdom come, Thy Will be done.

1727   London. Sir Isaac Newton died at 84. He had suffered from inflammation of the lungs and gout. Newton was buried in Westminster Abbey. Remembered for his scientific achievements concerning calculus, light, and gravity, Newton also spent twenty-five years secretly studying the occult. The story of the apple inspiring his theory about gravity was first told by Voltaire, who claimed he had it directly from Newton's niece. Newton's last words: "I do not know what I seem to the world, but to myself I appear to have been like a boy playing upon the seashore and diverting myself by now and then finding a smoother pebble or prettier shell than ordinary, while the great ocean of truth lay before me all undiscovered."

EM

– April 1 –

1984   Los Angeles. The day before his 45th birthday, Motown singer Marvin Gaye was shot to death by his father, Marvin Gaye, Sr., 70. The elder Gaye was charged with manslaughter. Neighbors said the pair had been arguing over the younger Gaye's birthday party plans. Gaye is known for "Heard It Through the Grapevine," "What's Going On" and "Ain't No Mountain High Enough."

– April 2 –

1988   Louisburg, North Carolina. Ivan Lester McGuire, 35, was an experienced parachutist who had become interested in videotaping fellow jump club members as they hurtled to the earth. He wore his camera on his helmet and was quite particular about how it was adjusted. On this date, he spent so much care on his camera that he forgot to put on his parachute. Neither he nor his companions noticed his lapse, and McGuire jumped. His videotape was salvaged. It shows the other jumpers holding hands, performing stunts, and then opening their chutes. It then shows the ground rushing up fast. McGuire fell 10,500 feet, hitting the ground at 150 m.p.h.

On August 26, 1989, Louis F. Pinick, 46, was similarly videotaping members of the Oz Parachuting Club over Kansas City, Missouri. Pinick made three 8,000-foot jumps. The first two went just fine. On the third, Pinick apparently forgot to activate either his main or his emergency chute and fell to his death.

1989   St. Louis. Joe Rutherford of Memphis, Tennessee, was flying to a training program in Sioux City, Iowa, and he was enjoying the trip. With three companions, Rutherford consumed quite a bit of liquor and, while changing planes at Lambert Airport in St. Louis, became excessively playful. According to police, he stole an electric cart and raced through the terminal "in a careless manner, scattering people." Airport personnel gave chase. Rutherford jumped from the cart and ran into a service room. Seeking escape, he jumped down a trash chute. His body passed through an electric eye that activated the motor of the trash compactor he landed in, where he was quickly crushed to death.

The training program Rutherford was traveling to dealt with how to operate heavy equipment safely.

– April 3 –

1882   St. Joseph, Missouri. While atop a chair feather-dusting and straightening a picture of a racehorse in his Lafayette Street home, Jesse James, 34, was shot behind the right ear for a $10,000 reward by Robert Ford, a member of his gang. The ball from the .44-caliber revolver was fired at a range of just three feet. James's last words were, "It's awfully hot today." James was buried in his mother's backyard in Kearney, Missouri. Offended by tourists, she moved the remains to Mount Olivet Cemetery in Kearney.

James and his brother Frank had served with Confederate guerrillas during the Civil War (his first killing was the murder of a Union officer). When peace came, they kept on raiding. Local citizens, whom Jesse plied with stolen cash, protected him from the law. They, and others since, saw him as a Robin Hood combating the banks and the railroads.

Ford received only a portion of the reward. He toured with a show reenacting the killing. Jesse-worshipers booed him from the stage till one outraged James fan in a Colorado mining camp blasted Ford in the neck with a sawed-off shotgun, killing him. The owner of the house Jesse was shot in sold every stick of furniture and smashed the bloody floor into splinters he peddled for twenty-five cents. James's mother sold tours of the family home. James's brother Frank (after obtaining a pardon) sold pebbles off Jesse's grave—replenishing the pile whenever it got low. James's relatives were the backers of the first Jesse James movie in 1920.

Hollywood made many films glorifying Jesse. The worst of these had a scene wherein poor, misused Jesse escapes the crooked lawmen by riding his horse off a cliff and into a river far below. The stunt was accomplished by forcing a horse to leap to its death while carrying a dummy. The incident led to more humane regulation of animal stunts.

– April 4 –

1841   Washington, D.C. William H. Harrison, 68, ninth U.S. president, died after thirty-one days in office. He was buried in Pioneer Cemetery in North Bend, Ohio. Harrison was the first U.S. president to die in office. He had refused to wear an overcoat or a hat for his inaugural address in a frigid drizzle and caught cold. The address was over 9,000 words long—the longest ever given (Washington's was 135 words). Despite his cold, Harrison attended three inaugural balls, where he danced and drank convivially. The cold developed into pneumonia. His doctors applied mustard plasters, bled him, and purged him. He had long suffered from ulcers, and the treatment caused intense pain. Just before he died, he addressed an unseen visitor: "Sir, I wish you to understand the true principles of government. I wish them carried out. I ask nothing more."

1968   Memphis. Civil rights leader Martin Luther King, Jr. 39, was shot through the neck when he stepped onto his motel room balcony. He died an hour later. Escaped convict James Earl Ray was identified as the assassin from possessions found in the building the shot had come from. Ray made his way via

Canada to Britain, where he was arrested. He pleaded guilty and was sentenced to ninety-nine years in prison. He soon recanted his confession and has since maintained that he was just a patsy for a mysterious, foreign, professional killer. Ray was certainly an inept crook. He once left his wallet behind while robbing a bank, and on another occasion managed to fall out of his getaway car. Nevertheless, it was widely rumored that a bounty had been offered for the assassination of King. Ray was precisely the kind of lowbrow crook that would take such rumors seriously and attempt to cash in on them.

King once observed, "Nothing in the world is more dangerous than sincere ignorance."

– April 5 –

1960   London. English publisher Peter Llewellyn Davies, 68, killed himself. As a child, he had inspired author James Barrie to write *Peter Pan*.

1976   En route to Houston, Texas, from Acapulco, Mexico. Billionaire aviation pioneer Howard Hughes, 70, died of kidney failure on his way by air to a Texas hospital. He had become eccentric, letting his hair and nails grow long, and weighed less than 100 pounds. For years it had been rumored that he was dead. Walter Kane wrote, "Hughes was the only man I ever knew who had to die to prove he had been alive."

Hughes's $2 billion fortune was tied up in the courts for eight years because he left no will and no widow. A will presented by a Utah gas attendant was thrown out of court. Some say that it was genuine, but that the gas attendant destroyed his case by the suspicious manner in which he advanced it. A claim by actress Terry Moore, who said she was secretly married to Hughes in 1949 during a cruise to Mexico, was settled when the family paid Moore $390,000. The remainder of the estate was split between the state of Texas, the federal government, Hughes's relatives, and many lawyers.

Hughes had inherited a tool company from his father. He expanded it tremendously, then went to Hollywood to produce movies, including *Hell's Angels* (1930), for which he won an Oscar, *Scarface* (1932), and *The Outlaw* (1941). *The Outlaw* was an ordinary Western till Hughes decided to highlight the chest of his leading lady, Jane Russell. He had a special seamless bra designed for a scene where she bent forward, but was unsatisfied, spending days retaking the shot again and again till he got exactly what he wanted. By the standards of that era, it was hot stuff. Film folk thought Hughes was nuts, but the effort paid off. The sensational gossip and a suggestive ad campaign made the movie a success. Years later, Jane Russell revealed the "hidden" story. She didn't like Hughes's uncomfortable bra. She said, "I put on my own bra and put Kleenex over the seams and I went out and Howard took a look and said, 'Okay,' and went right ahead and he never knew the difference."

Pundit Ted Morgan said, "Howard Hughes was able to afford the luxury of madness, like a man who not only thinks he is Napoleon but hires an army to prove it."

– April 6 –

1971   New York City. Composer Igor Stravinsky, 88, died of heart failure in his apartment. He was buried in the "Russian Corner" of San Michele Cemetery in Venice. His works included *The Firebird*, *Petrushka*, and *The Rite of Spring*. The last touched off a riot when it was first performed.

Stravinsky spent his life traveling from place to place performing. He had few longtime abodes. At the time of his death, he had just moved into a Fifth Avenue apartment. His last words were to his nurse as she gave him a wheelchair tour of the apartment: "How lovely. This belongs to me, it is my home."

1990   Redwood City, California. John James McDonald survived the San Francisco earthquake of 1906, but lost his parents. He was just six years old. A kindly couple took him in and he continued to live in the area. When the quake of October 17, 1989, struck, McDonald, now 90, was in his apartment in Belmont, just twenty-five miles south of San Francisco. McDonald suffered severe head injuries. He died of these injuries on this date.

– April 7 –

1891 Bridgeport, Connecticut. P. T. Barnum, 80, died of heart disease. His first success was in 1835, when he exhibited a slave woman whom he claimed was the 161-year-old nurse of the infant George Washington. When the rush to see the woman slowed, scathing letters calling her a fraud appeared in local papers. The controversy renewed ticket sales. Barnum had written the letters.

Barnum continued to exhibit novelties that proved his principle that "a sucker is born every minute." Typical of these was the "Feejee Mermaid." Thousands swarmed to see what was actually a dead monkey sewn to a big fish. When Irishmen packed his museum on St. Patrick's Day, Barnum placed a sign reading THIS WAY TO THE EGRESS over the back door. Curious customers went through expecting to see some strange creature, only to find themselves in the street with the sudden knowledge that an "egress" is an exit.

Barnum had his failures, however. His attempts to purchase the birthplace of William Shakespeare (he planned to disassemble it and move it to America), the ruins of Pompeii (same plan), and Niagara Falls (he was going to put a fence around it and charge admission) all fell through. In 1855, Barnum lost his fortune when he was swindled in a business venture. To make things worse, his underinsured museum burned. His friends, including the midget Tom Thumb, rescued him, and Barnum regained his fortune. He became a Republican member of the Connecticut legislature, where he fought railroad monopolies and backed the Fourteenth Amendment, which gave blacks citizenship. He was nearly nominated for the vice presidency in 1864 by the Republicans. Had he been, he would have succeeded the assassinated Lincoln as president of the United States.

Barnum had been seriously ill for some time and was so certain he would die that he let the New York *Evening Sun* run his obituary early so he could read it himself. He died in just a few weeks. The great showman's last words: "How were the circus receipts tonight at Madison Square Garden?"

1955 Los Angeles. Silent film star Theda Bara, 65, died of cancer. She was the epitome of the Hollywood "vamp." Her studio said she was of French and Arab descent and had been born in Egypt. Actually, she was Theodosia Goodman, the daughter of a Jewish tailor in Chillicothe, Ohio.

— April 8 —

1887   The Charity Hospital of Louisiana, New Orleans. A 45-year-old patient was recorded as dying from masturbation.

1950   London. Russian ballet dancer Vaslav Nijinsky died at nearly 60, following a brief illness caused by nephritis. He had been in a coma but roused long enough to make the sign of the cross and say "Good-bye" to his wife and family.

Nijinsky gave his last professional performance in 1917 in Montevideo. Two years later, he was sent to a Swiss sanitarium for treatment of schizophrenia, where he remained till 1940. His wife, Romola, credited over 271 insulin shock treatments with improving his mental state enough for him to leave, although he remained mentally ill till his death. Nijinsky and his wife wanted to go to the United States via Italy, but World War II prevented this. They settled in Budapest, but the bombing of that city forced them into the countryside. When the Russian Army arrived in 1945, Nijinsky, who hadn't heard his native language in years and who usually communicated in grunts, welcomed them. While visiting a Russian barracks, he danced to the sound of balalaikas and an accordion. Nijinsky and his wife moved to Egham in Surrey, England, where he spent his last days. Upon his death, doctors dissected his feet, hoping to discover what gave him his dancing skill. They found them completely ordinary.

1973   Mougins, France. Painter Pablo Picasso, 91, died of pulmonary edema at his hilltop villa of Notre Dame de Vie. He had been ill for weeks. His second wife, Jacquèline Roque, 47, was at his bedside. His last words were: "Drink to me."

Fernande Olivier lived with Picasso for seven years when he was a struggling artist. When she left in 1912, she spurned the portraits he had painted of her and took just a small, heart-shaped mirror as a keepsake. She thought his abstract portraits of her were unflattering. In 1966, she died in poverty. A few years after this, one of Picasso's portraits of her sold for

$790,000. Picasso himself was once so poor that he had to burn his canvases to keep from freezing.

Picasso said, "Computers are useless. They can only give you answers."

– April 9 –

1626   The earl of Arundel's house, near Highgate, London. English philosopher, writer, and scientist Sir Francis Bacon died at 65. He had wondered if cold would preserve meat and experimented by having a chicken stuffed with snow. He discovered that cold did slow putrefaction, but he also contracted a fatal case of bronchitis. Bacon is credited with introducing gunpowder bombs to Europe and predicted the automobile, airplane, microscope, and telescope. It has been rumored that Bacon was the son of Elizabeth I, and some believe Bacon wrote the plays credited to Shakespeare. Bacon's last words, "My name and memory I leave to man's charitable speeches, to foreign nations and to the next age."

1991   Tampa, Florida. Supermarket worker Joseph LaRose, 31, was unloading a six-foot rack from the back of a truck. The rack slipped, falling upon LaRose and crushing his skull under 500 pounds of "Nutty Buddies" ice cream bars.

– April 10 –

1909   Putney, England. British poet Algernon Charles Swinburne died five days after his 72nd birthday. He had written his friend A. H. Bullen comparing himself to Shakespeare's King Lear, who died after wandering madly around the heath in a storm. Swinburne, perhaps matching his own metaphor, also went frolicking around the heath in a storm. He wound up with double pneumonia. By the following day, Swinburne was delirious, raving in Greek. He died surrounded by cables and cards congratulating him on his birthday.

Swinburne had a fetish for babies and while at Eton had developed a passion for flogging. He also liked monkeys and servant boys. One boy claimed to have visited Swinburne while he was living in a tent with a monkey dressed as a woman. The boy said that Swinburne tried to seduce him and that the monkey, envious of these attentions, attacked the boy. The boy left but was persuaded to return for lunch. Swinburne served grilled monkey.

1919   Cuautla, Mexico. Emiliano Zapata, 39, anarchist, revolutionary, bandit, and butcher, had lost much of his support, so he was interested when an enemy colonel offered to switch sides. The colonel proved he was sincere by attacking his former allies and executing prisoners. Convinced, Zapata, with ten men, entered the colonel's fort, where the colonel had his men drawn up for review. The colonel raised his sword, ordered his men to present arms to the rolling of drums, and lowered his sword. The troops fired, blasting Zapata and associates to ribbons. The colonel collected a $50,000 reward and was promoted to brigadier general.

– April 11 –

1926   Santa Rosa, California. Horticulturalist Luther Burbank, 67, died of natural causes. His last words were: "I don't feel good." On an earlier occasion, he pronounced, "Men should stop fighting among themselves and start fighting insects."

– April 12 –

A.D.   Rome. The Roman philosopher Seneca had been tutor and
65   adviser to the emperor Nero, but after a falling out, Nero commanded Seneca to kill himself. Seneca, who was about 61, invited several friends to his house, where he calmly slit his veins and took poison. Because the effect was slow, Seneca sat in a hot bath to speed the bleeding. He chatted with his friends as he waited for death. Nero's soldiers grew impatient, so they carried Seneca to the stove that heated the bath water and suffocated him with steam.

Seneca believed that there was no afterlife. In *Troades* (as translated by John Wilmot, earl of Rochester), he wrote, "Dead, we become the lumber of the world, / And to that mass of matter shall be swept / Where things destroyed with things unborn are kept."

1945   The "Little White House," Warm Springs, Georgia. Franklin Roosevelt, 63, thirty-second U.S. president, died of a cerebral hemorrhage. His last words, before collapsing into a chair, were, "I have a terrific headache." He had been in declining health for years, his heart weakened by polio and heavy smoking. Roosevelt was carefully embalmed and placed in an expensive, handcrafted, copper-lined coffin. His Washington funeral procession and service were elaborate and emotional. He was buried at his Hyde Park home. Later, his wife, Eleanor, discovered funeral directions in his papers. He hadn't wanted embalming or a big procession, only a simple grave marker, which he got, although Congress immediately began planning a memorial structure similar to Lincoln's or Jefferson's. This memorial is still in the planning stage.

Dean Acheson worked for Roosevelt but didn't relish the experience. He said, "It didn't flatter me to have the squire of Hyde Park come by and speak to me familiarly, as though I were a stable boy and I was supposed to pull my lock and say, 'Aye, aye, sir.'"

– April 13 –

1956   Arlington, Virginia. Samuel J. Seymour, 96, died of natural causes. He was the last eyewitness to the assassination of Abraham Lincoln. He was five when his parents brought him to Ford's Theatre to see the president. His mother lifted him high so he could get a view. He thought Lincoln "looked stern because of his whiskers." He didn't understand what had happened when Booth killed Lincoln, but he saw Booth jump to the stage. He thought Booth had accidentally fallen and tugged on his mother, urging her, "Hurry, hurry, let's go help the poor man who fell down."

– April 14 –

1685   A public house in the Minotries, England. Poet Thomas Otway, 33, had fallen on hard times and was starving.

Supposedly, he was given some bread, but he so eagerly swallowed it that he choked and died.

1861   Fort Sumter, South Carolina. The bombardment of Fort Sumter on April 12, 1861, started the Civil War, but during the thirty-four-hour exchange, no one was killed. The Confederates destroyed most of the fort's guns and stores, making it impossible to continue resistance. During the surrender, Union soldiers fired a salute to the American flag as it was lowered. One of the guns exploded, and Gunner Daniel Hough, Battery E, First U.S. Artillery, became the first man killed in the Civil War.

1912   The North Atlantic. H.M.S. *Titanic* sank after hitting an iceberg. Fifteen hundred died. Her captain, wishing to set a crossing record, had ignored ice warnings. As the alarm was sounded, few realized their danger. One of the radio operators jokingly suggested to his colleague John Philips, "Why not send out this new call, SOS—it might be your last chance to send it." It was.

Fourteen years earlier, Morgan Robertson had written a novel called *Futility* about an ocean liner of the same size and design as the *Titanic*. The fictional liner was luxurious and supposed to be unsinkable, and it sailed the same route as the *Titanic*. It also struck an iceberg and sank with great loss of life. The name of the fictional ship was *Titan*.

The crew and passengers of the *Titanic* reported seeing the lights of a ship nearby when the *Titanic* was sinking. Signal rockets were fired, but the ship disappeared. Investigators later identified the vessel as the S.S. *Californian* under the command of Captain Stanley Lord. Lord denied it, claiming that he had been twenty-three miles away, had seen nothing, and couldn't have responded soon enough if he had. The authorities and the public condemned him for not rescuing the *Titanic's* passengers. He died in 1962, still under this stigma.

Recently, an autobiography of a Norwegian sea captain, Hendrich Næss, revealed that another vessel was probably the ship that was spotted by the *Titanic*. Næss wrote that he served as first officer on a Norwegian seal hunting ship, the *Samson*. The crew were illegally taking seals when they saw a large vessel approaching, just ten nautical miles away. When this vessel fired rockets, they were certain it was a revenue vessel calling for reinforcements to trap them. Fearing prison,

they fled. With no radio, they never heard the *Titanic*'s SOS.
They returned to port a month later to discover they'd run
from the *Titanic*. In 1926, the Norwegian press reported the
incident, but the non-Norwegian press ignored it. Næss said
that the *Samson* could have easily taken aboard all of the crew
and passengers of the *Titanic*.

1934   Hollywood. Actor Karl Dane, 48, was, aptly enough, Danish.
He got his big break in 1925, when he played a heroic soldier
in King Vidor's hit *The Big Parade*. He made more films, but
when the talkies came, his career ended. Dane had a thick
Danish accent. He wound up selling hot dogs near the
entrance of the studio where he had starred. On this date,
Dane spread out all his clippings, reviews, and contracts, lay
down upon them, and shot himself.

– April 15 –

1865   Washington, D.C. Abraham Lincoln, sixteenth U.S. president,
died at 56. He had been shot in the back of the head by John
Wilkes Booth the previous evening while attending a performance of *Our American Cousin* at Ford's Theatre. With him
were his wife Mary Todd Lincoln, a young officer named
Major Henry Rathbone (a distant relative of Basil Rathbone),
and Rathbone's fiancée, Clara Harris. Mrs. Lincoln eventually
went mad. Rathbone and Harris were married, but years later,
while in Europe, Rathbone, whom Booth had stabbed, killed
his wife. He spent the rest of his life in a Swiss insane asylum.

Lincoln, who became a successful lawyer, had little formal
schooling (as a result, he moved his lips when he read). Yet his
Gettysburg Address remains one of the finest orations in the
English language. At the time of its delivery, the fashion was
for long, ornate, bombastic speeches. Many thought the
address was insultingly short and unartistic. The *Patriot* of
nearby Harrisburg pompously observed, "The President acted
without sense...so let us pass over his silly remarks." The
Chicago Times declaimed, "The cheek of every American
must tingle with shame as he reads the silly, flat utterances of
the President." The *Times* of London grandly pronounced,
"Anything more dull and commonplace it wouldn't be easy to
produce."

Lincoln's body was carefully embalmed for the long train trip back to Springfield, Illinois. Along the route, people gathered to watch the black-draped funeral train pass. Lincoln was buried in Springfield's Oak Ridge Cemetery. In 1876, grave robbers unearthed the coffins of Lincoln and his wife but were caught before they could get away. Because Illinois had no law against body-snatching, the thugs were sentenced to just a year in jail for breaking and entering. It was necessary to verify that the bodies were inside the coffins. Officials discovered Lincoln to be remarkably well preserved. The bodies were reburied. In 1901, a new marble tomb was constructed, and Lincoln's son Robert Todd Lincoln directed that the coffins be sealed within six feet of solid concrete.

Years before the assassination, Edwin Booth, John Wilkes Booth's brother, saved a young gentleman who had fallen from a railroad platform. Edwin hauled the fellow back just before a train would have struck him. The young man was Robert Todd Lincoln.

1962   Hollywood. Actress Clara Blandick, 80, appeared in many films, including *Tom Sawyer*, (1930), *Anthony Adverse* (1936), *Gentleman Jim* (1942), and *A Stolen Life* (1946). Her most famous role was Auntie Em in *The Wizard of Oz* (1939). Clara suffered from crippling arthritis and failing eyesight. On this date, she got her hair done, donned her best dress, looked through some souvenirs, and took an overdose of sleeping pills. To be sure that she would die, she secured a plastic bag around her head.

1982   City Park West Municipal Golf Course, New Orleans. Michael Scaglione, 26, was on the thirteenth hole when he made a bad shot. He furiously hurled his club against his golf cart. The club broke in two, and the club head whirled back, its sharp shaft stabbing him in the neck. Scaglione's jugular vein was severed. He might have survived, but he pulled the club head from his neck, letting his blood flow unhindered. He soon died.

– April 16 –

1828   Bordeaux, France. Spanish painter Francisco de Goya, 82, died following a stroke. Prior to a mysterious illness at 46, Goya had been a conventional artist with a penchant for quaint subjects. The illness, which left him chronically depressed, deaf, and partially blind, wrought a massive change in his art. It became emotionally charged, original, and of such power that it still seems fresh. His work was so magical that even his famed nude Maja series withstood the Inquisition, which thought it obscene. Modern medical authorities suspect that Goya's illness may have been a rare virus or the consequences of his exposure to toxic metals in his paints.

Goya was buried in the Cemetery of the Chartreuse, in Bordeaux. Seventy-one years later, when his bones were moved to the Church of San Antonio de la Florida in Madrid, his movers discovered that Goya's friend Martin Goscoechea had been buried in the same tomb. It was impossible to tell whose bones were whose, and, curiously, only one skull was present. The movers decided to transfer all the remains, and Goya, entombed in a sarcophagus beneath frescoes he had himself painted, retains his "roomie."

– April 17 –

1790   Philadelphia. Benjamin Franklin, 84, died of a lung abscess that had burst a week earlier. He had been ill from a bladder stone and injuries to his arm following a fall. To deal with the pain, Franklin took morphine. Despite his being unable to walk, he remained active, inventing bifocals when he was 83.

On this date, Thomas Jefferson was describing the ongoing French Revolution to Franklin when Franklin began having trouble breathing. Franklin's daughter asked him if adjusting his position in bed would help him breathe more easily. His last words were, "A dying man can do nothing easy." He fell into a coma and died at eleven o'clock that evening. Franklin had had the habit of sleeping with the window open and, upon waking, sitting naked by it for about an hour. His doctor claimed that this caused the lung problem. Twenty thousand attended his funeral, which is thought to be the largest public gathering in America to that date. He was buried at Philadelphia's Christ Church burial ground. At 22, Franklin wrote his own epitaph:

The Body of
B. Franklin,
Printer;
Like the Cover of an old Book,
Its Contents torn out,
And Stript of its Lettering and Gilding,
Lies here, food for Worms.
But the Work shall not be wholly Lost:
For it will, as he believed, appear once more,
In a new & more perfect Edition,
Corrected and amended
By the Author.

Franklin was known for his amorous proclivities. He sired some two dozen illegitimate children. In a letter of advice to a young man, Franklin recommended older women, saying they were discreet, experienced, and grateful.

1987 University of California at San Diego. Madcap comic Dick Shawn, 57, delivered a punchline, then fell to the stage facedown. His audience thought this was part of the show, and it was several minutes before the comic's son called for help. A doctor administered cardiac massage, but Shawn died forty-five minutes later. Shawn's films included *It's a Mad Mad Mad Mad World* (1963) and *The Producers* (1968) (he played a hippie version of Adolf Hitler).

– April 18 –

1906 5:12 A.M., San Francisco. A fierce earthquake struck. Over 2,500 died, but the damages were underreported so as not to upset Eastern bankers and ruin the city's credit rating.

1955 Princeton, New Jersey. Albert Einstein, 75, died from a heart condition. A German, his last words were naturally in that language. Unfortunately, none of those at his side understood German, so his last words are unknown. Earlier, Einstein had directed that no stone be set up over his grave. His brain was removed for scientific examination and is still preserved.

Einstein loved music, and his idol was Mozart. At one time he was offered the presidency of Israel. He once said, "It is a sad fact that Man does not live for pleasure alone." He also said, "Only two things are infinite, the universe and human stupidity, and I'm not sure about the former."

– April 19 –

1824 Missolonghi, Greece. Romantic poet George Gordon Noel, 36, Lord Byron (sixth Baron Byron of Rochdale), died in his sleep of the delayed effects of malaria contracted while training troops for the Greek rebellion against the Turks. He had fought off the original attack, but a horseback ride in a storm a year later brought a fatal recurrence. The attending physicians bled Byron repeatedly. His last words were given the day before: "I want to sleep now. Shall I sue for mercy? Come, come, no weakness. Let me be a man to the last."

Byron affected great artistic sensitivity, poetic oddity (for example, he kept four pet geese that he took everywhere, including social gatherings), and wild hedonism. Coleridge said he was "a wicked lord, who, from morbid and restless vanity, pretended to be ten times more wicked than he was." The duke of Wellington said, "I hate the whole race of them, there never existed a more worthless set than Byron and his friends." John Constable said, "The world is rid of Lord Byron, but the deadly slime of his touch still remains." His onetime lover Lady Caroline Lamb said he was "mad, bad, and dangerous to know."

Unlike the stereotypical Byronic hero, Byron fought a lifelong battle against obesity with dieting and drugs. He was also clubfooted. He so hated this condition that he once sought to have the foot amputated. Perhaps as compensation, as Byron's autopsy revealed, he had another physical peculiarity—an overlarge sexual member. He put this asset to extensive usage, especially after he obtained literary fame, which brought him plenty of the nineteenth-century equivalent of groupies. In addition to these, Byron claimed to have slept with 200 prostitutes. He also enjoyed boys, and had a child by his half-sister. At the time of his death, he was rumored to have raped a 13-year-old girl, to have had an affair with an older woman who was the mother-in-law of one of his mistresses, and to have sodomized his wife just weeks before she was to give birth.

Because of these rumors, Westminster Abbey refused Byron's body. His heart and lungs are buried in Greece. His family placed the remainder in the family vault in Hucknall Torkard Church, near Newstead, Nottinghamshire.

1882 Downe, Kent, England. Charles Darwin, 73, died following a heart attack. His last words were, "I am not in the least afraid to die." He was interred at Westminster Abbey. Shortly after his death, Lady Hope, the evangelistic widow of an English admiral, told students at the Northfield Seminary in Massachusetts that she had visited Darwin on his deathbed and that he had recanted his theory. Darwin's daughter Henrietta was furious. She said, "Lady Hope wasn't present during his last illness, or any illness." Nevertheless, the lie has endured and was cited as recently as 1985 in a television sermon by Jimmy Swaggart.

Darwin wrote, "There is grandeur in the view of life, with its several powers, having been originally breathed into a few forms or into one; and that, while this planet has gone cycling on according to the fixed laws of gravity, from so simple a beginning endless forms most beautiful and most wonderful have been, and are being, evolved."

– April 20 –

1759 London. On April 6th, while conducting a performance of his *Messiah*, German composer George Frideric Handel, 74, collapsed in the orchestra pit. He had been feeble and blind for years. He died on this date. He was buried in Westminster Abbey. George III was a fan and encouraged memorial concerts.

Handel, like his contemporaries, often reused pieces. One love song of his, called "No, I Won't Trust You, Blind Love, Cruel Love," he reused in his greatest work, the *Messiah*. It was retitled "For Unto Us a Child Is Born."

1889 Braunau, Austria. Adolf Hitler was born. The following was written about Hitler in Communist China. It provides interesting insight into how one totalitarian state views another and itself:

Adolf Hitler was five feet, six inches tall and weighed 143 pounds. He was renowned for his spell-binding oratory, relations with women and annihilation of a minority people. In his last years, he suffered from insanity and delusions of grandeur. Chairman Mao is taller and heavier.

—"National Construction"
The Chinese Communist Quarterly,
1960

– April 21 –

1910   Redding, Connecticut. Samuel Clemens, known as Mark Twain, died at 75. Halley's Comet was in the sky, just as it had been the day he was born. Clemens had predicted he would "go out" with the comet.

Clemens had had a heart attack in June of the previous year and had never fully recovered. He suffered from chest pains that could be blocked only by hypodermic injections of morphine. He asked his doctor, "Can't you give me enough of the hypnotic injunction to put an end to me?" He traveled to Bermuda in January 1910, hoping the climate would improve his health. It didn't, and he sailed for home on April 12. The morphine caused him to dream of receiving unwanted honorary degrees and of fruitlessly looking for a general manager for a play. When he returned home, the injections continued. Just before falling into a coma, he spoke his last words to his daughter: "Good-bye...If we meet..."

Clemens's funeral was at the Brick Presbyterian Church in New York. Thousands attended. A laurel wreath was set upon the casket, and Clemens was buried in one of his trademark white linen suits.

Clemens once said, "Under certain circumstances, profanity provides a relief denied even to prayer." Of death he wrote, "Whoever has lived long enough to find out what life is, knows how deep a debt of gratitude we owe to Adam, the first great benefactor of our race. He brought death into the world."

– April 22 –

1915   Skyros, Greece. British poet Rupert Brooke, 27, died of
        septicemia. He was buried in an olive grove on that island. In
        spite of a nervous breakdown, Brooke had enlisted in the
        Royal Navy at the beginning of World War I. In "The
        Soldier," he wrote,
                    If I should die, think only this of me,
                    That there's some corner of a foreign field
                    That is forever England.

– April 23 –

1616   Stratford-upon-Avon, England. William Shakespeare, 52,
        died at his birthplace on what is his accepted birthday. He was
        buried at Stratford's Holy Trinity Church. That church's
        vicar, John Ward, wrote that following a drunken outing with
        playwright Ben Jonson and poet Michael Drayton, Shake-
        speare died of a fever.
            After Shakespeare's death, his plays were altered to make
        them more popular. For example, *Romeo and Juliet* was given
        a happy ending. By the late eighteenth century, they were
        incredibly corrupted. Meanwhile, American actors had begun
        performing his works using the original texts. They didn't
        have newer versions. When an American company happened
        to perform in England, the English were amazed. Shake-
        speare's works underwent a revival in their original form.
            A. L. Rowse has observed that Shakespeare's plays are
        "devotedly, passionately heterosexual—perhaps more than
        normally for an Englishman." Tolstoy was unimpressed. He
        said of Shakespeare, "Crude, immoral, vulgar, and senseless."
        Robert Graves differed: "The remarkable thing about Shake-
        speare is that he really is very good, in spite of all the people
        who say he is very good." Of the controversy over whether
        Shakespeare's plays were written by Bacon, James Barrie gave
        the best comment: "I know not, sir, whether Bacon wrote the
        works of Shakespeare, but if he did not it seems to me that he
        missed the opportunity of his life."

– April 24 –

1967   Kazakh, U.S.S.R. Soviet cosmonaut Vladimir Komarov, 40, became the first death in the exploration of space when the parachute for his capsule snarled and he fell over four miles to earth. There are rumors that previous Soviet space fatalities were concealed, but the publicity surrounding Komarov's mission made cover-up impossible.

1989   Kansas City, Kansas. According to police, while standing before a blood donation center, Michael Pugh and Arthur Davis argued over an unpaid debt that Davis owed Pugh. Davis refused to pay, so Pugh stabbed him to death. The sum involved was $3.65.

1989   Flushing Meadows, Queens. An unidentified woman wearing only a flannel shirt climbed to the top of a 120-foot foul pole in empty Shea Stadium and jumped to her death.

– April 25 –

1792   Paris. Nicolas Jacques Peletier, a highwayman, became the first man guillotined. Other guillotine-like devices had been used previously, but this device was the first perfected head-removal machine. Named after Dr. Joseph Ignace Guillotin, it was actually two other men, one a harpsichord builder, who built the machine. Guillotin persuaded the French government to adopt it as the official means of execution. It is commonly thought that Guillotin was himself guillotined. However, he died at 76 in his own bed of an infected carbuncle on his shoulder.

     During the Reign of Terror, 2,498 people were processed by what was ruefully called "the National Razor." The Nazis also used the guillotine, but they added the novelty of having the victim positioned face upward so he might watch the blade descend.

1901   Clayton, New Mexico. Train robber and killer Black Jack Ketchum, 35, took the steps two at a time as he climbed the scaffold where he was to be hanged. As the noose was fitted around his neck, he gamely cried, "I'll be in hell before you start breakfast, boys!" When all was ready, he yelled, "Let her rip!" The sheriff did, but due to misplaced weights, the effect was indeed "ripping." Black Jack's head was torn from his body.

1972   Castelldefells, Spain. Russian-born actor George Sanders was known for his roles as an urbane cad. His many films included *The Moon and Sixpence* (1942) and *All About Eve* (1950). Sanders had said, "I will have enough of this earth by the time I am 65. After that I shall be having my bottom wiped by nurses and being pushed around in a wheelchair. I won't be able to enjoy a woman anymore, so I shall commit suicide." On this date Sanders killed himself with Nembutal. His suicide note read: "Dear World: I am leaving because I am bored. I am leaving you with your worries in this sweet cesspool." He was 65.

– April 26 –

1865   Garrett Farm, Virginia. John Wilkes Booth, 27, was shot by Union troops in a burning barn. Booth was dragged to a farmhouse porch, where he spoke his last words: "Tell my mother I died for my country...I thought I did for the best...Useless! Useless!" Booth was first buried in a prison cellar. Later, his family claimed the body and reburied it with family members in an unmarked grave in Green Mount Cemetery, Baltimore, Maryland. Booth had written of Lincoln: "...This man's appearance, his pedigree, his coarse low jokes and anecdotes, his vulgar similes and his frivolity, are a disgrace to the seat he holds."

Some historians claim that a look-alike was killed in Booth's place. The dead man had sandy, reddish hair and freckles, according to a surgeon who examined the body. Booth was fair with black hair. Yet the surgeon knew Booth, and his report states the body was Booth. It has been suggested that the actor tinted his hair to disguise himself or that the fire and/or decomposition altered his complexion.

Reports of Booth sightings were made for years, ranging from the western frontier to India. A fellow named John St. Helen claimed to be Booth. St. Helen killed himself in an Enid, Oklahoma, boarding house in 1903 using wine laced with strychnine. The body was mummified and toured with sideshows for many years. In 1931, an autopsy was performed on it and many similarities to Booth were detected, including a healed fracture of the same leg Booth had broken jumping from Lincoln's theater box.

Sergeant Boston Corbett, the soldier who claimed to have shot Booth, was a religious fanatic who had castrated himself to prevent himself from sinning. He became sergeant-at-arms of the Kansas legislature. He later killed himself.

1989   Dhaka, Bangladesh. According to the *New York Times*, just forty minutes after the country's people answered their president's call for prayers to end a two-month drought, terrific rainstorms with two tornadoes and flooding lashed rural Bangladesh. About 500 died, and thousands were injured or left homeless after 20 villages and 5,000 homes were destroyed.

– April 27 –

1865   Mississippi River. The worst marine accident in U.S. history occurred when the steamboat *Sultana,* crammed with Union soldiers going home after the Civil War, blew up. Many were survivors of horrific Confederate prison camps. Over 1,700 were killed, and many were injured.

1882   Concord, Massachusetts. Writer Ralph Waldo Emerson, 80, died of pneumonia. He had become senile in his last years. He was buried near Henry Thoreau and Nathaniel Hawthorne in Sleepy Hollow Cemetery.

In 1855, Emerson proposed to the Anti-Slavery Society of New York a solution to the issue of slavery. He suggested that $200 million be raised by the government to purchase the freedom of all the slaves in the South. It was a huge figure for the time. Slaveholders dismissed the idea because it would remove their labor force. Abolitionists were against the idea because it would reward slaveholders and turn the U.S. government into slave dealers, thereby legitimizing slavery. When war came, 364,000 Northerners and 134,000 Southerners died; far more money was spent on war materials and lost to destruction.

Herman Melville, who was less successful during his lifetime, said, "I could readily see in Emerson, not withstanding his merit, a gaping flaw. It was the insinuation that had he lived in those days when the world was made, he might have offered some valuable suggestions." Emerson once said, "A child is a curly, dimpled lunatic."

1932   Off the Florida coast. While returning from Mexico by ship, poet Hart Crane, 32, leapt overboard in his pajamas. After a year in Mexico on a Guggenheim Fellowship, he had produced just one poem. While there, he unsuccessfully tried to kill himself by drinking iodine. Before jumping, Crane angrily complained to his traveling companion of how the sailors had treated him the previous night when he was drunk. He had made a pass at one of them, and they had roughed him up. His last words were, "Good-bye, everybody."

Crane's father invented the Life Saver candy, but sold it in 1913 for just $2,900. The buyer made a fortune large enough to purchase the American Broadcasting Company in 1943 for $8 million in cash.

– April 28 –

1944   Off Slapton Sands, Devon, England. Exercise Tiger, a rehearsal for the invasion of Europe, was staged using 25,000 American soldiers and many of the large landing craft called LSTs. The LSTs were supposed to be guarded by two British destroyers, but only one British vessel showed up—a slow tug. At 2:00 A.M., German torpedo boats discovered the unprotected convoy. They torpedoed three LSTs. Heavily loaded with troops, ammunition, and fully-fueled vehicles, the vessels blazed. One sank quickly. A second went down more slowly. A third managed to beach itself.

On board the stricken ships, hundreds burned to death. There were too few lifeboats. Some frightened soldiers had to be forced to jump into the water. Many inflated their life preservers without discarding their field packs. When they hit the water, their packs pulled them over, drowning them. Men passed out from exposure in the 44-degree water and drowned. The other vessels had standing orders not to stop to pick up survivors if the convoy came under attack. Nevertheless, one of the slow LSTs turned back. Miraculously, the Germans had left, and the vessel saved many. Seven hundred and forty-nine died. When light came, hundreds of drowned soldiers floated ashore at Slapton Sands.

The town of Slapton Sands had been evacuated to keep the exercise secret, so there were no civilian witnesses. The surviving troops were sworn to secrecy and promised a court-martial if they spoke. Burial parties hastily gathered the dead. Many couldn't be identified and were buried anonymously at Cambridge, England. Families weren't told how their men had died. Six weeks later, the Normandy invasion was made. Vicious resistance was faced at Utah Beach, but the number killed in Exercise Tiger outnumbered the Allied dead there. The Exercise Tiger disaster may have saved some lives by illustrating the dangers of amphibious operations.

If the disaster had been made public before D-Day, the story could have caused panic during the actual landings. The failure of the Royal Navy to protect the helpless American convoy might have engendered anti-British feeling harmful to the war effort. The Germans would certainly have made much propaganda of the disaster. But why the secret was kept after the war is less obvious. Perhaps reputations were at stake. In 1954, the U.S. government erected a monument at Slapton Sands thanking the locals for their evacuation, but the dead soldiers weren't mentioned. The truth emerged in 1970. Ken Small, an area innkeeper, grew curious when he discovered U.S. Army belt buckles, bullets, and even a few American silver dollars on the beach. There were stories of trucks loaded with dead GIs from local people, and fishermen complained of catching their nets on a submerged object. Small arranged for divers to investigate. Under sixty feet of ocean, they discovered a Sherman tank. The publicity brought out the truth. Small salvaged the tank, turning it into the only memorial to Exercise Tiger. It sits upon the beach at Slapton Sands, under an American flag, gun facing out across the Channel.

1945   Near Dongo, Italy. Benito Mussolini, 62, was executed. His last words to the Italian partisan officer who shot him were, "But...but...Colonel..." Mussolini's mistress was offered her life but chose to die with him. After death, the pair were hung by their heels at a gas station for crowds to abuse and mutilate. They were buried in an unmarked grave.

Mussolini was a great womanizer, despite his seldom bathing and his having contracted syphilis early in life. He nearly killed himself when he discovered he had the disease, but a friend talked him out of it. He was never cured. A symptom of the illness is megalomania.

Mussolini once said, "The history of saints is mainly the history of insane people."

– April 29 –

1836   Logan City, Ohio. American frontiersman Simon Kenton died in his 81st year. A scout for Daniel Boone and soldier in the Revolution and the War of 1812, he helped hundreds of settlers, giving them land he had claimed for himself. Despite his generosity, lawyers tied him up in court over land boundaries and whittled his holdings down to a tiny plot.

– April 30 –

1879   Philadelphia. Magazine editor Sarah Josepha Hale, 90, reputed author of "Mary Had a Little Lamb," died of natural causes. She was buried in Laurel Hill Cemetery. Actually, John Roulstone wrote the poem about a real incident in Sterling, Massachusetts, in 1816. His neighbor, ten-year-old Mary Sawyer Tyler, had a pet lamb that "followed her to school one day." Mary's brother talked her into hiding the lamb under her shawl and sneaking it inside. When the teacher called upon Mary to recite the day's lesson, the devoted sheep followed her to the front of the class. The teacher wasn't amused. Roulstone recorded the incident in his famous poem. Hale "borrowed" it, appended a couple of moralistic stanzas, and printed it in her magazine. It became so famous that when Thomas Edison invented the phonograph, the first thing that occurred to him when he tested it was the poem. "Mary Had a Little Lamb" became the first sound ever recorded.

In later years Mary married and moved to Cambridge, where she spent her life working with the mentally ill. She died in her 83rd year, in 1889. The lamb, however, had an unhappy ending. It was attacked and killed by a cow. Mary's mother turned the wool into two pairs of socks.

1900 Vaughan, Mississippi. John Luther Jones, 36, known as "Casey Jones," had volunteered for a double shift and was stubbornly fixed on bringing his passenger train, the Cannonball Express, in on time, despite having started seventy-five minutes behind schedule. He hit 100 m.p.h. at times and averaged 60 m.p.h. through a foggy night. Jones was just two minutes behind schedule, running at full speed, when he missed a flagman's signal that a freight train was stopped on the tracks, waiting to be shunted aside for Jones. He saw the caboose lights just 150 yards ahead.

Jones bravely stayed aboard his engine, "Old 382," trying to stop the collision. He slammed on the air brakes, jammed the engine into reverse, and sounded the whistle. His last words were to his fireman, "Jump, Sim!" The freight's caboose and two cars were shattered. Jones's engine toppled and exploded. A large bolt pierced Jones's neck, but he succeeded in slowing his engine enough so that only he died. His courage inspired a black engine-wiper to write the famous ballad that immortalized his demise.

1945 Berlin. Adolf Hitler, 56, shot himself in his bunker. His wife of one day, Eva Braun, 32, took poison. In accordance with Hitler's command, the bodies were soaked with gasoline and burned.

Hitler had wanted to be an artist, but the Vienna Art Academy turned him down. The youthful dictator lived as a vagrant, supporting himself with odd jobs and by painting postcards. When World War I began, swept up in the patriotic fervor, he enlisted, becoming a corporal and winning the Iron Cross (seldom given to enlisted men). After the war, the prospect of returning to the streets prompted him to join military intelligence. He was assigned the task of infiltrating an obscure organization called the National Socialist Workers' Party. He discovered he liked politics and became the party's leader.

Nazi propaganda boss Dr. Joseph Goebbels said of Hitler, "The whole nation loves him, because it feels safe in his hands, like a child in the arms of his mother."

– May 1 –

1873   Chitambo, Barotseland (now Zambia). Explorer and missionary David Livingstone, 60, the subject of Henry Stanley's
search, died. Livingstone suffered badly from hemorrhoids
but spurned corrective surgery in 1864 because he feared he
would become an invalid and wouldn't be able to continue his
expeditions. It was an unfortunate decision, for Livingstone
was killed by the hemorrhoids. His men removed his heart
and viscera, which were buried on the spot. They embalmed
his body, wrapped it in bark and sailcloth, tied it to a pole, and
toted it out of the jungle. It was buried in England.

1987   Orlando, Florida. A skywriting airplane crashed into another
small airplane, killing four. The skywriter was drawing a
giant "happy face."

1991   Anthon, Iowa. In 1922, farmer Charlie Osborne was slaughter-
ing a hog. He began hiccuping. He continued hiccuping every
1.5 seconds for the next sixty-eight years. Osborne tried every
remedy known to man, even offering $10,000 for a cure. On
June 5, 1990, Osborne moved in with his daughter Melissa.
Three days later, his hiccups stopped. The reason was
unknown. Osborne didn't enjoy his cure long. Just eleven
months later, on this date, he died at 98 of ulcer complications.

– May 2 –

1519   Cloux, France. Leonardo da Vinci died of a stroke shortly after his 67th birthday. His last words were reportedly: "I have offended God and mankind because my work didn't reach the quality it should have." He had earlier written, "As a well-spent day brings happy sleep, so a life well used brings happy death."

Leonardo was buried in France, and during the Revolution an angry mob looting "aristocratic" graves threw his bones into a pile with others. They were never separated, although a large skull found in the grisly litter was presumed to be his.

1972   Washington, D.C. John Edgar Hoover, 77, FBI chief for forty-eight years and under eight presidents, died of a heart attack in his bedroom. He was discovered by his housekeeper. Hoover established the FBI as one of the world's foremost law enforcement agencies. His greatest successes were achieved during World War II, when the FBI contained enemy activity in the United States. His eccentricities in later years undermined his earlier achievements. For example, he maintained files on prominent politicians detailing their sex lives. Lyndon Johnson used to take pleasure in reading these and purportedly used them to coerce cooperation with his policies. Johnson tried to charm Hoover, saying, "I'd rather have him inside the tent pissing out, than outside pissing in."

Hoover was devoted to his mother, living with her in his childhood home till she died in her 80th year. He once gave her an exceptional gift—a canary bred by the Birdman of Alcatraz.

– May 3 –

1950   New York City. Psychoanalyst Paul Federn, 79, the last living student of Sigmund Freud, killed himself.

1991   New York City. Polish-born writer Jerzy Kosinski, 57, committed suicide by locking himself in his bathroom, getting in his bathtub, and tying a plastic bag over his head. He had a debilitating heart condition and felt he would become a burden upon his family and friends. Kosinski had survived a childhood in Nazi-occupied Poland to become an award-winning author in America. His best known works were *Being There* and *The Painted Bird*.

In the 1980s, a young author, tired of perfunctory rejections from publishers, conducted an experiment. He retyped *The Painted Bird* and mailed it under his own name to the publisher who had originally published the work. The publisher not only failed to recognize the work, but also rejected it, suggesting several modifications to improve it.

– May 4 –

1975   Hollywood. Moe Howard, 78, last of the original Three Stooges, died of cancer. Moe was born Moses Horwitz in Brooklyn and, with his brothers Curly and Shemp, established the Stooges as vaudeville, then Broadway, stars. In 1934, they began making films. They made 190 shorts over twenty-three years.

1991   New York City. Publisher/philanthropist George T. Delacorte, 97, died in his sleep of natural causes. Delacorte founded the Dell Publishing Company but is remembered for his gifts to New York's Central Park. These included the Delacorte Theatre, where the Shakespeare in the Park festival is held, the animated Delacorte Clock at the Children's Zoo, and the bronze Alice in Wonderland statue group by the Conservatory Pond. The last, erected in 1959, was a memorial to his first wife, Margarita, who often read the book to their children.

Delacorte loved walking in Central Park. In 1985, while strolling there with his second wife, Delacorte was mugged at knife point. He lost his cash and his wife lost her mink. Despite this, Delacorte continued his walks.

Delacorte preferred to donate money to material improvements. He didn't wish to help the poor, observing, "People are poor because they're dumb or because they're lazy. If you feed them you just keep them in the same strata." He also refused to fund medical institutions, saying, "I hate hospitals."

– May 5 –

1821   Island of St. Helena. Napoleon Bonaparte, 51, died in exile of stomach and liver cancer. It is rumored that British agents poisoned him to prevent his causing another European war, which he had done after escaping his earlier exile to the island of Elba. Samples of his hair, which he had directed be shaved from his head and distributed among his friends, have been analyzed and show signs of antimony, lead, and arsenic. These substances were actually medicines prescribed by his doctors (St. Helena's soil and Napoleon's wallpaper also contained arsenic he could have absorbed). Napoleon had been vomiting blood from his stomach ulcer. His doctors gave him a poisonous emetic mixed with lemonade to induce more vomiting, which they believed to be palliative. It was so horrifically painful and Napoleon's desperate state so obvious, that one doctor deliberately gave the ex-emperor a fatal dose of a mercury-based laxative to end his suffering. Napoleon's last words were, "France! Army! Head of the Army! Josephine!"

Napoleon exhibited homosexual behavior and became impotent at 42. His autopsy revealed glandular problems that had caused a feminization of his body. Earlier in life, he had been a womanizer. While campaigning in Egypt, he became infatuated with the wife of one of his officers. He sent the officer back to France while he took up with the wife. The British captured the officer and, to irk Napoleon, returned him to Egypt, where he ended his spouse's close-order drill.

During Napoleon's autopsy, an onlooker took a very personal souvenir—the emperor's penis, which had been diminished by his illness. It was recently offered for auction in Paris. In 1840, Napoleon was removed from his St. Helena grave and entombed in Paris.

Napoleon was born on Corsica, which had fought for years for independence from France. Napoleon's father, Carlo, was friendly with rebel leaders, and when the French threatened to jail the rebels, Carlo was urged to flee to England. Carlo decided not to leave and ingratiated himself with the invaders to the extent that his son, Napoleon, was sponsored by a French general to a military academy. Had Carlo fled, Napoleon might have wound up in a British military academy and ultimately in the British Army.

1945   Oregon. The Japanese developed a plan whereby high-flying balloons carrying incendiary bombs would float across the ocean and ignite U.S. forests. No large fires were started, but one bomb exploded when a woman and five children examined it. They were the only U.S. war casualties within the forty-eight contiguous states. It was a dry year, and if more balloons had been sent, the Japanese might have destroyed America's western forests.

1968   Hollywood. Actor Albert Dekker, 62, best known for starring in *Dr. Cyclops* (1940), was found dead in his bathroom, bound, handcuffed, wearing ladies' lingerie, and hanging from his shower rod. Obscenities were scrawled on his body in red lipstick. The bathroom was locked from the inside, and it is presumed he died during an autoerotic activity gone awry. Dekker had also played in *Death of a Salesman* (1951), *East of Eden* (1955), and *Suddenly Last Summer* (1959).

Near-strangulation provides some people with an orgasmic feeling. Often, these efforts result in death. Authorities, wishing to spare the feelings of family and friends, commonly announce the death as a suicide. Most associates of the deceased would probably prefer the truth rather than imagine they had instigated the "suicide" through some failing.

Autoerotic deaths aren't limited to hangings. The Black Museum of Scotland Yard is said to contain a broom that killed its owner. He was inserting its handle in his anus and decided to stand upon a chair to facilitate this. He slipped, impaling himself. Transvestite James Kubicek of Olmsted Falls, Ohio, reportedly died in a more spectacular autoerotic effort. He tied himself to a railroad track where he masturbated, perhaps thrilled by the danger. Before Kubicek could untie himself, a locomotive ran him down.

– May 6 –

1862   Concord, Massachusetts. Transcendental philosopher and naturalist Henry Thoreau, 44, died after suffering for years from tuberculosis. A friend, noting his nearness to death said, "I almost wonder how the opposite shore may appear to you." Thoreau responded, "One world at a time." When his aunt asked him if he had made his peace with God, he replied, "I did not know we had ever quarreled." His last words were unintelligible, but "moose" and "Indian" were discerned.

Thoreau is remembered for his book *Walden* and for his essay *Civil Disobedience,* which inspired Mahatma Gandhi. Thoreau once observed, "Every generation laughs at the old fashions but religiously follows the new."

1919 Los Angeles. Writer L. Frank Baum, 62, known for *The Wizard of Oz*, died at home of heart disease. He had bought a great deal of real estate in Los Angeles with the idea of setting up what would have been the first theme park. Walt Disney would be successful with a similar idea, but Baum wasn't as lucky. He died in financial distress.

Years later, the costume designers for the movie version of *The Wizard of Oz* were looking for a worn topcoat for Frank Morgan, who played the snake oil salesman who becomes the Wizard. They found one in a secondhand store. During filming, Morgan found the name of the previous owner written in the pocket by the name of the tailor. A check with the tailor and with the widow of the owner verified that the coat had originally belonged to L. Frank Baum.

– May 7 –

1915 Near the Irish coast. The Cunard liner *Lusitania* was torpedoed by a German U-boat. The ship immediately listed at a steep angle. Crewmen refused to lower some of the lifeboats because of this. One passenger forced them at gunpoint to lower one. The tilting, heavy lifeboat slipped and crushed dozens. The gunman survived the sinking. Close to 1,200 were killed, including 128 Americans. American outrage led to U.S. involvement in World War I.

Some think that the *Lusitania* was sacrificed by then Lord of the Admiralty Winston Churchill to get U.S. support for the British in World War I. The liner was in an area where a submarine had been reported, and a warship steaming to escort the liner was ordered away. Years later, it was revealed that the liner was carrying munitions.

– May 8 –

1903 Atvona, Hiva Oa, Marquesas Islands. French painter Paul Gauguin, 54, died of a heart attack. He was destitute and wracked with syphilis. He had been a stockbroker in Paris till one day he decided to chuck it all and live a life of ease in the South Seas. When he got there, he found that it wasn't Eden.

He had to scratch out a living as a clerk, and while he did find exotic island girls, the idyllic scenes he painted of them contained a large element of fantasy. Gauguin said, "Life being what it is, one dreams of revenge."

1989   Lawrence, Kansas. Lance Foster, a 23-year-old student at the University of Kansas, put fifty cents in a Pepsi machine but didn't get a soda. He rocked the machine, hoping to shake loose a can. The 1,000-pound machine fell on him. He died on this date of his injuries, two weeks before he was due to graduate. Similar cases include:

> 1988, Safety Harbor, Florida. Daniel Erickson attacked a soft drink machine after it cheated him for a second time. It fell over, crushing him.
>
> May 28, 1987, Seattle, Washington. A 17-year-old boy was crushed after rocking a soda machine.
>
> March 3, 1988, Texas. A Navy enlisted man was crushed and suffocated by a soda machine he is presumed to have rocked.
>
> July 31, 1988, San Diego, California. A young U.S. Marine was fatally injured after rocking a soda machine at a recruit depot.
>
> October 29, 1988, New Orleans, Louisiana. A college student was crushed by a candy machine he was hitting in an attempt to retrieve his money.
>
> November 11, 1988, Arden, North Carolina. Three boys were rocking a soda machine in hopes of getting free sodas. One was crushed to death.
>
> December 19, 1988, New Baltimore, Michigan. A young man died after a soda machine fell on his neck.
>
> February 27, 1989, West Allis, Wisconsin. Trying to steal a soda, an 11-year-old placed one foot in a soda machine's dispensing well to make rocking it easier. When it overturned, he was crushed.

Antitheft devices, which make it difficult to shake loose sodas, have reduced deaths by reducing the motivation to rock machines.

– May 9 –

1657   Plymouth, Massachusetts. William Bradford died at 67. Organizer of the one hundred Pilgrims who sailed on the *Mayflower,* he helped write the Mayflower Compact. He was also the first governor of Plymouth Colony and was reelected thirty times.

1864   Spotsylvania, Virginia. Union Major General John Sedgwick, 51, was warned against peering over a parapet lest Rebel sharpshooters plug him. He replied: "They couldn't hit an elephant at this dist––."

– May 10 –

1863   Guiney's Station, Virginia. Confederate General Thomas Jonathan "Stonewall" Jackson died at 39. He received the nickname "Stonewall" at the First Battle of Bull Run, when, at a critical moment, his men stood firm. A dying Confederate officer said: "See, here stands Jackson like a stone wall." On May 2, following a battle near Chancellorsville, while passing through Confederate lines, one of his own soldiers shot Jackson. His left arm had to be removed. When he awoke nauseated, cold towels were applied to him. Pneumonia and delirium followed. Morphine was administered, but it was clear he was dying. His doctor told him this and Jackson, who was noted for his fanatic Christianity, said, "It is the Lord's Day, my wish is fulfilled. I have always wanted to die on Sunday." His last words: "Let us cross over the river and sit under the shade of the trees." Before the battle, Jackson had ordered his sentries to shoot first and ask questions later. They did.

1977   New York City. After several years of suffering, actress Joan Crawford, 73, died from stomach cancer. She refused diagnosis and treatment because she was a Christian Scientist. However, her last words, addressed to her housekeeper, who was praying for her, were: "Damn it––don't you dare ask God to help me."

Mercedes McCambridge said of Crawford: "I kept my mouth shut about her for nearly a quarter of a century, but she was a mean, tipsy, powerful, rotten-egg lady." Bette Davis and Crawford worked together but didn't get along (some say it was because Davis was interested in Crawford's husband Franchot Tone). Davis said, "Joan Crawford—I wouldn't sit on her toilet!" and "The best time I ever had with Joan Crawford was when I pushed her down the stairs in *What Ever Happened to Baby Jane?*"

1987   Seoul. When South Korea switched to daylight savings time, many forgot to set their clocks ahead. The wife of one businessman missed preparing her husband's lunch for a company picnic. She was so embarrassed that she hanged herself.

– May 11 –

1984   Six Flags Great Adventure, Jackson Township, New Jersey. Dozens of teenagers were jammed into a "Haunted Castle" constructed of a series of connected trailers when a young man lighted his cigarette lighter to find his way in the spooky darkness. The lighter set fire to the decorations, and soon the trailers were blazing. Eight teenagers died. The lighter-bearer got out unharmed.

1988   Moscow. Harold "Kim" Philby, 76, died of unannounced causes. The Soviets memorialized his death by issuing a stamp with his portrait in 1991. Philby nearly became head of the British intelligence service before two Communist double agents, Donald Maclean and Guy Burgess, defected to the Soviets in 1951. This stirred suspicion of their friend Philby. Nevertheless, British authorities asserted his innocence. He was still working for MI6 in 1963 when he was exposed as the man who had warned the spies. Philby fled to Russia. The threesome, who had spied for thirty years, were united by homosexual romances dating back to their university days. One of the secrets the spy ring filched was the decision by Truman to not carry the Korean War northward. The Soviets passed this on to the Chinese, who, confident that the war wouldn't escalate, delayed truce talks. Thousands of U.N. soldiers were killed and maimed during the stalemate.

Many sympathized with Philby's "exile," and a film was made depicting his travails. In it, an Australian actress meets her old pal Philby while touring Russia. He asks her to help him get English clothing. She vilely browbeats London clerks into providing poor Philby, via mail, with clothing of a quality fit to his taste. The film ends with Philby, dapperly outfitted, striding through Moscow to the Gilbert and Sullivan air "He Remains an Englishman." The film failed to report that Philby was provided with the best the KGB could offer. He was given a headquarters job, where he continued his work subverting Britain, and was made a "Hero of the Soviet Union," its highest honor. He lived outside Moscow in a villa complete with servants and chauffered limousine. He was also provided with Western products, pipes, magazines and even the London *Times*.

– May 12 –

1957 Paris. Austrian-born director Erich von Stroheim, 71, died of a spinal ailment. In Hollywood during the 1920s and 1930s, von Stroheim became a legend, staging elaborate and costly orgy scenes. He eventually went to Europe to make films, but returned to Hollywood to appear as the faithful servant in *Sunset Boulevard* (1950). He was nominated for a Best Supporting Actor Academy Award for that role.

1960 Suresnes, France. Playboy and diplomat Prince Aly Khan, 48, died following a car crash. Heir to the Aga Khan III of India and destined to be the religious leader of 20 million Muslims, he preferred a life of sensuality. He won many women, but his most famous amour was Rita Hayworth, whom he married. Another conquest was Lady Thelma Furness, the companion of Edward VIII of England. The disappointed Edward turned to American divorcée Wallis Simpson, for whom he abdicated the throne.

– May 13 –

1865   Palo Pinto, Texas. The last battle of the Civil War was fought. Confederate forces won the day but still lost the war. Union Private John J. Williams of the Thirty-fourth Indiana became the last battle death of the Civil War, although pointless skirmishes that cannot be regarded as part of any war campaign continued to produce deaths (see 5/22/1865).

1961   Hollywood. Actor Gary Cooper (Frank James), 60, died of spinal cancer. He was a real cowboy from Montana but was educated in England. He began his career as a stunt man and sometimes played both cowboy and Indian in the same picture. Later, he won two Oscars.

     Cooper was extremely successful with his leading ladies, including Clara Bow and Patricia Neal, despite, or perhaps because of, a reserved style of which George Burns noted, "George Raft and Gary Cooper once played a scene in front of a cigar store, and it looked like the wooden Indian was overacting."

     Hollywood historian Jim Bacon wrote of a visit he made to the Movieland Wax Museum in Buena Park after Cooper's death. It contained a likeness of Cooper as he appeared in *High Noon* (1952). Bacon noticed an elderly woman sitting in front of it. An employee told him that she was in her nineties and that she visited once or twice a month to sit by the likeness for hours. The woman was Cooper's mother.

– May 14 –

1976   London. Keith Relf, 33, was the lead singer of the 1960s blues-rock band the Yardbirds. On this date, Relf died as he had lived—he was electrocuted by his electric guitar.

1987   New York City. Actress Rita Hayworth, 68, died of Alzheimer's disease. Hayworth's career was ruined by the disease, whose early symptoms were taken for alcohol abuse. Her loving daughter, Princess Yasmin (Prince Aly Khan was her father) cared for her till her death. Hayworth's real name was Margarita Cansino; she Anglicized her Hispanic name in order to avoid typecasting. Ironically, she sometimes played Hispanic ladies in her films.

– May 15 –

1886   Amherst, Massachusetts. Poet Emily Dickinson, 55, died of Bright's disease, a kidney illness. She'd spent her last two decades as a recluse, affecting ghostly white gowns. She rarely shared her poetry, publishing only seven poems while she was alive. Dickinson's reclusiveness has been attributed to an unhappy love for a married minister, but some think it was related to a misalignment of her eyes, which gave her an unusual appearance. Her last words were: "I must go in, for the fog is rising."

1978   Doyle, California. Joe Marsters, alias Cowboy Joe, died at 83. He was the last surviving member of the Butch Cassidy gang. He joined them as a boy and served as Cassidy's horse wrangler. He later became a rodeo star and claimed that in 1915, long after Cassidy was reported dead, Cassidy visited him after a performance.

– May 16 –

1984   Los Angeles. Comic Andy Kaufman, 35, who played Latka Gravas on TV's "Taxi," died of lung cancer. Kaufman's offbeat stand-up routines included Elvis impressions, lip-synching with children's records, and wrestling with women. In 1982, after many appearances on "Saturday Night Live," the show held a live phone-in poll to ask viewers if Kaufman should be banned from the show. Viewers voted to ban him. Jerry Lawler said of Kaufman, "I think that when Andy was born, his father wanted a boy, his mother wanted a girl, and they were both satisfied."

1985   Salisbury, Connecticut. Actress Margaret Hamilton, 82, the Wicked Witch of the West (and Miss Gulch) in *The Wizard of Oz* (1939), died of a heart attack. Hamilton's schoolmarmish ways were naturally acquired; she had studied kindergarten teaching before she became an actress in the 1920s. Her acting career spanned Broadway, movies, and television commercials, where she played a storekeeper who seemed to sell nothing but Maxwell House Coffee.

     During the shooting of *The Wizard of Oz*, Hamilton was hardly a witch off-camera. She and Judy Garland staged gossipy tea parties. Hamilton wore green makeup for her role. It rubbed off on anything she touched, so an assistant was hired to help her go to the bathroom. The makeup also caused her great suffering following an accident. Hamilton was supposed to disappear in a puff of smoke, but her costume caught fire, and she was burned on the face. The pain of her injury was compounded when doctors had to use alcohol to remove her makeup. Fortunately, she wasn't scarred.

Hamilton said, "I hope when I die someone has the presence of mind to say, 'Ding Dong, the Witch is *really* dead.'"

1990   New York City. Puppeteer Jim Henson, 53, creator of Kermit the Frog and dozens of Muppets, died of pneumonia. When admitted to the hospital on the fifteenth, he was suffering acute respiratory distress, a virulent bacterial infection, heart and kidney failure, and shock. Henson's life might have been saved had he gotten to the hospital just a few hours earlier.

Henson's career began in the early 1950s, when his Muppets appeared on a Washington, D.C., television show. He made the original Kermit out of his mother's old green coat and a halved Ping-Pong ball. Henson went on to devise Rowlf the Dog for "The Jimmy Dean Show," create "Sesame Street," and launch "The Muppet Show," which had an audience of 235 million. "Sesame Street" treated the alphabet and numbers like commercial products and explained the world to children with charming humor. Many educators complained that Henson made learning "too much fun," causing children to be disappointed with duller public schools. In typical bureaucratic style, they sought to eliminate the competition rather than improve their own efforts.

In an interview with the *Boston Globe* in 1989, Henson said, "I think it's good to be your own person. But individuality is a mixed blessing. People who are 'different' are isolated. I always felt that I was not a part of things in general. I've always been outside of things."

Miss Piggy, a Henson creation, is a superstar sow with an attitude. She has a weight problem, but still gives sage diet advice. She counsels, "Never eat more than you can lift."

1991   Canton, Georgia. Retired poultry worker Carl Hulsey, 77, wanted a watchdog. He decided a goat could fill the job. He procured one, christened it "Snowball," and for an entire year regularly beat the animal to make it mean and fearful of humans. On this date, he went out to continue Snowball's education, but Snowball decided he had had enough. The 100-pound animal butted Hulsey twice, knocking him flat. Hulsey crawled onto his five-foot-high porch. Snowball followed and butted him off. The infuriated goat tried to butt Hulsey again, but Hulsey's wife, Alma, tied the creature to a post. Hulsey died of a ruptured stomach. Animal control authorities seized the goat. Alma expressed the desire that the goat be prepared for her freezer, but officials placed it with a kindly "foster family."

– May 17 –

1849   St. Louis. A disgruntled sailor set fire to the steamship *White Cloud*. The blaze destroyed twenty-five ships and the waterfront, with a loss of $4 million. The crowding that followed induced a cholera epidemic. Hundreds died.

– May 18 –

1981   Fresno, California. Writer William Saroyan, 72, died of cancer. He is remembered for his novel *The Human Comedy* and his play *The Time of Your Life*. The latter won a Pulitzer Prize, which he refused. Five days before his death, he called the Associated Press and stated: "Everybody has got to die, but I have always believed an exception would be made in my case. Now what?"

– May 19 –

1795   London. James Boswell, 54, died from gonorrhea. Condoms made from animal intestines didn't save him from the results of continual debauchery. He had at least nineteen bouts of urethritis due to gonorrhea. Herbs, bloodletting, cauterization of the sores, irrigation of the urinary tract with vitriol, nitrous acid, mercury salts and lead, and periodic dilation of his penis by the insertion of metal rods didn't cure him.

    Boswell is known for his exhaustive biography of Samuel

Johnson, which he based on their friendship. It did much to assure Johnson's place in history, but Boswell's constant company occasionally grew tiresome. Johnson once said, "You have but two topics, yourself and me, and I'm sick of both."

1864   Plymouth, New Hampshire. Author Nathaniel Hawthorne died at 59. His most famous works were *The Scarlet Letter*, *Twice-Told Tales,* and *The House of the Seven Gables*. The last dealt with the dark legacy of a witch-hunting Salem judge. Hawthorne had such an ancestor and had added a *w* to his last name to distance himself from this relative.

As a boy, Hawthorne was overly indulged. Once, upon meeting a strange woman, the infant aesthete wailed, "Take her away! She is ugly and fat, and has a loud voice!" Hawthorne's first published work was an anonymous essay on fruit tree pests. With his sister Elizabeth, he wrote a world history for the "Peter Parley's Universal History" series in 1836. It sold over a million copies. They received $100. In 1858, Hawthorne visited Florence, where he turned away from Titian's *Venus,* which was "reclining on a couch, naked and lustful." He preferred Botticelli's more demure *Venus,* which "has a dimple in her chin." Hawthorne once became involved in a back-to-nature utopian community called Brook Farm. He soon left, saying, "I cannot endure being chambermaid to a cow."

Hawthorne hated doctors and refused to see one when he became ill in April 1864. On May 12, he traveled with his friend ex-president Franklin Pierce to Concord. On this date, around 3:30 A.M., Pierce found Hawthorne in his room, dead.

Hawthorne once said, "What we call real estate—the solid ground to build a house on—is the broad foundation on which nearly all of the guilt of the world rests."

1935   Clouds Hill, Dorset, England. Thomas E. Lawrence, 46, better known as Lawrence of Arabia, died from injuries received in a motorcycle crash. He enjoyed beatings so much that he invented a fictional guardian who would write letters demanding that Lawrence be punished. Lawrence persuaded acquaintances to do the beating by showing them the letters. He also had a questionable relationship with a young donkey drover called Dahoum, whom he met in Turkey while on an archaeological expedition. He brought Dahoum back to England and had a nude statue of the boy displayed in his home. Lawrence said of heterosexual sex: "For myself, I haven't tried it, and hope not to."

1987 Brooklyn's Prospect Park Zoo. After sneaking into the closed zoo, 11-year-old Juan Perez tried to talk two friends into swimming in the pool within the polar bear cage. The bears were secluded within their cave, and Juan assured his friends that polar bears were afraid of people and didn't like water. He got his friends to disrobe, but they were afraid to go farther. Juan threw their clothing inside the cage, but they still didn't wish to try their luck. Juan squeezed through the bars to retrieve his clothes, and one of the boys timidly followed. When a 900-pound polar bear emerged, Juan began teasing it and throwing sticks and bottles at it. Another 1,600-pound polar bear emerged. While Juan's friend escaped, the two bears ate Juan. Police killed the bears so that they could search the cage. They received hundreds of calls protesting the killing of the bears.

– May 20 –

1886 Sidney, Australia. Eliza Donnithorne died. She is thought to be the basis for Dickens's Miss Havisham in *Great Expectations*. Miss Donnithorne was left standing at the altar. She marked the event by stopping the clocks in her mansion, leaving the wedding cake to rot, and remaining in her wedding gown for the next thirty years.

1913 West Palm Beach, Florida. Henry Morrison Flagler, 83, helped found Standard Oil. His railroad converted Florida from a rustic swamp into a tourist and agricultural powerhouse. With his earnings, he built an elaborate mansion in West Palm Beach, featuring automatic doors that closed behind passers-through. Flagler, on his way to the bathroom, passed too slowly through one of these doors. It smacked into him, sending him tumbling down a set of stairs. He broke his hip and, after two months of suffering, died on this date.

1989 Los Angeles. Comedienne Gilda Radner, 42, best known for her five-year role on TV's "Saturday Night Live," died of ovarian cancer. Her husband, Gene Wilder, was at her bedside. She had suffered from the disease since 1986, enduring months of chemotherapy, surgery, and radiation treatment. In her book about her illness, *It's Always Something*, she observed, "I'm a comedienne, and even cancer wasn't going to stop me from seeing the humor in what I was going through. The last thing that I wanted was to be tragic...The three weeks I spent at the hospital recovering from surgery, I amused myself by making the nurses laugh and racing up and down the halls with my IV stand while Gene chased me. How could I be happy under the circumstances? I don't really know—except that I discovered that I have a strong spirit and a powerful will to survive." Radner died at 6:20 A.M. on a Saturday morning.

– May 21 –

1506   Valladolid, Spain. Christopher Columbus, 58, died of heart failure. He had been promised a tenth of the revenue from the lands he discovered, but King Ferdinand and Queen Isabella reneged after Columbus failed as an administrator of Spain's new colonies. He had been severely ill for two years following his last voyage to the New World.

Many medical historians believe that syphilis and rheumatoid arthritis were diseases native to the New World and not the Old (see 11/24/1494). Columbus is thought to have suffered from both of these illnesses contracted during his voyages. He had the joint pain, swelling, and heart problems associated with arthritis. He suffered from mental illness and hallucinations, which may have been caused by syphilis, which also damages the heart. In his last days, he heard heavenly voices and believed that he was God's special ambassador sent to lead a new Crusade to recapture Jerusalem. His last words upon setting out on his final, eternal voyage were: "Into thy hands, O Lord, I commend my spirit."

Columbus was buried in Valladolid but was soon moved to Seville, Spain, and then, in 1542, to Santo Domingo. In 1795, when Santo Domingo became French, he was moved to Havana. When Cuba ceased to be Spanish, he was moved to Seville again. In 1877, workmen in Santo Domingo discovered a casket that is now believed to contain the real bones. It is thought the wrong bones were transported in 1795. So we have a choice of resting places for Columbus—one in the Old and one in the New World.

Columbus once said, "The farther one goes, the more one learns."

1924   Chicago. Nathan "Babe" Leopold, Jr., 18, had a millionaire father, who gave him a car and a $125 weekly allowance. Richard "Dicky" Loeb, 17, had a millionaire father, who gave him $250 a week. This at a time when five cents bought a loaf of bread. Leopold spoke seventeen languages and was bound for Harvard Law School. Loeb was one of the youngest students to graduate from the University of Michigan. Despite these advantages and talents, the pair, who became homosexual lovers at 14, were consumed with a desire to prove their superiority to others by committing successful crimes. They began with petty theft and went on to arson and vandalism. Then Loeb decided that a "perfect murder" would be fun.

The pair planned a kidnapping to cover the murder. They composed a ransom note that demanded $10,000, leaving its address blank because they hadn't chosen a victim. They settled upon John Levison because he was too small to put up a fight and was playing near the street. The murderers didn't know his address for the note, and when they returned from checking a drugstore phone book, John had gone home. They spotted Bobbie Franks, 14. Franks was a relative of Loeb's, so he trustingly got into their car.

As Leopold drove, Loeb stabbed Franks in the head four times with a chisel, stuffed rags into the unconscious boy's mouth, and wrapped him in a lap robe. Franks bled to death. The murderers stopped for hot dogs, then went to a restaurant for a larger meal, while waiting for darkness. They then drove to a swamp. To make identification difficult, they stripped the body and poured acid in its face. Leopold shoved the body in a culvert. His exertions caused him to remove his coat. When he put it back on, he didn't notice that his glasses had fallen from his pocket. He also left one of Franks's feet protruding from the culvert. By telephone, Leopold told Bobbie's mother that her son had been kidnapped. The note arrived the next morning. The killers smashed the typewriter used to type it, burned the bloody robe, then dispatched another note. Franks's father was gathering the money when a workman spotted the exposed foot. Despite the acid, the boy was identified.

Police scoured the city for clues. Loeb followed them, making suggestions. Once he said, "If I were going to pick out a boy to kidnap or murder, that's just the kind of cocky little son-of-a-bitch I would pick." Then the glasses were found. Police traced the design to three customers. One was touring Europe. The second answered the door with her pair on her nose. The third was Leopold, who claimed he'd lost the glasses while bird-watching. Reporters found notes for a law class typed by Loeb that matched the ransom note. Confronted with all this, the murderers confessed.

Loeb was disowned by his father, who died two months later. Leopold's father sought out Clarence Darrow, the foremost defense lawyer of his day, and, on his knees, offered Darrow $1,000,000 to keep his boy out of the death house. Claiming they were mentally ill and that execution was uncivilized, Darrow saved the killers. They were sent to prison for life. Leopold's father paid Darrow just $30,000, saying, "The world is full of eminent lawyers who would have paid a fortune for a chance to distinguish themselves in this case."

The pair's wealth bought them a luxurious prison life style. They used the officers' showers, dined privately, had expensive furniture, and kept their own hours, and their cells were seldom locked. They were permitted to visit each other freely, take walks outside the prison, see visitors when they wanted, make phone calls, and purchase booze and drugs. Most disturbingly, it has been reported that Loeb often raped other prisoners while guards looked away.

In 1936, Loeb cornered prisoner James Day in a bathroom. Loeb removed his clothing and produced a razor. He demanded Day take off his clothing, but Day kicked Loeb in the groin, took the razor, and slashed Loeb fifty-six times. Loeb's mother rushed the family surgeon to the prison, but Loeb died. Leopold was at his bedside. Loeb's last words were, "I think I'm going to make it." Supposedly, a newspaper ran the story of his death with the lead, "Richard Loeb, a brilliant college student and master of the English language, today ended a sentence with a proposition."

Leopold was paroled in 1958. He died in 1971 in Puerto Rico (see 8/28/1971).

– May 22 –

1802   Mount Vernon, Virginia. Martha Washington, 69, wife of
       George Washington, died of a bilious fever. Her husband died
       in 1799. His will stated that his slaves would be freed upon the
       death of Martha. Martha irrationally started to believe that the
       slaves were consequently plotting to kill her by poison or by
       letting the fire in her room die out and thereby inducing a
       fatal cold. She would bolt her door and refuse to eat. It was a
       sad closing, for she had been an intelligent, gracious woman.

1865   Floyd, Virginia. A Confederate soldier called Bordunix and
       two of his buddies refused to accept that the South had lost
       the war. They hid in a courthouse and ambushed 560 federal
       cavalrymen. Two of the surprised troopers fell wounded. The
       rebels ran, but the troopers cornered them in a graveyard. The
       rebels were killed there and buried where they fell. They
       were the last official casualties of the American Civil War.

– May 23 –

1701   Newgate. Pirate Captain William Kidd, a citizen of New
       York City, the son of a Scottish Presbyterian minister, and a
       former businessman, had been promised a pardon, but the
       British hanged him anyway. He arrived drunk for his
       execution. It was a custom for bystanders to offer liquor to the
       condemned en route to the execution. The rope broke twice
       but held on the third attempt. Kidd was about 56. His last
       words: "This is a very fickle and faithless generation." Kidd
       was condemned on six counts of piracy and for murdering
       "one Moore, the gunner of the *Adventure.*" Kidd admitted to
       killing the gunner by walloping him on the head with a
       bucket, but claimed the gunner had been rebellious.

1868   Fort Lyon, Colorado. Explorer, trapper, Indian fighter, and
       respected Indian agent Christopher "Kit" Carson, 58, had
       long suffered from indigestion and difficulty in breathing.
       The cause was diagnosed as an aneurysm compressing his
       pneumogastric nerve. When, in April 1868, Carson lost his
       wife following the birth of his seventh child, grief aggravated

his condition. Swallowing food became an agony relieved only by the administration of chloroform.

On May 22, the aneurysm burst. Oddly, Carson slept well that night. On this date, he had a meal of black coffee and buffalo steak. He spent the rest of the day smoking his favorite clay pipe, but that afternoon, he began bleeding at the mouth. He quickly bled to death. His last words were to a friend helping the doctor, *"Adios, compadre!"*

Carson was buried in a pine box lined with the only good-quality material handy, the wedding dress of a soldier's wife. The women of the desert fort, unable to find natural flowers for the service, collected all the artificial flowers from their dresses and hats. Carson wanted to have his and his wife's bodies buried in Taos, New Mexico. A year later, they were moved there. In 1908, local Masons erected monuments over their graves. Carson's bears the words "He led the way."

1906   Oslo. Norwegian poet and playwright Henrik Ibsen, 78, died following his third stroke. His last words, when his wife told him he would get better: "On the contrary."

1934   Bienville Parish, Louisiana. Bonnie Parker, 23, and Clyde Barrow, 24 (it was the day before his 25th birthday), were shot to death. Police, not wanting a shoot-out with the murderers, ambushed their Ford sedan, blasting it into metallic Swiss cheese. Two shotguns, ten automatic pistols, and two machine guns were found in the crooks' car with 1,500 rounds of ammunition.

The duo were hardly the romantic crooks legend portrays. They were inept thieves, their targets were penny-ante (Barrow had started out as a chicken thief), and their love life was bizarre. Clyde was bisexual and shared his boyfriends with Bonnie. Both were fame-hungry. Bonnie wrote maudlin poems about their exploits, which were eagerly printed by a press that pandered to the public's unhealthy glorification of gangsters. Their fourteen killings were invariably brutal and never involved much risk. For example, they once asked a traffic cop for directions. After the officer politely answered, they cut him down with a shotgun blast. These blood-crazy louts were reglorified by Hollywood in 1967. Their victims, however, weren't glorified by anyone.

The duo's bullet-riddled death car is displayed in a casino in Las Vegas.

– May 24 –

1964   Lima. A Peru-Argentina Olympic soccer elimination match
       in Lima's National Stadium turned into a riot over a disputed
       call that gave Argentina the game on a last-minute goal.
       Three hundred were killed and 500 were injured in soccer's
       most deadly game. This horrible incident wasn't the worst
       sports row: Fourteen centuries ago a chariot race in Con-
       stantinople's Hippodrome ended when an unpopular call
       started a riot. Most of the city was leveled, and 30,000 died.

– May 25 –

735   Jarrow, England. The Venerable Bede died in a monastery at
       about 62. According to his student Cuthbert, Bede had been
       suffering from a "tightness of breath" but had kept up his
       lectures and his work translating the Gospel of St. John into
       English. He finished it in time to participate in the Feast of
       the Ascension, dying while chanting the "Gloria Patri" with
       his fellow monks. His last words were "the Holy Ghost."
           Bede was buried at Jarrow but didn't rest peacefully. In the
       first half of the eleventh century, a priest named Alfred stole
       the bones for his church in Durham. In the Middle Ages,
       churches were tourist traps for pilgrims. A church with an
       important set of saintly bones drew larger crowds, making
       more money for its clergy and local merchants. Alfred put
       Bede's bones in the coffin of St. Cuthbert. In 1104, they were
       placed in a fine (perhaps too fine) gold casket, which was soon
       stolen, and Bede's bones were lost.

1927   The Ford Motor Company stopped production of the Model
       T. It had made 15,007,003 of the "Tin Lizzies" in nineteen
       years.

1935   Forbes Field. Baseball star Babe Ruth hit his last home run. It
       was his 714th. He was playing for the Boston Braves. Ruth
       died of cancer at 53 in New York City on August 16, 1948.

1979   Near O'Hare Airport, Chicago, Illinois. An American Air-
       lines DC-10 crashed, killing 272 passengers and three people
       on the ground. It was the worst U.S. air accident.

1980   Oral Roberts saw a 900-foot Christ.

– May 26 –

1703   Clapham, England. Diarist Samuel Pepys died at 70 at a
        friend's country home of bladder and kidney stones worsened
        by hardening of the arteries. At 22, without benefit of
        anesthetics or sterile instruments, a surgeon had removed a
        two-ounce bladder stone from Pepys, but the painful and
        dangerous operation didn't cure his affliction. Although Pepys
        served as first secretary of the Admiralty, he is remembered
        today for his six-volume intimate diary, which, in addition to
        the details of his sex life and hemorrhoids (which he thought
        would kill him), covered Charles II's reign, the Plague, and
        London's Great Fire. The diary was written in shorthand and
        used many foreign terms so as to increase its secrecy. It wasn't
        till 1825 that it was translated and published.

1868   Michael Barrett became the last criminal publicly hanged in
        England. He was convicted of helping kill 13.

1984   Edenton, North Carolina. Mary Bradham Tucker died at 81.
        She was the first Pepsi Girl in the 1900's. Pepsi-Cola was
        invented by her father Caleb Bradham, a druggist.

– May 27 –

1777   St. Catherine's Island, off Savannah, Georgia. Signer of the
        Declaration of Independence Button Gwinnett, 42, quarreled
        with General Lachlan McIntosh over the conduct of a
        campaign against the British in Florida. When McIntosh
        publicly called Gwinnett "a scoundrel and a lying rascal,"
        Gwinnett was compelled to challenge the general to a duel.
        Both were wounded in the leg. They were going to continue
        the duel, but their seconds persuaded them that honor had
        been satisfied. General McIntosh recovered, but Gwinnett
        contracted gangrene and died. He was buried near Savannah,
        but the site was lost—it is said that his marble tombstone was
        stolen and used as a top for a bar.
            Gwinnett signed few documents other than the Declara-
        tion, and because of this, his signature is very valuable today.

1949   New York City. Robert Ripley, 55, died of a heart attack. He
        had started *Ripley's Believe It or Not*, his column about the
        strange and spectacular, in 1918. It was carried in 326

newspapers in 38 countries. Ripley had been ill and was in the hospital at the time of his death. He called a friend and said, "I'm just in for a checkup, and I'll be out to the farm to see you tomorrow." He hung up and fell back in his bed, dead—believe it or not.

– May 28 –

1960   A sanatorium in South San Gabriel, California. Actor George Zucco, 60, was renowned for the evil villains he played. Reportedly, Zucco began taking his roles to heart and was committed to an asylum. He was certain that the monstrous god of H. P. Lovecraft's horror fiction, the "Great God Cthulu," was hunting him. On this date, in the middle of the night, Zucco died of terror. His wife and daughter killed themselves the next night.

1972   Paris. The duke of Windsor, 77, once King Edward VIII, who gave up the English throne for the woman he loved, died of throat cancer. That woman, American divorcée Wallace Warfield Simpson, said of him, "He was born to be a salesman. He would be an admirable representative of Rolls-Royce. But an ex-King cannot start selling motor-cars." Alistair Cooke said, "The most damning epitaph you can compose about Edward—as a Prince, as a King, as a man—is one that all comfortable people should cower from deserving: he was at his best only when the going was good."

Following his wife's death in 1986 at 89, numerous books examining their lives were written. It was revealed that Edward had never forgiven the royal household for not accepting his wife, referring to them in letters by satiric nicknames. Queen Elizabeth II, for example, was "Shirley Temple."

– May 29 –

1911   Harrow Weald, Middlesex, England. Sir William Gilbert, 74, of Gilbert and Sullivan fame, died of a heart attack after saving a young woman drowning in his private lake. His last words were to her: "Put your hands on my shoulders and don't struggle." He enjoyed entertaining women in a special room of his house that he called "the Flirtorium." When he was an infant, while his family toured Italy, Gilbert had been kidnapped. He was ransomed for about $125. An acute critic as well as dramatist, he deemed Sir Herbert Beerbohm Tree's performance as Hamlet, "Funny without being vulgar." Of himself, Gilbert said, "I know how good I am, but I do not know how bad I am."

1942   Hollywood. Actor John Blythe Barrymore, 60, died of dissipation. He had wanted to be an editorial cartoonist but kept getting fired. In his last years, he married Elaine Jacobs, a "groupie" nearly thirty years his junior. He appeared in a Broadway play called *My Dear Children* with Jacobs. Audiences flocked to see it because Barrymore was always ad-libbing, forgetting his lines, calling for louder cues, or swearing. His last words were directed to his old friend Gene Fowler: "Tell me, Gene, is it true that you're the illegitimate son of Buffalo Bill?" He earlier said, "For a man who has been dead for fifteen years I am in remarkable health."

1957   Hollywood. Director James Whale, 60, killed himself by jumping headfirst into the shallow end of his swimming pool. Among his films were *Showboat* (1951), *Frankenstein* (1931), *The Bride of Frankenstein* (1935), and *The Invisible Man* (1933). His best film, *The Road Back* (1937), was butchered by Universal Studios to appease Nazi censors. In 1956, Whale suffered a series of strokes and was given shock treatments. Afterward, he couldn't drive or even read a book. Depression led to suicide.

– May 30 –

1431   Rouen, France. Joan of Arc was burned as a witch in her 19th year. She asked for a cross to look at during the execution, and a monk, using a pole, held one high in the air so she wouldn't watch the rising flames. When they reached her, she screamed, "I have great fear you are going to suffer by my death...Jesus! Jesus!" When the flames had burned away her garments, the executioners raked away the fire so that the crowd could see that the sentence had been carried out. Joan was dead, probably from suffocation or shock. The fire was then rebuilt and Joan's body completely burned. The ashes were dumped in the Seine.

Some think a stand-in was executed, as there are records of Joan's appearance after she was supposed to have died. The reason for the switch was that Joan was said to be of royal blood and thereby immune from execution, as her death would be an attack on the king. The French Armoises family claims to have documents proving that Joan was imprisoned for a time and that after her release she married their ancestor Robert des Armoises and spent the rest of her life in Metz.

Twenty-five years after the burning, Joan was retried. She had helped install the dauphin as king of France, and her heresy was a threat to his legitimacy. He had failed to aid her at the first trial, but at the second, when he was himself partially on trial, she was cleared of all charges. The clergy who had burned her were admonished as hasty.

Joan had been largely forgotten by the eighteenth century, but Napoleon, looking for a heroic folk figure for propaganda, decided Joan was just perfect. She became a hero of French nationalism. She was canonized in the twentieth century.

1788 Paris. Writer François-Marie Arouet de Voltaire, 83, died of complications of uremia. He had dealt humorously with religion, and on his deathbed, he was asked if he recognized the divinity of Christ. His last words: "In the name of God, let me die in peace!" A different account gives his last words when seeing a bedside lamp flare up brightly as "The flames already?"

Voltaire had been ill for a long time. When offered Communion, he refused, saying his bloody coughing would spoil the sacrament. This, plus his criticisms of the Church, outraged Paris's Archbishop. It became clear that he would refuse Voltaire burial in consecrated soil. After Voltaire died, his body was dressed and transported by coach to the nearby town of Ferney, where local priests weren't aware of the controversy. Voltaire was safely tucked under by the time word came to refuse him burial. But perhaps the archbishop got his way. In 1864, when Voltaire's tomb was opened, it was found empty.

Voltaire once said, "A clergyman is one who feels himself called upon to live without working at the expense of the rascals who work to live."

– May 31 –

1889   Johnstown, Pennsylvania. A flood killed 2,295 and caused $17 million in damages. Heavy rains had filled an old dam, which collapsed, releasing 20 million tons of water behind a 35-foot wall. It crushed part of the town and hurled the debris against a mountain. The backwash from this impact roared down another valley, destroying Johnstown's downtown and piling up the wreckage against a bridge, which formed a dam. Hundreds were saved by the presence of this dam, which let people who had sought safety on the roofs of floating houses climb to solid ground. However, many people were trapped in the debris dam, and at least eighty burned alive when it caught fire. Fifty undertakers were needed to bury the dead, and bodies were still being found in 1906.

Historians blame the disaster on the South Fork Fishing and Hunting Club, an organization of wealthy sportsmen that had purchased the dilapidated dam for recreational use. To prevent the escape of game fish, they had placed screens on the spillway. Trash clogged these screens, preventing the water from exiting, which could have relieved the stress on the dam. The sportsmen had refused to make repairs despite warnings. They never paid a penny in damages for the flood.

1974   Palos Verdes, California. Health-food expert Adelle Davis, 70, who said, "You are what you eat," had long blamed cancer on bad nutrition, so she was surprised when, despite her healthful diet, she developed bone cancer. She died of it on this date.

– June 1 –

1868   Lancaster, Pennsylvania. James Buchanan, 77, fifteenth U.S. president, died after contracting a cold that affected his lungs. His last words were in a whisper, "Oh Lord God Almighty, as Thou wilt!" He was buried at Lancaster's Woodward Hill Cemetery. Buchanan was the only unmarried U.S. president, and it was rumored by political rivals that he was homosexually involved with his vice president.

1879   Ulundi, Zululand, Africa. The prince imperial of France, Napoléon-Eugène-Louis Bonaparte, 23, son of Napoleon II, had been exiled with the imperial family upon the reestablishment of the French Republic. The English Crown extended its protection to the family and, perhaps to say "thanks a bunch," or just for the adventure, the prince joined the British forces fighting Zulus in South Africa. He did much charging about, waving a sword inherited from the original Napoleon. This weapon proved ineffective when a surveying party he was accompanying was ambushed. During their retreat, the prince was tossed from his horse and speared seventeen times. The Zulus admired the fight he had made, so they refrained from disemboweling his corpse. The British officer in charge of the party was court-martialed but remained in the service till

1883, when he was fatally injured in Karachi by a horse's kick to the groin.

– June 2 –

1941 New York City. Baseball star Lou Gehrig died seventeen days short of his 38th birthday. He hadn't missed a game in fourteen years and was consequently known as the "Iron Man" of baseball. In 1939, he went into a batting slump. He was diagnosed as suffering from amyotrophic lateral sclerosis, a progressive, fatal paralysis. He left baseball after an emotional leave-taking wherein he called himself the "luckiest man in the world" because of his many friends and fans. Since then, the disease has been known as "Lou Gehrig's disease."

1961 New York City. Playwright George S. Kaufman died at 71— quite old, considering that his diet consisted largely of chocolate. He had been ill since suffering a stroke in 1958. He suggested as his epitaph: "Over my dead body."

Although married, the successful playwright was a ladies' man. His most public affair was with actress Mary Astor, known for *The Maltese Falcon* (1941). It broke up her marriage. Astor's diary was introduced in divorce court, and one passage created a sensation: "He fits me perfectly...20—count them, diary, 20...I don't see how he does it...he is perfect." The papers called him "Public Lover Number One," and $10,000 was offered by one paper for any picture of him in swimming trunks.

– June 3 –

1861 Chicago. Stephen Douglas died at 48. He had been the Democratic candidate for president against Lincoln, had defended slavery, and had once been Lincoln's rival for Mary Todd Lincoln, but when war came, he strove to get Democrats to back Lincoln and persuaded some Southern sympathizers to change sides. Douglas figured prominently in Lincoln's inaugural, holding Lincoln's hat and cane while Lincoln was sworn in and escorting Mrs. Lincoln in the Grand March at the Inaugural Ball. But his efforts exhausted him, and he was killed by a fever. Some suggest that if he had lived, he would have been vice president in Lincoln's second term. He would then have become president after Lincoln's assassination. His last words, while delirious: "Stop, there are twenty against me, the measure is defeated!"

1924 Kierling, Austria. Writer Franz Kafka, 40, died of tuberculosis. His last words, after ordering his books burned, were, "There will be no proof that I ever was a writer." His works survived. Kafka had once said, "In a fight between you and the world, bet on the world."

1953 Tallahatchee Bridge. Billie Joe McAllister killed himself by jumping into the Mississippi River.

– June 4 –

1798 Dux, Bohemia. Venetian adventurer Giovanni Jacopo Casanova, 73, died while working as a librarian. On his deathbed, he observed: "Life is a wench that one loves, to whom we allow any condition in the world, so long as she does not leave us." Following the last rites, he gave his last words: "Bear witness that I have lived as a philosopher and die as a Christian." He was buried in the town cemetery, but when his headstone was discovered in 1922, his remains weren't beneath it.

Casanova suffered eleven bouts of venereal disease despite practicing the eighteenth-century version of "safe sex"—a condom made of waxed cloth and a diaphragm of half a lemon (the citric acid acted as a spermicide). The toxic mercury treatments he received for his venereal infections probably helped kill him. Medical historians believe they wrecked his urogenital tract and that he died of an infection of the prostate.

The illegitimate son of an Italian actress, Casanova had been sent to a seminary to train for the priesthood, but a homosexual romance with a priest ended his studies. His sexual partners were varied and included males, nuns, extremely young girls, and even his daughter (producing a son/grandson). His activities and consequent illnesses caused him to burn out sexually at 40. He spent the rest of his life writing his 4,545-page autobiography.

1923   Belmont Park, New York. Horse trainer Frank Hayes, 35, wanted to be a jockey. On this date, he convinced his employer to let him ride in a steeplechase. His horse, an old bay mare named Sweet Kiss, was a twenty-to-one shot, but she led all the way and won. Hayes didn't enjoy the victory. Sometime during the race, he died of a heart attack. Mounted on Sweet Kiss, his corpse won the race.

1982   Pisa. Umberta Giorgia Carli Piglia, a 30-year-old woman of Turin, leapt to her death from the 180-foot Leaning Tower of Pisa.

– June 5 –

1910   New York City. Writer O. Henry (William Sydney Porter), 47, died of diabetes, cirrhosis, and a heart condition (some accounts say tuberculosis). His last words were, "Turn up the lights; I don't want to go home in the dark." In 1886, he was convicted of embezzling and fled to Honduras. When he heard his wife was dying, he returned and was imprisoned for three years. He began writing while in jail.

1990   Niagara Falls, Ontario. Jessie Sharp, 28, of Ocoee, Tennessee, was confident of his kayaking ability, which he had honed navigating whitewater rivers. He was so confident that on this date he attempted to paddle his red kayak over Niagara Falls. While police and tourists watched, he waved his paddle in the air, then disappeared over the 182-foot falls on the Canadian side. He wore neither helmet nor life jacket. His paddle and his dented kayak were found, but Sharp wasn't.

– June 6 –

1799   Red Hill, Charlotte County, Virginia. Patriot Patrick Henry died at 63. He had been very ill, and his doctor decided on a last measure—a dose of poisonous mercury. He told Henry that it would either cure or kill him. Henry pulled his nightcap over his eyes, prayed for his family, his country, and, finally, himself, then swallowed the mercury. The doctor ran outside, weeping. When he composed himself enough to return, he found Henry dying. Henry's will left his money to his wife, providing she didn't remarry. Despite this, she remarried, then broke Henry's will in court.

1832   London. Philosopher and jurist Jeremy Bentham died at 84. Because he believed everything should have a utilitarian purpose, he willed that his body be preserved so no statue would need to be made. Bentham called such a displayed corpse an "auto-icon." His funeral service was in a medical amphitheater, as directed by his will. Following the eulogy, the body was dissected (at the time illegal). The skeleton was dressed in his clothing, his cane placed in its hand. The head was damaged by the dissection, so a wax duplicate was made. The body wound up in a closet at University College, with the removable head placed between its feet. In recent years, he has been assembled and put on exhibit.

Bentham's last words: "I now feel that I am dying. Our care must be to minimize pain. Do not let the servants come into the room and keep away the youths. It will be distressing to them and they can be of no service."

1961   Küsnacht on Lake Lucerne, Switzerland. Psychologist Carl Jung, 85, creator of analytical psychology, died of heart and circulatory problems. He invented the terms "extrovert," "introvert," and "inferiority complex." He was a friend of Freud's till 1913, when they bitterly disagreed. Jung was more interested in mythology than in Freud's sexology. They reconciled and would meet to discuss their dreams, once talking for twelve hours straight. Tall, coarse-humored, and temperamental, Jung was nevertheless popular with his female patients, keeping one as his mistress for forty years. His son said Jung loved cooking, detective books, winning at games (he would cheat), and dogs. Jung said, "Show me a sane person and I'll cure him for you."

Over the door of Jung's home, there is the motto, "Called or not called, God is present."

– June 7 –

1937   Los Angeles. Jean Harlow (christened Harlean Carpentier), 26, died of kidney failure. She was a protégé of Howard Hughes, and her saucy manner and bleached hair made her a film favorite, especially when matched with Clark Gable in

such classics as *Red Dust* (1932) and *China Seas* (1935). Critic
Graham Greene wasn't favorably impressed. He commented,
"There is no sign that her acting would ever have progressed
beyond the scope of the restless shoulders and the protuberant
breasts; her technique was the gangster's technique—she
toted a breast like a man totes a gun."

Harlow's death may have been related to her unhappy
marriage. In 1932, on their wedding night, she was badly
beaten by her husband, Paul Bern. He bruised her kidney, but
she refused treatment and suffered kidney pains for the rest of
her life. Bern killed himself two months later (see 9/5/1932).
In 1936, she was enduring a bad case of the flu and a general
infection, but her MGM contract obliged her to begin
Saratoga. During filming, she was severely sunburned. A
throat infection followed, forcing her to leave the set. In early
June, she was vomiting and semiconscious, but her mother, a
Christian Scientist, refused medical help. When Harlow was
brought to a hospital a week later, it was too late, and she died.
Saratoga (1937) was completed using a double hidden under a
floppy hat.

At Harlow's funeral, Gable was an usher and pallbearer.
Jeanette MacDonald sang "The Indian Love Call," and
Nelson Eddy finished the service by singing a favorite of
Harlow's, "Ah Sweet Mystery of Life." Harlow was buried at
Forest Lawn Cemetery in Los Angeles. Gable said of Harlow,
"She didn't want to be famous. She wanted to be happy."
Harlow suggested as her own epitaph:

"Of this quiet and peace
I'm very fond;
No more remarks—
She's a platinum blonde."

1967   New York City. Humorist Dorothy Parker, 73, died of heart
failure. Parker was known for her acidic comments; Quentin
Crisp referred to her era as "that far-off time when Dorothy
Parker was alive and bitching." For example, she said of a
book, "This is not a novel to be tossed aside lightly. It should
be thrown with great force." She also commented, "I don't
care what is written about me so long as it isn't true." Parker
died in a shabby hotel room short of cash. Mislaid checks for
thousands of dollars were found among her effects.

Parker suggested her own epitaph: "Excuse my dust." She
was cremated, and her will requested that her friend Lillian
Hellman handle the disposition of the ashes. Hellman never

bothered to do so. When Hellman died in 1984, her will said nothing about Parker's ashes, leaving them in a legal limbo. However, Hellman's will left her estate, including Parker's remains, to the NAACP. They interred Parker's ashes in a memorial garden in Baltimore.

Parker wrote:

> Guns aren't lawful;
> Nooses give;
> Gas smells awful;
> You might as well live.

1988   Chelmsford, England. The lost cat of Ann Edmunds, an 80-year-old widow, missed her dearly. When it found its way home after a month, it was so happy to see its mistress at work in her garden that it ran over and jumped up to greet her. Unfortunately, the cat severed a vein in Mrs. Edmunds's leg, the bleeding couldn't be controlled, and Mrs. Edmunds died. Her neighbors took the hapless cat in.

– June 8 –

1809   New York City. Revolutionary Tom Paine, 72, known for his essay "Common Sense," died in poverty and probably of drink. He drank three quarts of rum each week. His doctor, observing Paine's physical condition, said, "Your belly diminishes." Paine replied, "And yours augments." He then died.

Paine was disliked because of his religious views, and he wasn't permitted to use stages or taverns in New York. He wasn't allowed to vote, and when he died, a Quaker cemetery refused his corpse. Only six people attended his burial. In 1819, an Englishman dug up Paine's bones and brought them to England, where he wanted to build a monument to Paine. He died before he could do so. The bones were sold to a furniture dealer and disappeared.

On his deathbed, Paine, an atheist, was pressed for his religious views. He replied, "I have no wish to believe on that subject."

1845   Hermitage, Nashville, Tennessee. Andrew Jackson, 78, seventh U.S. president, died of dropsy and consumption. His body had greatly swollen, and he coughed up blood continually. One lung had ceased functioning, and the other was barely working. This didn't prevent his singing "Auld Lang

Syne" over and over, nor stop him from smoking a silver pipe.
His last words: "I hope to meet each of you in heaven. Be
good children, all of you, and strive to be ready when the
change comes."

Jackson's lungs had been injured years earlier.
Unknowingly, his wife, Rachel Donnelson, hadn't received a
final decree of divorce from a previous husband when she
married Jackson in 1791. The exposure of this caused her to
suffer a nervous breakdown and die before Jackson took
office. Jackson fought a number of duels in defense of her
reputation. During one, he was wounded. The bullet remained in his chest, and the wound wouldn't heal, despite
periodic painful draining. Jackson agreed to have the bullet
removed (without anesthesia), but the wound still wouldn't
heal. He survived but remained in increasingly poor health
till he died.

Jackson is remembered for the Battle of New Orleans in
1815, wherein a force of militia, frontiersmen, and pirates
under his command slaughtered British forces (many of
whom had recently fought more successfully at Waterloo).
Due to communication delays, the battle was conducted after
a peace treaty had been signed. It is doubtful, however, that
the British would have returned New Orleans had they been
victorious.

1969   Chu Lai, South Vietnam. Nurse Sharon Lane, 25, became the
first American servicewoman killed in the Vietnam War. A
hunk of steel from a North Vietnamese rocket tore through
her heart. She bled to death in minutes. Lane had written
home telling her folks how proud she was that her medical
battalion had treated 10,000 patients. She was awarded a
number of posthumous medals, and a statue of her stands in
the courtyard at Aultman Hospital in Canton, Ohio, where
Lane obtained her nursing degree. Lane's mother observed
sadly, "She just thought she was a nobody, you know, just an
ordinary person, and everybody tries to make a hero out of her
now."

– June 9 –

A.D.   Near Rome. Roman emperor Nero commited suicide in his
68   31st year rather than be captured by pursuing cavalry after

being deposed. His last words: "What an artist perishes in me!" and then, quoting Homer, "The galloping of speedy steeds assails my frighted ears." It is a common debunker's statement to say that Nero didn't actually fiddle while Rome burned because he was thirty-five miles away at the time. It is true that he wasn't in Rome when the fire started, but he rushed back to see the flames and to command the firemen about. It took days to extinguish the blaze, and one night Nero was seen standing on the roof of his pavilion, which was outside the danger area. Observers say he picked up a fidicula (a sort of lyre) and sang a few words about the spectacle. After the fire, Nero expanded his palace. It was suspected that he had set the blaze to create the room.

Nero also liked playing the bagpipe, an instrument that didn't originate in Scotland. It was at one time popular throughout Europe and has been traced to ancient Asia.

1870　Gadshill, England. Writer Charles Dickens, 58, died of a stroke he had suffered the night before while sitting at his dinner table. He had spent the day working on *The Mystery of Edwin Drood*. At the table, he complained of headache and confusion, then he stood, declaring he must visit London at once. Before he could take a step, he grabbed his head, collapsing. His sister-in-law tried to carry him to a sofa, but Dickens said, "On the ground." These were his last words. He fell into a coma from which he never woke. A recent book claims Dickens died at the home of his mistress and that he was then transported to his own home.

Dickens's will provided for his children, his wife, and his mistress. It also directed a modest burial, but his funeral was virtually a state occasion. He was buried in the Poet's Corner of Westminster Abbey.

Dickens is best remembered for *A Christmas Carol*, which described the miraculous conversion of the miser Scrooge. Scrooge's clerk, Cratchit, is depicted as a poor man, but economics professor Procter Thomson claims Cratchit was actually well paid. He received thirty-nine pounds a year. In the 1840s, the average annual English wage was thirty pounds, so Cratchit was in the upper half of the wage pool. Only one of the Cratchit kids worked, whereas it was common for all the children in a lower-class family to work. Great Britain was a prosperous nation, and Cratchit's income was about double the per capita income in America.

Of one of Dickens's most famous characters, Oscar Wilde said, "One must have a heart of stone to read the death of Little Nell by Dickens without laughing."

1911   Leavenworth, Kansas. Saloon-smashing temperance leader Carry Nation, 64, died following what had probably been a stroke in January.

Nation was first jailed in 1900. She had barged into the barroom of Wichita's Carey Hotel to scold the drinkers there when she spied a painting titled *Cleopatra at the Bath* above the bar. Witnesses said she "screeked," then shouted to the bartender, "Disgraceful! You're insulting your mother by having her form stripped naked and hung up in a place where it is not even decent for a woman to be when she has her clothes on!" Nation returned the following day with a hatchet and smashed everything she could reach. As she was led to jail, she said, "You have put me in here a cub, but I will come out roaring like a lion, and I will make all hell howl." This she did. Nation traveled the country attacking saloons and, when arrested, used money earned by selling tiny souvenir hatchets to pay her fines.

Nation was married twice. Her first husband died from alcohol abuse. Her second was a minister who divorced her on the grounds of desertion. She spent all her time traveling for her cause. Thus, her first marriage was ruined by love of liquor, and her second was ruined by hatred of liquor. Carry Nation's daughter gained little from her mother's virtue; she died in an insane asylum, an alcoholic.

Nation once said, "Men are nicotine-soaked, beer-be-smirched, whiskey-greased, red-eyed devils."

– June 10 –

1967   Beverly Hills. Actor Spencer Tracy, 67, died of a heart attack. His health had been weakened by years of heavy drinking. He was the longtime amour of Katharine Hepburn (twenty-nine years), who left films in 1963 to care for the nearly invalid Tracy.

In 1991, Hepburn published her autobiography, *Me*. In it she described Tracy's death. He had gone to the kitchen to make a cup of tea but hadn't returned. She found him on the floor, dead, spattered with the tea. She wrote, "Oh lucky one. That's the way to exit. Just out the door and—gone." His grave is in Los Angeles's Forest Lawn Cemetery. Hepburn didn't attend his funeral. Tracy had been unable to divorce his wife, and Hepburn, not wanting to embarrass the widow, stayed home.

When Hepburn first met Tracy, she commented to Hollywood mogul Joseph Mankiewicz, "I'm afraid I'm a little tall for Mr. Tracy." She was 5 foot 7½ inches (in heels), while Tracy was 5 foot 10 inches. Mankiewicz replied, "Don't worry, Kate, he'll cut you down to his size." Tracy and Hepburn made nine films, including *State of the Union* (1948), *Adam's Rib* (1949), *Desk Set* (1957), and Tracy's final film, *Guess Who's Coming to Dinner?* (1967).

Tracy starred in many movies and won Oscars for *Captains Courageous* (1937) and for *Boy's Town* (1938); yet he observed, "Why do actors think they're so goddam important? They're not. Acting is not an important job in the scheme of things. Plumbing is." As a young actor, Burt Reynolds haunted the set of Tracy's *Inherit the Wind* (1960), hoping to learn more about acting. Tracy confronted Reynolds. "Who are you? Why are you always hanging around?" Reynolds explained himself. "An actor, huh?" Tracy said and added with a wink, "Just remember not to ever let anyone catch you at it."

– June 11 –

1979   Los Angeles. Actor John Wayne, 72, died after a fifteen-year battle with cancer. Just two months earlier, Wayne had appeared at the Academy Awards ceremony. His daughter Aissa Wayne has recently written that Wayne had purchased a smaller-sized tuxedo for the occasion because his cancer had caused him to lose a great deal of weight. However, on the night of the ceremony, even this tuxedo proved too baggy. To hide his thinness, Wayne wore a diver's wet suit under the tuxedo. The assembly of film folks gave Wayne a standing ovation.

Wayne's real name was Marion Michael Morrison. Wayne's nickname, "Duke," was derived from a dog he had as a boy. In 1928, Wayne was attending the University of Southern California and took a summer job as a prop man for Fox studios.

Director Raoul Walsh noticed Wayne moving furniture and cast him in a Western called *The Big Trail* (1930). Wayne starred in several low-budget films and serials till he got his first major role in *Stagecoach* (1940). Thereafter, he made feature after feature (totaling nearly 200 films). Wayne won his only Oscar for *True Grit* (1970), a self-parodying role.

Wayne's death may have been related to his most unusual role, as Genghis Khan in Howard Hughes's *The Conqueror* (1956). The movie was filmed in 1955 in Utah near an atomic test ground in Yucca Flat, Nevada. Wayne, the film's director, Dick Powell, and costar Agnes Moorehead all died of lung cancer. The leading lady, Susan Hayward, died of a brain tumor. Co-star Pedro Armendariz killed himself after being diagnosed with terminal cancer (see 6/18/63). Of the 220 film crew members, 91 contracted cancer, and thus far 46 have died from it.

– June 12 –

1831   Bath, New York. Moses Alexander and his wife, Frances, were discovered in their bed dead. Moses was 93 and Frances 105. They had been married the day before.

1983   Woodland Hills, California. Actress Norma Shearer, 80, died of pneumonia. A Canadian, at 14, Shearer sold her family's dog and their piano and used the money to travel to New York City. She worked as a model there. Once, while posing for a magazine, the artist asked her how she could bear to smile for so long. She acutely replied, "I can't help smiling when I think I'm getting paid for it." Shearer moved to Hollywood, where she married producer Irving Thalberg and became one of the highest-paid film actresses.

– June 13 –

323   Babylon. Alexander the Great died of a fever at 33. His last
B.C.   words, when asked who should succeed him, were, "The strongest." His body, preserved in honey, was taken to Egypt

and buried there. Centuries later, Caligula desecrated the tomb and went about in Alexander's armor.

Alexander once visited Diogenes the Cynic, who lived in an old barrel. Diogenes' philosophy shunned material things. Alexander stood in front of the barrel opening and asked if there was anything Diogenes might want. To the conqueror of the entire known world, Diogenes replied, "Yes, I should like you to stand out of my light."

1979   Hollywood. Child star Darla Hood, 48, died of unknown causes. She was born in Liddy, Oklahoma. Her mother hated Liddy and started training three-year-old Darla for the stage. Darla was spotted by a talent agent during a visit to New York, and she was soon the "leading lady" in the *Our Gang* comedies. She liked the cast, excepting the dog Pete and Alfalfa. She thought Pete, who sported a black circle around one eye, was a mutt, and Alfalfa tormented her (see 1/21/1959).

Darla endured a difficult adolescence but went on to a singing career dubbing for other stars and in television commercials. She was the voice of the Chicken-of-the-Sea mermaid for many years. The *Our Gang* films were revived for television in the 1950s, earning millions, but because their parents had signed away any rights to residuals, the kids got nothing. In addition, when Darla grew up, she discovered that her parents had spent nearly everything she had earned.

– June 14 –

1801   London. Benedict Arnold, 60, died of dropsy, a lung disease. He had fought bravely and skillfully for American Independence but had received little recognition. He had, for example, helped win the Battle of Saratoga. Officers with more political clout, most notably Gen. Horatio Gates, got the credit for his efforts. Embittered and encouraged by his ambitious wife, he changed sides and nearly managed to hand over West Point to the British. He evaded American authorities and served with the British Army, leading its troops against Americans, but never equalled his earlier achievements.

1991   Independence, Kansas. Edward Bell, 56, suffered from cancer. To free himself from the pain, he went to his garage, started his car, and crawled into a sleeping bag. Soon he was dead from carbon monoxide poisoning. He left a note apologizing to his three daughters. One of Bell's daughters, Susanne, 18, was asleep in her upstairs bedroom. The carbon monoxide gas entered the house and filled every room. Susanne died in her bed.

This isn't that unusual. Often, people who choose this means of suicide forget that the car will keep running long after they are dead. On June 8, 1990, in Peoria, Arizona, police found Ruth M. Goran in her car in her garage. She had killed herself with carbon monoxide. The gas had seeped out of the garage and into Goran's condominium, killing her room-mates, Claude R. Hillhouse, 42, and Gordon Gear, 32.

– June 15 –

1849   Nashville. James K. Polk, eleventh U.S. president, died at 53 of dysentery. Polk's campaign slogan in 1844 was "Fifty-four Forty or Fight," which referred to a dispute with Britain over the U.S.-Canadian border. He settled this and led a successful war with Mexico that established U.S. claims over Texas and California. Some thought cholera killed Polk, as that water-borne disease was in the area at the time and had similar symptoms. Texan Sam Houston observed of Polk's death, "A victim of the use of water as a beverage."

The practice of playing "Hail to the Chief" to announce the entrance of the president was started by Polk's wife. She had noted that her short husband was often ignored when he came into a room. The formal, musical salute guaranteed attention.

1904   East River, New York City. The steamer *General Slocum* burned. One thousand twenty-one of the 1,400 aboard died. The steamer had been rented for a church outing and was crammed with women and children (only 100 men were aboard). A boy discovered the fire in a barrel and fetched a crewman, who tried to extinguish it by throwing charcoal on it. It spread quickly. Rotted fire hoses burst. Life jackets had been wired to the walls to prevent theft. The few that could be ripped free were stuffed with sawdust instead of cork. Lifeboats couldn't be launched because years of paint glued them to the deck. Captain William H. Van Schaick ordered full speed for shore, hoping to beach the steamer. The speed spread the flames, and ships that tried to take off passengers couldn't keep up. After the *Slocum* beached, a ferryboat managed to take off 50 before it, too, caught fire—fortunately, her crew controlled their blaze. Prison inmates from Riker's Island rowed out to pull victims from the water. Patients from a hospital on the island also rushed to help. The disaster was over in forty minutes.

In 1906, Captain Van Schaick was convicted of manslaughter and sentenced to ten years in Sing Sing, but when the inspectors, who took bribes to certify the ship was safe, and the owners, who paid the bribes, weren't even charged, public outrage swelled. A quarter-million people signed a petition that caused President Taft to pardon Van Schaick on Christmas Day in 1911. He lived to celebrate his ninetieth birthday in 1927, then died the next day.

– June 16 –

1871   Ohio. During the Civil War, Clement L. Vallandigham, 50, had been banished to the Confederate states for treason, but when the war ended, he returned to Ohio and became a prosperous lawyer. He was retained to defend Thomas McGehan, who was charged with shooting a man in a barroom brawl. Vallandigham contended that in pulling the gun from his trousers, McGehan had unknowingly cocked the pistol and that it had gone off accidentally. Vallandigham demonstrated his views to other defense attorneys in his hotel room. He had a loaded and an unloaded pistol on hand for the purpose. Vallandigham said, "There, that's the way [he] held it." The gun fired. He had picked up the wrong pistol. "My God, I've shot myself!" he exclaimed. He died twelve hours later. Using the incident as an example, the defense secured McGehan's freedom.

1959   Los Angeles. George Reeves, 45, known for his role as Superman, shot himself with a 9-millimeter Luger. It was ruled suicide, but friends disagreed. Reeves had received telephoned death threats, including one just hours before he died. Gossip linked the threats to an affair with another man's wife—a man reputed to have underworld connections. Reeves was also involved in three near-accidents: His car was nearly caught between two trucks, a car swerved at him while he was walking, and he nearly crashed when the brake fluid mysteriously disappeared from his car.

On the night of his death, Reeves had been watching television and drinking with his fiancée, Lenore Lemmon, who lived with him in his Benedict Canyon home, and a houseguest, Robert Condon, who was writing an article about Reeves. The three retired. At about 1:30 A.M., three friends, who had also been drinking, hammered on the door. Reeves didn't like late-night guests, and an argument broke out. Reeves went to his bedroom. Lenore said, "Well, he's sulking; he'll probably go up to his room and shoot himself!" There was a shot, and Reeves was found dead.

There were no powder burns on Reeves, indicating that the gun wasn't pressed against his head. The bullet was found in the ceiling, suggesting a strange angle for suicide. Police didn't fingerprint the death room. Some suggest that Reeves was in the habit of faking suicide with blanks and that the jealous husband substituted real bullets.

It has been suggested that Reeves was unhappy with being typecast as Superman, especially since the show had been canceled. However, Reeves was booked to box light heavyweight champ Archie Moore and for a tour of Australia. He was to star in a movie he was going to direct. There would be more episodes of "Superman" filmed for syndication. There was also his impending marriage. When asked if he believed Reeves had killed himself, friend Gig Young, who would later shoot himself and his wife (see 10/19/1978), said, "No! Absolutely not. George could never take his life...everything was going his way."

– June 17 –

1986   Raleigh, North Carolina. Singer Kate Smith, 77, known for her renditions of "When the Moon Comes Over the Mountain" and "God Bless America," died of respiratory failure.

Smith was afraid of being underground. Even when New York City cabbies went on strike, she refused to use the subway. Her will called for her to be entombed in an aboveground, rose-colored mausoleum in the cemetery of St. Agnes

Catholic Church in Lake Placid, New York. Cemetery officials rejected the structure as too large and garish, and it took a year of negotiations before she was finally entombed.

During World War II, Smith sold $600 million worth of war bonds.

– June 18 –

1959   New York City. Actress Ethel Barrymore, 79, died of a heart condition. Her last words were "Is everybody happy?" She had been on the stage since 1894. As a young woman, she was a renowned beauty, tempting young Winston Churchill to unsuccessfully woo her. She was also friendly with Teddy Roosevelt. Like her famous siblings, Ethel had problems with alcohol. She once fell, drunk, onstage in Denver, and on another occasion, in London, she was jeered from the stage for performing while intoxicated. Fortunately, Ethel overcame her drinking problem.

1963   UCLA Medical Center, Los Angeles. Pedro Armendariz, 51, shot himself. He was Mexico's top film star before arriving in Hollywood, where he appeared in several John Ford pictures, including *Fort Apache* (1948) and *Three Godfathers* (1936). He was filming *From Russia With Love* (1963) when he died. He had suffered from kidney cancer for years and had just been told that he had terminal lymph cancer. He shot himself to avoid a lingering death. Armendariz may have contracted the disease during the filming of *The Conqueror* (1956) (see 6/11/79).

1979   Key West, Florida. B. P. Roberts died at age 50. His tombstone reads: I TOLD YOU I WAS SICK.

– June 19 –

1937   London. Scottish writer Sir James Matthew Barrie, best known for *Peter Pan*, died in his 77th year, of bronchial pneumonia. He had written, "To die will be an awfully big adventure."

Barrie once encountered the British author H. G. Wells and, in true Peter Pannish-style, asked, "It is all very well to be able to write books, but can you waggle your ears?" Barrie could. Wells couldn't.

1953 Sing Sing Prison, Ossining, New York. Julius, 41, and Ethel Rosenberg, 37, were executed for passing atomic bomb secrets to the Russians. Generations of sympathizers have claimed that they were victims of a witch-hunt because of their progressive views and that the information they passed was useless. In 1990, a transcript of a conversation with Nikita Khrushchev indicated that no less an authority than Stalin had recognized their efforts as atomic spies and that they were instrumental in providing the Russians with the atomic bomb.

– June 20 –

1830 Danville, Kentucky. In 1809, Dr. Ephraim McDowell made a sixty-mile house call to treat Jane Crawford, a frontier mother of six. She was expecting twins, but Dr. McDowell discovered she wasn't pregnant. She had a massive ovarian tumor. He suggested surgery. This was before anesthetics and antiseptics. In fact, no one had ever tried a surgical cure. If he failed, he might be tried for murder. Gamely, Mrs. Crawford agreed. She recited psalms during the half-hour procedure. Although a twenty-two-pound tumor was removed, Mrs. Crawford was on her feet in five days. The first successful major abdominal surgery had been performed by a backwoods country doctor.

Dr. McDowell performed two similar operations successfully. Other doctors tried to imitate his work in America and Europe but with less success. The horrible pain involved, the poor rate of recovery due to infections and blood loss (there were no transfusions), and the lack of anatomical knowledge delayed progress. It took decades for Dr. McDowell's work to become accepted. It was too late for Dr. McDowell. He died on this date at 58 of acute appendicitis. The first surgery in America for appendicitis was thirteen years later, and it would be fifty years before another would be performed in Kentucky. Mrs. Crawford survived her doctor by eleven years, dying quietly at 79.

1876 Mexico City. General Antonio Lopez de Santa Anna, dictator of Mexico and butcher of the Alamo, died in poverty and friendless at about 81 of natural causes. His wife had earlier converted his fortune to her own use and abandoned him.

In 1838, the French demanded that Mexico pay $600,000 worth of claims against Mexican merchants. One of these claims was made by a French baker who hadn't been paid for some pies. This caused the fracas to be called the "Pastry War." Santa Anna served as a commander during the war. He was asleep in his mansion in Vera Cruz one night when French marines landed. When they demanded the location of the commander, the nightshirted Santa Anna escaped by pointing upstairs and yelling "Up there!" Santa Anna later captured some French soldiers but quickly returned them when a French warship turned its guns on the city. When the French started to sail away, Santa Anna, now dressed in a splendid uniform and astride a white charger, dramatically stormed out of hiding and after them. The French aboard the warship were beyond the reach of his flashing saber. He, however, was within reach of their cannons. As he rode along the beach shouting insults, a cannonball killed his horse and tore off one of Santa Anna's legs. Santa Anna wrote an emotional "deathbed" letter that appeared in Mexican newspapers and he became a national hero. His leg was given an elaborate military funeral. But by the time the remainder of him died decades later, Santa Anna was scorned. His leg received a much better funeral than the rest of him. The Mexicans paid the claims.

– June 21 –

1527   Florence. Italian political writer Niccolò Machiavelli died at 58. His last words: "I desire to go to hell and not to heaven. In the former place I shall enjoy the company of popes, kings, and princes, while in the latter are only beggars, monks, and apostles." Nevertheless, he received the last rites.

– June 22 –

1969   London. Actress Judy Garland (born Frances Gumm) died shortly after her 47th birthday of an accidental overdose of sleeping pills.

Only one star of *The Wizard of Oz* (1939) was paid less than Garland—the dog Toto (a Cairn terrier). Garland was paid $500 a week. She was 17 when that film was made, but she was soon seeing a psychiatrist and, at 28, tried to commit suicide.

Of Garland, Joan Crawford said, "I didn't know her well, but after watching her in action a few times, I didn't want to know her well." Anita Loos said, "Judy's mental attitude may have been pathetic but it turned her into a great bore." Garland said, "Hollywood is a strange place when you're in trouble. Everyone is afraid it's contagious." Ray Bolger, the Scarecrow in *The Wizard of Oz*, said of her death, "She just plain wore out."

Garland has always enjoyed the affection of gay fans. She said, "When I die, I have visions of fags singing 'Somewhere Over the Rainbow' and the flag at Fire Island being flown at half-mast."

– June 23 –

1611   Hudson Bay. The English explorer Henry Hudson, his son, and six loyal crewmen were set adrift without water or provisions by the mutinous crew of Hudson's ship, the *Discovery*. They were never seen again. Hudson was about 61. The mutineers weren't hanged, as they claimed the ringleaders had been killed by Indians while foraging for food in Canada and, more important, because they said they knew a sea route to China—the "Northwest Passage." The search for such a route had been the purpose of the Hudson voyage, and the British government was keenly interested. In fact, the mutineers didn't know the way. Without a modern icebreaker or a submarine, there is no such route. One mutineer became a ship's surgeon, another became a boatswain's mate, and one actually became the captain of the *Discovery*.

1954   East Orange, New Jersey. Dentist William Lowell, 94, died after a short illness. He invented the golf tee in 1921. Prior to this, golfers made a little mound of sand and water to tee off from.

– June 24 –

1908   Princeton, New Jersey. Grover Cleveland, twenty-fourth U.S.
        president, died at 71. In 1893, he discovered a sore on the roof
        of his mouth. A doctor decided it was a cancer and prescribed
        surgery. The U.S. economy was in a precarious state, so the
        operation was kept secret. Under the guise of a cruise, the
        surgery was done aboard a yacht in Manhattan's East River.
        The surgical bed was a chair lashed to the mast. Most of
        Cleveland's upper jaw was removed. Only one of seven
        survived this kind of surgery, but Cleveland managed to walk
        off the yacht on his own. A second secret surgery was later
        performed, and Cleveland was fitted with a rubber, artificial
        jaw to restore his appearance. The press found out, but all of
        the facts weren't known till 1917, when the surgeon donated
        the removed jaw to a museum. Modern doctors suspect that
        the sore wasn't malignant and the radical surgery unneeded.
            Cleveland remained in poor health. His death has been
        variously attributed to heart failure, intestinal blockage, and a
        stroke. His last words: "I have tried so hard to do right."

– June 25 –

1876   Near 5:00 P.M. The Little Big Horn, Montana. Two hundred
        and eleven soldiers were killed in "Custer's Last Stand" by
        Sioux and Cheyenne Indians. Indian oral tradition credits the
        soldiers with fighting courageously, but notes that some
        soldiers killed themselves to avoid torture when it became
        clear that there was no hope. One suspects that some troopers
        also killed hopelessly wounded comrades. Their commander,
        George Armstrong Custer, 36, was last seen on all fours,
        bleeding at the mouth. Some claim he also killed himself.
            Custer had attacked Indian camps at high odds before and
        had succeeded by triggering a panic that made opposition
        piecemeal. However, this time the Indians rebuffed the initial
        attack and then swarmed over Custer's greatly outnumbered
        men. One supposed explanation is that Custer's men had
        callously ridden through a sacred hemp patch, and that

outrage at this caused the immediate defense. Others more reasonably credit Crazy Horse, who rallied the startled Indians. This failure to induce a stampede, Custer's premature attack before other forces could arrive (he may have thought he had been detected by the Indians and had no choice), and his division of his force into three smaller forces (perhaps to give the impression of a larger force) led to Custer's defeat. In addition, many of the Indians were armed with repeating rifles. The troopers carried single-shot carbines, which, while having longer range than the repeaters, were prone to jamming and delivered a much smaller volume of fire.

When the soldiers' bodies were discovered by troops sent to support Custer, they had been stripped and mutilated. Curiously, Custer, while naked, hadn't been mutilated, save for the piercing of his ears. This was supposedly to improve his hearing in the next world so that he would hear Indian complaints that the white man was breaking his word. It has been suggested that the reason Custer wasn't mutilated was that he had had an affair with an Indian woman that produced a child. The child died, but the woman and her relatives still considered Custer a family member and protected the body. Another explanation forms the basis for the suicide claim. Indians were known to leave the body of a suicide alone. Yet the other bodies, which almost certainly included suicides, were all mutilated. Possibly, the Indians simply respected Custer's body because of his reputation.

The dead troopers were quickly buried in shallow graves. With thousands of hostiles in the area, this is understandable. Custer and his brother Tom, who had died with him, were given the best burials. They were buried in an eighteen-inch-deep hole, covered with blankets, then a tarp, then with earth, and finally topped with an Indian stretcher heaped with rocks. While the other graves were despoiled by animals and the weather, Custer's and his brother's should have been left intact. Yet when the army sent a detail to retrieve Custer's bones, they couldn't find the stretcher. They chose one grave as the likely spot, but when they unearthed its skeleton, they found the shreds of a corporal's uniform. They moved to a nearby grave, where they found a skull, ribcage, and leg bone. Labeling these as Custer's remains, they dispatched them to

West Point, where they were reburied beneath an obelisk bearing brass plaques depicting the battle.

A lock of auburn hair was found in the battlefield grave. Custer's wife, Elizabeth, identified this as her husband's hair. Nevertheless, some historians believe the bones belong to an unknown enlisted man. The soldiers who gathered them expressed doubts to their commander, Captain Michael Sheridan, but he philosophically replied, "Nail the box up; it is all right as long as the people think so." An examination of the bones at West Point might end the mystery, but the Custer family, most notably great-grandnephew Colonel George A. Custer III, U.S. Army retired, declared "absolutely not." Coloniel Custer died in May of 1991 at Pebble Beach, California, but it is unlikely that the family's views will change. One fact is certain—since only part of the skeleton was transferred, some of Custer's bones must have been left at the battle site. So, at least in part, Custer will stay with his men.

1946   Near Joplin, Missouri. A bus hit a cow, crashed, and killed twelve passengers.

– June 26 –

363   Phrygia. The Roman emperor Julian the Apostate, 32, the last pagan emperor, died in battle against Persian enemies of the empire. He was killed by a cavalry spear to the side. Although educated in Christian monastic schools, he had abandoned Christianity and was trying to revive the traditional Roman deities. His last words were, "You have conquered, Galilean." He was referring to Christ. It has been suggested that the emperor was assassinated by Christian religious leaders.

– June 27 –

1829   Genoa. English scientist James Smithson, 64, died of natural causes. He disliked the treatment he had received from his countrymen because of his illegitimate birth. Consequently, he bequeathed his fortune to the United States for the creation of a museum, which became the Smithsonian Institution. Smithson was buried in the English cemetery in Genoa, but when this was demolished in 1903, he was moved to Washington, D.C., by the Smithsonian.

1844   Carthage, Illinois. Mormon founder Joseph Smith, 38, had been jailed on the twelfth after followers smashed the press of the Nauvoo *Expositor*, a newspaper critical of Mormons. On this date, a mob stormed the jail and killed Smith.

1957   Ripe, Sussex, England. British writer Malcolm Lowry killed himself in his 48th year. He had long suffered from alcoholism. His works weren't fully valued till after his death. Among them are *Ultramarine* and *Under the Volcano*. In the latter, he wrote, "How alike are the groans of love to those of the dying."

– June 28 –

1836   Montpelier Station, Virginia. James Madison, fourth U.S. president, died at 85 of debility, aggravated by difficulty in swallowing. His last words were "I always talk better lying down." Madison was the smallest U.S. President. He was five feet four inches tall and weighed about 100 pounds.

1914   Sarajevo, Bosnia-Herzegovinia. Archduke Ferdinand, 51, and his wife, Sophia, were assassinated. Moments before, they had avoided assassination by grenade, and they bravely insisted on continuing their tour. Their car took a wrong turn, and their driver paused to turn about in front of another assassin, who leapt out and shot them. Ferdinand's stoic last words: "It is nothing." The incident triggered World War I. The devastation from that war has been estimated at seven times the destruction of the 901 major wars preceding it.

– June 29 –

1933   New York City. In 1913, 266-pound assistant plumber Roscoe "Fatty" Arbuckle unplugged producer Mack Sennett's drain. Sennett cast him in a comedy. By 1921, Arbuckle had signed a $3 million contract with Paramount Pictures. He staged a celebration in San Francisco's St. Francis Hotel. It began September 2 and ended September 5, when Arbuckle took actress Virginia Rappe, 25, into a bedroom and locked the door. Screams and pounding were heard. Arbuckle emerged with Rappe's hat on his head and his pajamas torn. He giggled, telling the other girls present to get Rappe dressed because "she makes too much noise." Rappe kept screaming. Arbuckle: "Shut up or I'll throw you out of the window!" The girls found Rappe half-naked and in agony. Every piece of her clothing had been ripped. Later, in a private hospital, she said: "Fatty Arbuckle did this to me. Please see that he doesn't get away with it!" She died September 10.

A coroner discovered that Rappe's bladder had been ruptured by some form of great pressure and that death had resulted from peritonitis. Speculation blamed Arbuckle's weight or the violent use of some artificial object when the intoxicated comic couldn't perform naturally. No murder weapon was found. Arbuckle was charged with rape and first-degree murder. Headlines demanded justice. Women in Connecticut tore down the screen of a theater showing an Arbuckle film, while Wyoming cowboys shot up another. Everywhere, showings were canceled. Arbuckle's lawyers presented Virginia as a tramp. This, plus the muddled testimony of the drunken guests and the lack of a weapon, produced an acquittal after two hung juries.

Arbuckle thought he could go back to pie fights, but his contract was abrogated and his films scrapped. He worked as a gag writer but never acted again. He continued his drinking and died broke of a heart attack on this date at 46. As for the missing murder weapon, film historian Kenneth Anger in *Hollywood Babylon* relates how Arbuckle was pulled over for drunken driving in Hollywood in 1931. When the officer approached the car, Arbuckle heaved a bottle out. "There goes the evidence." He laughed.

1967   New Orleans. Actress Jayne Mansfield, 34, was beheaded when her car hit the back of a truck at high speed. Mansfield's first publicity coup was at the premiere of Howard Hughes's *Underwater!* (1955). The film was shown underwater, with the audience of press and critics wearing scuba gear. Mansfield wasn't even in the film, which starred Jane Russell, but she got the attention. Russell was supposed to appear for photographers in a skimpy bathing suit but was reluctant to do so. Mansfield got to the pool first in an even skimpier bikini and managed to lose her top just as the photographers gathered.

1978   Scottsdale, Arizona. Actor Bob Crane, 49, known for playing Captain Hogan on TV's "Hogan's Heroes" (1965–70), was murdered in a hotel room. An electrical cord was wound around his neck, and he had been beaten to death. Recently, new tests have been applied to a bloodstain found on a suspect's car, and a friend of Crane's, John Carpenter, has been charged with the murder. Reporters have suggested that police were sidetracked by numerous photographs and sexually explicit videotapes Crane had made of himself and a number of women.

Crane was married twice and had six children. His second wife was Sigrid Valdis, who appeared as Helga, Colonel Klink's blond-bombshell secretary. At the time of Crane's death, they were in the middle of a divorce. Valdis inherited most of Crane's half-million-dollar estate. His children received $5,000 each and a few personal effects. His son received the hat Crane wore as Colonel Hogan.

– June 30 –

1882   Old Capital Prison, Washington, D.C. Charles Guiteau, 41, the assassin of President James Garfield, was hanged (see 7/2/1881 and 9/19/1881). Guiteau acted as his own lawyer, with the assistance of his attorney brother-in-law, George Scoville. Scoville claimed Guiteau was innocent on the grounds of insanity. Guiteau objected to this defense, insisting that God had used his hand to conduct His divine will, and besides, Garfield's doctors had killed the President through malpractice. After a long trial full of nineteenth-century psychobabble (Guiteau's head was measured and proved lopsided), Guiteau's raving at all parties while playing to the press, and a long examination of Guiteau's disappointments in life (he had been cast out of a free-love commune because no woman would have him), the jury took five minutes to convict Guiteau of murder. He called them "low, consummate jackasses." The judge sentenced him to hang.

Guiteau had nightmares about the hanging and was reported sleeping with his blanket raised to protect his neck. His sister tried to smuggle him arsenic in some flowers so he could kill himself more comfortably, but guards discovered it. One army guard, disgusted with Guiteau, took a shot at him but missed, whereupon a congressmen called for an investigation of marksmanship training in the army. When Guiteau went to the scaffold, he recited a bizarre poem of his own writing that described a dying child's thoughts in baby talk. He mentioned that it would make a beautiful song, given the right tune. His last words were "Glory, hallelujah! Glory!"

The authorities removed the flesh from Guiteau's bones, bleached them, and prepared to exhibit them to the public free of charge as an object lesson on crime and consequence. However, this plan was canceled. It was said that the bones were privately disposed of by the U.S. surgeon general, but they may fill a drawer somewhere in the Army Medical Museum.

1971   Three Soviet cosmonauts from the *Soyuz XI* mission were found dead in their capsule upon its return to earth. Their mission had been successful, but during reentry their ventilation system opened too early. It was meant to admit earthly air automatically when the capsule was at six kilometers above the ground. Instead, it opened at 150 to 180 kilometers, where there is no air. As a Soviet space official admitted years later, "There was a vacuum inside, and that was the end of them. Their blood was boiling. So they died."

EM

– July 1 –

1860   New York City. Inventor Charles Goodyear, 59, died. He had patented the vulcanization process, which made rubber resistant to heat and cold. Goodyear spent years developing the process. He lived in poverty and was sent to debtor's prisons a number of times, where he gamely continued conducting experiments behind bars. A friend observed, "If you meet a man who has on an India rubber cap, stock, coat, vest, and shoes, with an India rubber money purse without a cent of money in it, that is he."

Goodyear's wife grew tired of the expense and time he devoted to the project. He was experimenting in the kitchen one day in 1839 while she shopped. When she returned early, Goodyear swept his materials into the hot kitchen stove so she wouldn't see that he was still experimenting. When his wife left again, Goodyear retrieved his materials and discovered that rubber, when blended with sulfur and heated, became heat-resistant. It was his only moment of triumph. His rights were infringed upon in the United States and weren't recognized in Britain and France. Goodyear employed Daniel Webster to assert his ownership and won in court, but collected little. When he went to press his claims in Europe, he ran out of money, and the French imprisoned him for debt. He was on his way to his sick daughter when he became ill. Before he could reach her, she died, and Goodyear died a few weeks later, $200,000 in debt. His last words: "God knows...God knows all."

1976   West Germany. Anneliese Michel, a student, died at 23 from malnutrition and dehydration caused by months of exorcism

1989   Arvada, Colorado. Pat Ryan was standing behind his six-year-old son Brian during a baseball outing to coach the boy on fielding, when a line drive slipped past the boy's glove and hit the youngster in the chest. He collapsed and was rushed to a hospital, but was pronounced dead on arrival. An autopsy revealed that the blow had caused heart failure. The batter who had hit the fatal line drive was the boy's mother.

– July 2 –

1778   Ermenonville, France. Philosopher Jean-Jacques Rousseau, 66, died of apoplexy. He believed man is good till civilization corrupts him. This notion of the "noble savage" has had great influence. His glorification of the primitive is actually racist. Rousseau stereotyped less technical civilizations, dismissing their variety, dehumanizing them by ignoring their faults. This patronizing attitude treats primitives as childish innocents too unsophisticated to understand big, bad civilization. An example of this attitude is the "Hiawatha Complex," which portrays American Indians as saintly ecologist-philosophers, trivializing the people it pretends to glorify.

Rousseau never lived among primitives, nor did he spurn the comforts of civilization. Rousseau was also a masochist who delighted in being humiliated. Once, when he grew attached to a beautiful prostitute, he sought a way to mentally distance himself from her because he found her career sordid. He discovered that one of her nipples was less than perfect. His love vanished, and he lectured the girl on her imperfection. He wrote, "I held in my arms some kind of monster rejected by Nature, man, and love." Perhaps this reveals something about how he came to his conclusions about civilization.

1961   Ketchum, Indiana. Nobel Prize-winning writer Ernest Hemingway, 61, took his life with a twelve-gauge shotgun. Hemingway had been in poor health and was depressed. His father had also committed suicide because of poor health. Hemingway once chose as his epitaph, "Pardon me for not getting up."

Harold Robbins, saying more about himself than about Hemingway, once complained, "Hemingway's stupid book comes out and they make a big fuss out of this old man and the stupid dead shark, and who cares?" E. B. White said, "Ernest Hemingway's writing reminds me of the farting of an old horse." Hemingway's own mother didn't like his writing. She refused to finish *The Sun Also Rises*. She said she couldn't make sense of "such vulgar people and such messy subjects." She added, "I can't stand filth."

– July 3 –

1937   Somewhere near Howland Island, South Pacific (this was July 2 in the United States). Aviator Amelia Earhart, 38, with her navigator, Fred Noonan, disappeared while attempting to fly around the world. Earhart, poorly trained in radio, had lost contact with a navy ship that was positioned to guide her. Navy radiomen reported distress signals for three nights. These could have been broadcast only if the aircraft was upright and able to run its engines. Nevertheless, an extensive search turned up nothing.

Rumors persist that Earhart crash-landed on an island held by the Japanese, who shot her as a spy. After World War II, a woman on Saipan, many miles from Earhart's planned course, claimed she saw a Caucasian woman shot by the Japanese. An American soldier who served there claims that he saw her aircraft there. He says military authorities told him to keep quiet, then burned the plane. Another soldier, also on Saipan, claims he found papers belonging to Earhart in a Japanese safe. He turned these over to an officer and never saw them again. Why American authorities would wish to hide a Japanese atrocity or a heroic spy mission remains unexplained, especially when it would have served as useful wartime propaganda.

One expert theorizes that a map error positioned Earhart's target, Howland Island, at the wrong latitude and longitude and that when she flew to that spot, there was no island there. She searched fruitlessly for the island, then crashed into the sea when she ran out of fuel. He believes the reported radio signals were false.

In 1991, Richard Gillespie of the International Group for Historic Aircraft Recovery announced that he had discovered a navigation book case on the tiny island of Nicumaroro (formerly known as Gardner Island). FBI scientists said the paint upon the case matched that used in 1930s aircraft. Search planes had reported signs of life on the island, but because it was far off Earhart's course the sighting wasn't followed up. Gillespie suggests that Earhart may have landed on the island's beach and that the distress calls were made from there till the tides pulled the aircraft into the sea. He believes that Earhart and Noonan died of thirst. There was no fresh water on the island.

In 1992, Gillespie returned to Nicumaroro and found part of a woman's shoe, a bottle cap, and a piece of aluminum that he identified as part of Earhart's plane. A shoe manufacturer matched the shoe to a 1930s model. The cap matched a stomach medicine of the 1930s. Earhart had been having stomach problems. However, several men who worked on Earhart's Lockheed Electra say that the piece doesn't match Earhart's aircraft. Gillespie responds that the fuselage was altered during repairs earlier in Earhart's flight, but workers who were there during the repairs disagree. It should be noted that the British unsuccessfully tried to establish a colony on Nicumaroro shortly after Earhart disappeared and, during World War II, an American weather station was set up on the island. The relics may date to their occupation.

Before leaving on her flight, Earhart wrote her husband, "Please know that I am aware of the hazards. I want to do it because I want to do it. Women must try to do things as men have tried. When they fail, their failure must be but a challenge to others."

1971   Paris. Jim Morrison, 28, member of the Doors, died of heart failure in his bathtub. He was buried in Paris's Père Lachaise

Cemetery along with such notables as Frédéric Chopin,
Getrude Stein, Edith Piaf, and Oscar Wilde. His marker
differs from theirs. It is liberally covered with the graffiti of
myriad fans.

– July 4 –

1826   Virginia. Thomas Jefferson, third U.S. president, died at 83.
He had spent his last years nearly bankrupt. These money
problems worsened the bouts of dysentery and rheumatism he
suffered. He refused the treatments his doctors prescribed—
bleeding and purging—but despite this good sense, he
weakened as the dysentery dehydrated him. He fell into a
stupor, awakening on the evening of the third to ask "Is it yet
the Fourth?" Informed that it wasn't, he held on to die after
dawn on the Fourth. He was buried at his home, Monticello.

Jefferson left his family destitute, but the legislatures of
Virginia and South Carolina gave his surviving daughter
$20,000 in gratitude to her father. This wasn't enough to save
Monticello, which fell into near-ruin until the 1920s, when it
was restored.

It has been claimed that Jefferson sired five children by
Sally Hemings, one of his slaves. Jefferson's affection for his
wife, Martha Wayles Skelton, was well known. He had
promised her on her deathbed not to remarry and he never
did so, but Sally Hemings was said to bear a remarkable
resemblance to Jefferson's late wife. It was even suggested that
she was the daughter by a slave of Jefferson's father-in-law.

Jefferson was the first president to wear long trousers. He
also ended the custom of bowing at the White House,
replacing it with shaking hands.

1826   Quincy, Massachusetts. John Adams, second U.S. president,
died at nearly 91. He had long suffered from rheumatism and
arteriosclerosis. To celebrate the Fourth, Adams had been
dressed and set by a window to observe the festivities.
However, he soon fell into a coma, dying that afternoon. His
last words were, "Thomas Jefferson survives." He was wrong:
Jefferson had died that morning.

The two patriots had quarreled over many issues, and

Jefferson had defeated Adams for the Presidency in 1800. Jefferson said of Adams, "He is distrustful, obstinate, excessively vain, and takes no counsel from anyone." Adams would respond in kind, but in 1812, Adams renewed their friendship with a letter. Thereafter they corresponded often, still differing, but with civility and with many pleasant memories of their Revolutionary days.

1831   New York City. James Monroe, fifth U.S. president, died at 73 of debility and probably tuberculosis. After leaving office, Monroe fell on hard times. He lost his home and had to live with his son-in-law. In his diary, John Quincy Adams sadly reflected on the "wretchedness and beggary" in which Monroe died. He was buried at Hollywood Cemetery, Richmond, Virginia.

– July 5 –

1944   New York City. Illustrator Frederick D. Steele died at 70. He illustrated many famous works by Kipling, Twain, and Conrad, but his best-remembered illustrations are those he drew for Arthur Conan Doyle's Sherlock Holmes stories. He helped create the image of Holmes. The cape and deerstalker cap were his idea.

1950   Korea. The first American soldier died in the Korean conflict. It wasn't till 1989 that a national memorial for Korean veterans was announced.

– July 6 –

1535   London. Sir Thomas More, 57, was beheaded for opposing Henry VIII's divorce of Catherine of Aragon. He was taken blindfolded to the scaffold, but the structure was rickety. He asked that the blindfold be removed, saying: "I pray you, I pray you, Mr. Lieutenant, see me safe up, and for my coming down let me shift for myself." After a statement and a few prayers, he addressed his last words to the headsman, "Pluck up thy spirits, man, and be not afraid to do thine office, my neck is very short. Take heed therefore thou shoot not awry for saving thine honesty."

More's head was placed on London Bridge, where it was intended to stay till ravens and decay had reduced it to a skull. Margaret Roper, his eldest daughter, was passing under the bridge on the fourteenth day of the head's display, and she prayed that the head, which had so often lain in her lap, would fall into it. Whether a bribe caused a bridge keeper to drop it or an angel answered her prayer by chucking it down is unknown, but the head did fall into her lap. She was jailed when she refused to return it but was soon freed. When she died in 1544 at 36, the head was entombed with her at St. Dunstan's Church, Canterbury. Later the head, diminished to a skull, was removed and displayed in a niche.

1893   Paris. French writer Guy de Maupassant, 42, died of syphilis in an insane asylum.

Diagnosed with syphilis at 24, Maupassant claimed to have had sex with thousands of women. He also claimed to be able to have sex dozens of times a day. When his friend Gustave Flaubert expressed disbelief, Maupassant hired an accountant to accompany him to a brothel. The accountant certified that Maupassant had enjoyed six women in a single hour.

Maupassant was insane by his thirties. After an attempt to kill himself, he was imprisoned for his own good. Denied female visitors, he relived past exploits while licking floors, seeing faces on furniture, and attacking attendants. Oddest of all, he became certain that anything emitted by his penis was precious beyond measure and therefore refused to urinate. Eventually, he lapsed into a coma and died.

1962   Near Oxford, Mississippi. Southern writer William Faulkner, 64, was thrown from a horse. He injured his back but remounted and put the horse through its paces, lest the animal think it had triumphed. Faulkner spent the next two weeks in pain from the injury and drinking heavily, then suffered a fatal heart attack on this date. His writing had won a Nobel Peace Prize and two Pulitzer Prizes. He once said, "If a writer has to rob his mother he will not hesitate; the 'Ode on a Grecian Urn' is worth any number of old ladies."

Faulkner had been postmaster at the University of Mississippi but was fired when it was discovered that rather than sort it, he was throwing mail into the trash.

– July 7 –

1930   Crowborough, Sussex. Sir Arthur Conan Doyle, 71, creator of
        Sherlock Holmes, died of a heart attack following a two-
        month illness. His family blamed the illness on exhaustion
        from a lecture trip in Scandinavia. Doyle's last words were to
        his wife, Lady Doyle, "You are wonderful."
            Doyle was an ophthalmologist before becoming a writer. In
        later years, he became interested in spiritualism, and his
        lectures at New York City's Carnegie Hall on the subject were
        so convincing that several people killed themselves so as to
        join the spirit world.

1973   Burlington, Vermont. Actress Veronica Lake (born Constance
        Ockleman), 53, died of acute hepatitis. Her trademark was the
        way her blond hair dipped mysteriously over one eye. Many
        girls copied her style, but when World War II came and these
        girls went to work in factories, the style caused accidents.
        Safety authorities asked Lake to alter her hair to a safer
        design. She did and the accidents stopped, but without this
        trademark, Lake's career suffered and she was reduced, for a
        time, to working as a barmaid. Her last film (she coproduced
        it) was titled *Flesh Feast* (1970). It was a bizarre work wherein
        Lake played a mad scientist who tortures to death Adolf
        Hitler.

– July 8 –

1822   Off the coast of Italy. Romantic poet Percy Bysshe Shelley had
        always been sickly. Thomas Carlyle said, "Poor Shelley always
        was, and is, a kind of ghastly object: colourless, pallid,
        tuneless, without health or warmth of vigour, the sound of
        him [is] shrieky, frosty, as if a ghost were trying to 'sing' to
        us..." In his last year, he was depressed by the death of Keats,
        and when a poem he wrote in honor of Keats was poorly
        received, he stopped writing. He even purchased poison to kill
        himself, but ironically, his poor health seems to have prevented
        his self-destruction: He was too weak to do the deed. While ill,
        Shelley dreamed that Allegra, the deceased illegitimate
        daughter of Lord Byron, rose from the sea and gestured for
        him to join her.

Shelley went abroad to rest. He was in Viareggio, Italy, when, on this date, to lighten his spirits, Shelley and his friend Edward Williams took a small boat out. Williams piloted while Shelley relaxed with a book of Keats's poetry. Biographer Edward John Trelawny, an experienced seaman and friend of six months, waved frantically at the pair. He had seen clouds piling up and knew a storm was brewing. Williams and Shelley didn't see him. Within half an hour, the storm sank their boat. Shelley's wife, Mary Wollstonecraft Shelley, author of *Frankenstein*, hoped they would be found alive, but after a few days, two bodies, disfigured by fish, were discovered. Trelawny identified them as Shelley and Williams. Shelley was 29.

In that part of Italy, corpses cast up by the sea had to be cremated, so on August 14, Williams's body was burned in a furnace assembled on the beach. The following night, Shelley was cremated in the same furnace, but the heart, as is sometimes the case, wouldn't burn. Trelawny snatched it from the flames and presented it to Shelley's wife. Mary Shelley carried it about with her wrapped in silk; then, in later years, kept it in a bottle upon her desk. Shelley's ashes were buried in Rome in the grave of their son William, who had died as a child. Trelawny built a pair of beautiful tombs in the same cemetery and had Shelley's ashes moved to one of them. He then informed Mrs. Shelley that the second tomb wasn't for her. It was for him. In 1889, the heart was buried with Shelley's son.

Shelley was so unpopular during his Eton school days that the other students formed a club dedicated to taunting him.

1939 Washbrook, Suffolk, England. Physician-psychologist Havelock Ellis, 80, died of a heart attack following throat problems. He was called the "Darwin of Sex" because of his writings. Ellis was impotent and didn't have sex successfully until he was 60. He once said, "The place where optimism flourishes most is the lunatic asylum."

1967 London. Actress Vivien Leigh, 53, who played Scarlett O'Hara in *Gone With the Wind* (1939), died of tuberculosis. She had suffered from the disease since 1945. A heavy work load, too much smoking, and a number of breakdowns worsened the illness. She willed her violet eyes to medicine, but because of her contagious tuberculosis, they were not taken.

Leigh was married to Laurence Olivier for a time. He said, "She wanted us to be like brother and sister. But, fortunately, occasional incest was allowed." Leigh once observed, "I'm not Scarlett; I'm not as brassy or bright as Scarlett. Actually, Scarlett is not one of my favorite people."

– July 9 –

1850   The White House, Washington, D.C. Zachary Taylor, twelfth U.S. president, died of bilious fever, typhoid, and cholera. He was 65. On the Fourth, he had laid the cornerstone of the Washington Memorial. It was a hot day, and Taylor drank a great deal of water. When he returned to the White House, he ate large quantities of cherries and berries washed down with water and iced milk. Shortly thereafter, he suffered cramps and continued to suffer them for days before dying. He said, "I regret nothing, but am sorry that I am about to leave my friends." He was buried in Louisville, Kentucky.

Recently, historian Clara Rising theorized that Taylor was given arsenic in the fruit and that his death was an assassination. A 1991 autopsy on Taylor's remains demonstrated that Taylor hadn't been poisoned.

Taylor didn't vote in any election till he was 62. He was a professional soldier and moved so often that he couldn't establish a legal residence. He couldn't even vote for himself when he ran for President. Taylor's wife said before his election, "His nomination [for President] is a plot to deprive me of his society and to shorten his life by unnecessary care and responsibility." She died two years after her husband.

– July 10 –

1941   Los Angeles. Jazz musician Jelly Roll Morton, 50, died of heart trouble and asthma. In the slang of the time, "jelly roll" referred to the sexual act. Morton's godmother, Eulalie Echo, was supposed to be a voodoo witch who had offered her godson to Satan as a sacrifice. As such, Morton was to accompany Eulalie to hell when she died. She died in May, and two months later Morton lay dying. His wife said that he died begging her to keep anointing his lips with holy oil.

1979   Brookline, Massachusetts. Arthur Fiedler, 84, conductor of the Boston Pops Orchestra for nearly fifty years, died of heart failure. On the evening of his funeral, the Boston Pops, as a tribute, played his signature piece, "The Stars and Stripes Forever," with no conductor.

1989   Los Angeles. Mel Blanc, 81, died of heart disease and other medical problems. He was the voice for hundreds of cartoon characters, including Woody Woodpecker, Speedy Gonzalez, Pepe Le Pew, the Tasmanian Devil, Road Runner, Foghorn Leghorn, Heathcliffe, Yosemite Sam, Daffy Duck, Tweety, Barney Rubble, Dino, Mr. Spacely, the Frito Bandito, Sylvester (for whom he originated "Thufferin thuccotash!"), Porky Pig (for whom he invented "Th-th-th-that's all, folks!"), and, most notably, Bugs Bunny (for whom he created the line "Eh, what's up, Doc?").

In 1961, Blanc came close to death after an auto accident. He was comatose for two weeks, and newspapers printed his obituary. His doctor tried one last thing to wake him. He asked, "How are you feeling today, Bugs Bunny?" Blanc answered in the voice of the cartoon rabbit, "Eh, just fine, Doc. How're you?"

– July 11 –

1929   Gillingham, Kent, England. Local firemen planned a demonstration of firefighting for the annual fête. A mock wedding party of nine young boys and six firemen would be rescued from a makeshift house. In error, instead of smoke bombs being detonated, the house was set afire. The blaze killed all the "actors" while the firemen ineffectually sprayed water. Spectators, who thought the victims were stuffed dummies, cheered.

– July 12 –

1804   New York City. Secretary of the Treasury Alexander Hamilton, 47, had established the nation on a firm economic footing and had helped avert war with France and England.

He had been a delegate to the Constitutional Convention and had written most of the Federalist Papers. During the Revolution, he had served in the Continental Army. On one occasion, Hamilton's division was about to be destroyed when a young major broke through the British lines and led the division to safety. The major was Aaron Burr.

By 1804, the two men had become enemies. Burr blamed Hamilton's influence for his defeat in his campaign to become governor of New York. He challenged Hamilton to a duel at the same spot in Weehawken, New Jersey, where Hamiliton's 19-year-old son had been killed in another duel. Hamilton agreed, and they met there at 7:00 A.M. on July 11. The weapons used were .544-caliber English dueling pistols with nine-inch barrels. Just before the order to fire, Hamilton paused to don a pair of spectacles. When the signal was given, they both fired. Hamilton was hit in the right side by Burr's shot. Hamilton's shot hit a tree. He had deliberately fired to miss. Hamilton fell, saying, "This is a mortal wound." He was taken to a friend's home, where he died on this date after great suffering. His last coherent words were to his wife. "Remember, my Eliza, you are a Christian." Burr was vice president of the United States at the time. He avoided a trial for dueling by returning to Washington, D. C., where he continued in office till the end of his term in 1805.

Hamilton was an illegitimate child. His beautiful mother despised her West Indian merchant husband and took a number of lovers. One was a Scot named James Hamilton, and it was his name that Alexander bore. Some historians note that George Washington was in the West Indies at the time of Hamilton's conception, and that Hamilton was a favorite aide of Washington's during the Revolution and was appointed treasury secretary by him.

1942 New York City. Max Geller, owner of the Green Parrot Bar, was murdered. The crime was solved with testimony provided by Geller's pet parrot, who kept repeating the killer's name. Twenty human bar patrons claimed to have seen nothing.

– July 13 –

1890 New York City. John Charles Frémont died at 77. He drew up the route of the Oregon Trail, explored the Northwest, and was key to the conquest of California. His writings made him a national figure, and he became a senator for California. The discovery of gold made him a millionaire. Frémont received the Republican presidential nomination in 1856 but lost the election. He served in the Civil War, but politics limited his role. From 1878 to 1883 he was governor of the Arizona Territory. By the time of his death, he had lost much of his fortune.

While returning by streetcar from a visit to a friend's grave, Frémont suffered a chill. A doctor diagnosed peritonitis or gastric ulcer. Early on the thirteenth, after vomiting, Fremont grew peaceful. To his doctor he said, "If I continue as free from pain, I can go home next week." The doctor asked where he meant. "California, of course," he replied, and died. He never went home. He was buried in Piermont, New York, overlooking the Hudson River.

– July 14 –

1904   Badenweiler, Germany. Anton Chekhov died from tuberculosis at 44. His doctor prescribed champagne. "I haven't had champagne for ages," said Chekhov, drinking a glass. He then turned onto his left side and died.

Maxim Gorky wrote a scathing account of the funeral in Moscow. Chekhov's coffin was carried from the rail station to the graveyard in a green wagon bearing the motto, "Oysters." The body of a general arrived on the same train. It was treated with greater respect, and many of Chekhov's mourners mistakenly followed it to the general's grave. There, they were amazed to see a military band and an honor guard. When they discovered their mistake, Gorky claims, they broke into sniggering laughter. Meanwhile, only a hundred mourners followed the correct body. Gorky wrote that they exhibited banal vulgarity throughout the service.

Chekhov once said, "Doctors are just the same as lawyers; the only difference is that lawyers merely rob you, whereas doctors rob you and kill you, too."

1976   Traves, France. Former SS Colonel Jochen Peiper, 61, had spearheaded the German assault during the Battle of the Bulge and was responsible for the massacre of over eighty

American soldiers at Malmedy. He spent thirteen years in prison for the murders. After several unsuccessful jobs, Peiper settled in Traves, working as a translator of military books, but many didn't forget or forgive. On this date, which is Bastille Day in France, unknown parties surrounded his house and opened fire. Peiper's body was found in the burned ruins with an empty Colt pistol and an empty hunting rifle.

– July 15 –

1881   Fort Sumner, New Mexico. Sheriff Pat Garret killed Henry Bonney, 21, better known as Billy the Kid. Garret had crept near to the house where Billy was staying. Billy heard Garret and came out, pistol in hand, to investigate. Billy's last words were, "Who's there? Who's there?" Garret, knowing Billy's deadliness, shot him down without warning.

Born in New York City, Billy came west as a child in the early 1860s. His father died, and his mother contracted tuberculosis. He nursed her for two years before she, too, died. Billy became a drifter. In 1877, he killed his first man (Billy claimed a lifelong total of 21), a blacksmith who had teased Billy. Billy shoved a pistol in the unarmed fellow's side and pulled the trigger. He fled to become a cattle rustler till a kindly rancher took him in. When rustlers killed the rancher, Billy ambushed and killed the local sheriff, who had been bribed to look the other way, then returned to rustling. Eventually, Garret caught him, but Billy escaped, killing two guards. Garret tracked him down again and shot him. Billy was buried in an army cemetery in Fort Sumner. For years, traveling side shows exhibited a mummified corpse claiming it to be Billy's and to have gotten it from grave robbers. There is little reason to think that his body was disturbed.

Garret was a bad man turned lawman who knew Billy well, having rustled cattle with him. He said Billy "drank and laughed, rode and laughed, talked and laughed, fought and laughed, and killed and laughed."

1984   Karlsruhe, West Germany. A hippocidal elephant reached through its cage's bars with its trunk and turned a valve that eleased 140-degree water into the neighboring hippopotamus tank. Three hippos were killed.

A nonfatal elephant incident was chronicled by Florida's *Journal Herald*. Robert Burris, who trained animals for the Hoxie Brothers Circus, was knocked down by an elephant while unloading a group of the creatures from a truck. The fall didn't injure him significantly. However, he *was* significantly injured when one of the circus elephants proceeded to do a headstand on the recumbent trainer's chest.

1988   St. Petersburg, Florida. Pinellas County assistant school superintendent Douglas Tarrant, 41, had been charged with sexually abusing a 15-year-old schoolgirl. On this date, he videotaped a denial, then killed himself in his car with carbon monoxide. Tarrant didn't know that two days earlier, the girl's mother had told authorities the girl had admitted the charge was false. Neither the authorities nor the mother bothered to let Tarrant know.

– July 16 –

1676   Paris. Marie-Madeleine d'Aubray, 46, was beheaded. She was an aristocrat who married a wealthy marquis. When she tired of him, she took up with Godin de Sainte-Croix. Her father had Sainte-Croix sent to the Bastille to break up the affair. In prison, Sainte-Croix learned all about poisons, and when he was released, he instructed Marie. She practiced by poisoning dozens of poor patients in a public hospital. When she was confident of her skill, she poisoned her father's soup and inherited his estate. She soon spent this, so she poisoned her two brothers for their money. She had many lovers, but she loved Sainte-Croix and wished to marry him. Chronicler Madame de Sevigne wrote of the situation, "...she often gave her husband poison. Sainte-Croix, not desiring so wicked a woman for his wife, gave antidotes to the poor husband..." Her husband became an invalid but survived. Others didn't. Marie poisoned the coffee of a woman who made a snide remark at a reception. Another woman who spilled a drink on Marie's gown soon died. Sainte-Croix continued his own research, but forgot to wear a protective mask when mixing fuming drugs and inadvertently poisoned himself.

Authorities became suspicious, and a valet informed on Marie after being broken on the wheel. Marie escaped, hiding for three years. She was found in a convent and brought back to Paris by a cavalry escort. On the way, she tried to kill herself three times, once by ingesting broken glass. Many testified against her, and she was condemned. As was the custom, she was placed on the rack to extract a final confession and later, at the Cathedral of Notre Dame, she made a public confession. After she was beheaded, her body was burned. The crowd eagerly snatched the remnants of her corpse, since the remains of murderers were considered good-luck charms. Marie had murdered nearly 100.

1918 Ekaterinburg, Russia. The Communist secret police shot Czar Nicholas II, 50, his wife, his children, his doctor, his valet, the empress's maid, and their cook. The bodies were dismembered, burned, drenched in sulfuric acid, and dumped down a mine shaft. The Communists denied the execution, but the White Russian Army discovered the remnants and the Communists, seeking to distance themselves from the murder, arrested twenty-eight people and blamed it on them. Five were executed. In 1924, Ekaterinburg was renamed Sverdlovsk in honor of the planner of the murders, Jakov Sverdlov. Sverdlov didn't get to enjoy this honor. After giving a speech urging the workers in a factory to the Communist cause, the workers stomped him to death. In 1990, the Russian government admitted that Lenin himself had ordered the murders.

Years after the killings, a girl claimed to be Anastasia, one of the czar's children. Her claim was never proved, but an expert on ears, which are said to be as unique as fingerprints, has since backed her claim. The girl said a servant had rescued her.

In 1992, forensic experts who examined the remains of the Czar and his family couldn't match any of the remains to Anastasia. Even more curiously, they couldn't match any of the remains to her brother Alexei, either. A Russian author has suggested that while Anastasia, 17, escaped, Alexei, 14, who would have inherited the throne, spent the rest of his life in an insane asylum.

– July 17 –

1903 London. Painter James McNeill Whistler, 69, best known for "Whistler's Mother," died after a long illness. It was the first painting by an American placed in the Louvre. Ironically, his brother was closer to their mother. Whistler entered West Point in 1851 but was discharged for a poor chemistry grade. He later claimed, "Had silicon been a gas, I would have been a major general." A Southerner, he would have been drafted into the Confederate Army during the Civil War, except he, with his mother, ran the Union blockade from Charleston and went to England.

Whistler once observed, after hearing too much bemoaning of the artistic past, "Listen! There never was an artistic period. There never was an Art-loving nation."

1928 Mexico City. Mexican President Alvaro Obregon, 48, had avoided an assassination plot that called for a young girl to inject him with poison by pressing close while dancing, but when an artist begged him to pose, he wasn't so lucky. "I hope you make me look good, kid," Obregon remarked. The artist shoved a pistol into the president's face and with five shots made him look very bad indeed.

1959 Metropolitan Hospital, New York City. Jazz singer Billie Holiday died at 44. She had been a prostitute as a teenager. By the time she was 20, she was touring as a singer with Count Basie and Artie Shaw. Her success didn't prevent her becoming addicted to heroin. By the 1950s, her health was precarious, and alcoholism compounded the evil effect of heroin. In May of 1959, she went into a coma and was hospitalized for liver problems and cardiac failure. On June twelfth, police found heroin in her hospital room. She died five days later. She had seventy cents in her bank account but had taped $750 to her legs. The 1960 royalties for her recordings exceeded $1,000,000.

– July 18 –

1792 Paris. U.S. naval hero John Paul Jones was born John Paul in Scotland, but while captaining a vessel in the West Indies, he settled a mutiny by killing a man. He was forced to change his name and flee to America, where he took up the American cause during the Revolution, sinking several British ships and capturing others. He even raided an English port. His most notable action was when he took the *Bonhomme Richard* (a near-hulk named by the French after *Poor Richard's Almanac*) and a few other ships and defeated a superior force of English warships.

After the war, Jones was sent to Russia to help Catherine the Great as a friendly gesture. He fought his last battle in the Black Sea against the Turks for the Russians. The Russians weren't grateful. Palace intrigues stole the credit he deserved and subjected him to a trial for abusing a 10-year-old girl. He was cleared by Catherine but decided to leave Russia (some suggest she instigated the plot because of jealousy over Jones's romance with one of her ladies-in-waiting, who bore him a child). The journey homeward ruined his health. Prematurely gray, Jones died on this date in Paris at 45.

Jones's body was treated with alcohol, sealed in a lead coffin and buried in Paris's St. Louis Protestant Cemetery. The graveyard was forgotten and housing was built upon it. It was rediscovered during slum clearance in 1899. U.S. Ambassador to France Horace Porter, using his own money, sank shafts into the area and dug tunnels searching for Jones's coffin. Five coffins were retrieved before Jones's was discovered. His remains were so well preserved that an autopsy could detect that he had suffered from chronic kidney inflammation, high blood pressure, and pneumonia. The pneumonia had caused a fatal heart attack.

In 1905, by order of President Theodore Roosevelt, a squadron of U.S. warships brought Jones's body home. He is entombed at the U.S. Naval Academy in Annapolis.

1817   Winchester, Hampshire, England. Following a long illness, author Jane Austen, 41, died of Addison's disease, which is the progressive atrophy of the adrenal cortex. It leads to very low blood pressure, severe backache, weight loss, debility, and blackening of the skin. Despite her pain, she worked hard, finishing *Persuasion*, and nearly finishing *Sanditon*, which mocked nineteenth-century medicine. Her last words, when asked if she wanted anything, were, "Nothing but death." She died on this date with Cassandra, her elder sister, by her side. She was buried in Winchester Cathedral. Cassandra, her executrix, burned many of Austen's papers and censored much of what she let survive.

Mary Russell Mitford wrote of Austen, "Mamma says she was then the prettiest, silliest, most affected, husband-hunting butterfly she ever remembers: and a friend of mine, who visits her now, says that she has stiffened into the most perpendicular, precise, taciturn piece of 'single blessedness' that ever existed, and that, till *Pride and Prejudice* showed what a precious gem was hidden in that unbending case, she was no more regarded in society than a poker or a fire-screen, or any other thin upright piece of wood or iron that fills its corner in peace and quietness. The case is very different now: she is still a poker—but a poker of whom everyone is afraid." Austen noted of herself, "...as I must leave off being young, I find many Douceurs in being a sort of Chaperon, for I am put on the Sofa near the fire & can drink as much wine as I like."

1899   South Natick, Massachusetts. Writer Horatio Alger, 67, died of respiratory problems. The writer of rags-to-riches (or at least, rags-to-middle-class) stories had himself gone from rags to riches to rags. A few years earlier, after a breakdown, he had amused himself by writing epitaphs for himself. One read: "Here lies a good fellow who spent his life while he had it."

– July 19 –

1969   Chappaquiddick Island, Massachusetts. Senator Edward Kennedy drove off a bridge, killing Mary Jo Kopechne, 28. Kennedy's ten-hour delay in informing the police, the lack of an autopsy, and the use of Kennedy family clout to limit investigation produced unsavory speculation. State Police Detective-Lieutenant George Killen, whose investigation of the incident was suppressed, said, "[Kennedy] killed that girl the same as if he put a gun to her head and pulled the trigger." Kennedy was reelected to the Senate just four months later and nearly became the Democratic presidential nominee in 1980.

Recently, on the television show "Current Affair," Kopechne's cousin Georgetta Potoski broke the silence the Kopechne family had maintained for twenty-two years. She said the girl's parents had asked her to speak for them. She said Kopechne's parents had trusted Ted Kennedy and believed his story. She also said they hadn't been bribed to keep quiet. They had received a settlement of $150,000, mostly from Kennedy's auto insurance, and lawyers had taken 40 percent of this. Potoski said the parents lost their trust in Kennedy three years after the incident when the diver who removed their daughter from the sunken auto told them that Mary Jo had suffocated, not drowned. She could have lived from forty-five minutes to three hours breathing air trapped in the car. The Kopechnes were also troubled by Kennedy's failure to express regret to them. At one point the television interviewer asked Potoski if she thought Kennedy was a liar. She replied, "Yes. We all do. Don't you? Do you believe it? I don't know of anyone who does."

Mary Jo Kopechne called her parents before leaving for Chappaquiddick to tell them of her seaside vacation plans. Her mother remembers her last words to Mary Jo as, "Honey, be careful of the water."

One wag has suggested that if Kennedy ever wins the nomination and runs for president, there will be in every crowd he addresses "some guy in a frogman's suit" with a "Chappaquiddicans for Kennedy" sign. But perhaps the sharpest cut came from a 1979 "Saturday Night Live" sketch. Bill Murray, portraying Senator Kennedy, arrives late for an address soaking wet and complaining of confusion. Jane Curtin, portraying Kennedy's wife, chides him for being late and calls him "Flipper."

1991   Bensalem, Pennsylvania. Michael J. Klucznik, 31, and Marc J. P. Cienkowski, 25, were playing Monopoly in Cienkowski's home when they began arguing over the rules. Klucznik angrily left. Cienkowski got a bow and arrow and followed. He fatally shot Klucznik in the chest (see 11/2/1991 for another Monopoly murder).

– July 20 –

1919   Parral, Mexico. Pancho Villa, 45, was assassinated while riding in his new Dodge touring car. His last words were, "Don't let it end like this. Tell them I said something." A lover of sardines, peanut brittle, and candy, Villa killed with little regret and once had a man executed for having the look of a traitor in his eye. He killed eighty women and children in his own camp because they were slowing the movements of his guerrillas. He raided some villages for the exclusive purpose of raping the village women. Villa once had a father tied to a chair and then raped the man's daughter in front of him.

– July 21 –

1796   Dumfries, Dumfrieshire, England. Scottish poet Robert Burns, 37, died of rheumatic fever. His last words concerned a bill collector who had been harassing him, "That damned rascal, Matthew Penn!" Burns wrote affectingly of true friendship: "I want someone to laugh with me, someone to be grave with me, someone to please me and help my discrimination with his or her own remark, and at times, no doubt, to admire my acuteness and penetration."

1991   Myrtle Beach, South Carolina. Ronald Turner, 17, and his sister decided to take a Ferris wheel ride. They chose to ignore the ride operator's instructions to not swing their cab. They swung and rocked it so much that the cab tipped over, initiating a chain-reaction accident that knocked a second girl out of her cab and tangled a third girl's cab in the wheel's structure. Turner's sister, the second girl, and Turner himself fell thirty feet to the ground. The girls were seriously injured, and Turner died.

– July 22 –

1934   Outside the Biograph Theater, Chicago. John Dillinger, 31, was shot to death by FBI agents. He had just seen the movie *Manhattan Melodrama* (1934) with two women. One was "the Lady in Red," who had informed the FBI that Dillinger would be attending the film. In the movie, Clark Gable plays a criminal sent to the electric chair. Before his execution Gable laments that he didn't meet a quick, violent death, but is pleased he won't have to linger in prison for years.

Some claim the dead man wasn't Dillinger. Perhaps this was because Dillinger had undergone a face-lift, burned his fingerprints with acid, dyed his hair, grown a mustache, and plucked his eyebrows. In 1991, a death mask of Dillinger fetched $10,000 at auction.

1962   Cape Canaveral. The $18.5 million *Mariner I* was launched. It was meant to zoom past Venus, but a missing minus sign in its programming caused it to zoom into the ocean four minutes after blast-off.

– July 23 –

1885   Mount McGregor, New York. Ulysses S. Grant, eighteenth U.S. president, died at 63. His real name was Hiram Ulysses Grant, but when he enrolled at West Point he was listed as Ulysses S. Grant. He decided to keep his military-issue name.

As a boy, Grant had been nicknamed "Useless." It must have haunted him throughout his life. He did poorly at West Point and left the service after a short, disappointing career (he served for a time with Robert E. Lee in the Mexican-American War). He did little better as a civilian, barely supporting his wife as a ribbon clerk and by selling firewood on street corners. When war came, he was refused a commission in his state militia but eventually got into the regular army and, by just refusing to be defeated, won larger and larger victories till Lincoln gave him command of all Union forces.

After the war, Grant was elected president, but his administration was burdened by corruption, which made him unpopular. Bad investments after he left office impoverished him. He had placed his money in a bank looted by one of its owners. Grant borrowed $150,000 to help save the bank. The man he gave the money to ran off with it. Grant insisted on repaying the loan and wound up with just $80. To make matters worse, he was diagnosed as suffering from terminal cancer of the tongue and tonsils. Despite severe pain, Grant wrote his autobiography, hoping to provide for his family; however, he had trouble finding a publisher. It took the help of former Confederate Samuel Clemens (Mark Twain) to get the work into print. Grant worked day and night to finish it, even though he was in pain, had lost the power of speech, couldn't swallow solid food, and couldn't even sit up. By the time he finished, four days before his death, Grant weighed under 100 pounds. The book earned Grant's family nearly $500,000. And it wasn't a hack job. Gertrude Stein said that Grant had the finest American prose style.

Grant's last wish was to be buried in New York City, where he had been befriended in his last days. Over 300,000 lined up to view his body lying in state in New York's City Hall. He was buried in the landmark Grant's Tomb.

– July 24 –

1862   Kinderhook, New York. Martin Van Buren, 79, eighth U.S. president, died of asthma in his mansion, Lindenwalk. He had been healthy till his last year. His last words dealt with the importance of religion in the face of death: "There is but one reliance." Van Buren was the first native-born American president.

– July 25 –

1834   Highgate, near London. English poet Samuel Taylor Coleridge, 61, died. An autopsy failed to indicate the cause of death. His best known work, *Kubla Khan,* which describes Kubla Khan's opulent pleasure palace, Xanadu, was reportedly inspired by a drug-induced dream. Halfway through writing it, someone rapped on his door. He let the person in and returned to his poem only to discover he'd forgotten the rest of the dream. The poem was never finished.

Coleridge once said, "He who begins by loving Christianity better than truth will proceed by loving his own sect of church better than Christianity and end in loving himself better than all." On another occasion, "Our quaint metaphysical opinions, in an hour of anguish, are like playthings by the bedside of a child deathly sick."

– July 26 –

1925   Dayton, Tennessee. William Jennings Bryan, 65, who had unsuccessfully run three times for president as the Democratic candidate, died of diabetes mellitus. He had been President Wilson's secretary of state but resigned the day after the *Lusitania* was sunk. An isolationist, he thought the sinking was a setup to get U.S. participation in World War I. Bryan was part of the successful prosecution at the Scopes trial and began a speech-making tour afterward. Exhaustion brought on his death. His last words were to his son, as Bryan went up to his bedroom for the night: "Seems there's hardly time enough for resting and none at all for dying."

Bryan was a populist; that is, he loudly campaigned against the wealthy. He claimed, "No one can earn a million dollars honestly." This played well with farmers, who blamed Eastern bankers for their problems.

1947   Grandview, Missouri. Martha Ellen Truman, 94, the mother of President Harry Truman, died of natural causes. A daughter of a Confederate family, she was placed in an internment camp during the Civil War. Consequently, she refused to sleep in the Lincoln bedroom when she visited her son in the White House. When she broke her hip at age 92 and Harry visited her, she said, "I don't want any smart cracks out of you. I saw your picture in the paper last week putting a wreath at the Lincoln Memorial."

1984   Central State Hospital for the Criminally Insane, Wisconsin. Mental patient Edward Gein died quietly in his seventy-eighth year, of natural causes. The staff referred to him as "harmless," but Gein had hardly been harmless in 1957. In November of that year, in the tiny farming town of Plainfield, Gein achieved superstardom in the world of maniacs.

Gein lived alone on a derelict farm. His father, brother, and, finally, his highly religious mother had all died. He did odd jobs such as running errands, delivering goods, and baby-sitting. His neighbors also thought him harmless, although he did grin too much. And he was always talking about female anatomy. And he claimed to have a shrunken head collection. Nobody thought anything was seriously amiss till storekeeper Bernice Worden disappeared. Police found bloodstains on her floor. A record of an antifreeze sale to Gein was also found, so authorities went to Gein's farmhouse to question him.

Inside Gein's rundown farmhouse, trash clogged every room except the parlor and Gein's mother's room. Both were clean, and both had their doors nailed shut. They found more than trash in the kitchen—human shinbones, lips strung together, a human-skin purse, human-skin–covered chairs, a cup of noses, a human-skin drum, a soup bowl made from a skull, five women's faces (with rouge and powder) made into masks and tacked to the wall, ten female heads, a vest made from the skin of a woman's torso, a heart in a pot on the stove, and a freezer full of human organs. Hanging by the heels in a shed, headless and disemboweled, were the remains of Bernice Worden.

Gein was arrested. Police suspected him of the torture-murders of at least ten women. He admitted to only two murders—Worden's and the shooting of a female tavern owner. The rest of his collection he said he had gathered by grave-robbing. He confessed to wearing the skins of his victims and claimed he just wanted to see "how things worked." As if to demonstrate his meekness, Gein claimed never to have shot a deer. His neighbors were left to wonder where he had obtained the "venison" he had given them as gifts. Disturbed by the prospect that the murder house would be turned into a tourist trap, his neighbors burned the place down.

Gein was committed for life. His story became the inspiration for Robert Bloch's book *Psycho*. Alfred Hitchcock brought it to the screen in 1960, and no one has felt safe in a motel shower since.

– July 27 –

1946   Neuilly, a suburb of Paris. American writer Gertrude Stein, 72, died during cancer surgery. As she was wheeled into the operating room, she asked her constant companion Alice Toklas, "What is the answer?" Toklas said nothing, so Stein nodded and said, "In that case, what is the question?"

   Stein ranked herself with Einstein as the only two creative minds of the century. She was stout and dour, and it was said that if Hollywood did her life story, her role would be played by Spencer Tracy.

1988   Los Angeles. Child actress Judith Barsi, 11, had starred in fifty commercials, the movie *Jaws IV: The Revenge*, and the TV movie *Fatal Vision*. In the last, a father kills his wife and daughters. On this date, Judith's father, Jozsef Barsi, 55, shot

Judith and her mother, Maria, 48, doused their bodies with gasoline, set them afire, and then went to their garage, where he shot himself in the head.

— July 28 —

1794   Paris. French revolutionary Maximilien Robespierre, 36, who had sent many to the guillotine, was himself guillotined. His foes were afraid his eloquence would sway the populace against them, so they had Robespierre shot through the jaw. He was executed with his nearly detached jawbone tied to his head with a bandage. With his death, the Reign of Terror ended.

1945   New York City. Lt. Col. William F. Smith, 27, freshly stateside after flying 100 combat missions, was flying an Army Air Corps B-25 bomber from New Bedford to Newark. Two servicemen accompanied him. Halfway through the trip, air traffic controllers advised Smith that fog had rolled in over Manhattan and suggested that he land at La Guardia instead of Newark. At that time, a pilot was deemed the final authority in such decisions. Smith felt he could continue safely. When he thought he was near Newark, he lowered his landing gear and descended. He broke through the thick fog only to discover that he was zooming down New York's Fifth Avenue at 250 m.p.h., just 450 feet above the sidewalks. Smith frantically pulled the plane's nose up but smashed into the side of the 1,400-foot Empire State Building.

The plane hit the building 915 feet above the street, at the seventy-eighth-floor level. All three men aboard the twelve-ton bomber and eleven people in the building were killed. Six floors were flooded with burning gasoline. Several people in the building managed to flee the flaming gas and found safety in fireproof stairwells. Others were caught as they ran or as they hid in offices. Paul Dearing, 37, jumped from his office window. He hit a seventy-second-floor ledge and was killed. One of the aircraft's 1,500-pound engines punched clear through the building, falling to Thirty-third Street, below. The other engine cut through the two-inch, braided steel cable of an elevator. Elevator operator Betty Lou Oliver had stopped her car between the seventy-sixth and seventy-seventh floor to take her break. It was her last day at work, her soldier-husband had returned from overseas. She was sitting on the floor, singing the "St. Louis Blues," when she heard an explosion and her cage began to fall. It reached 200 m.p.h. in the four seconds it took to fall 1,000 feet. Oliver became weightless, floating in mid-air before the cage crashed into the bowels of the building. Her back was broken in two places, her right leg was shattered, and she nearly lost an eye, but she survived and, after a year, recovered.

The crash had two aftereffects besides the deaths. First, air traffic controllers were given the authority to order planes down. Second, in repairing the building, some of the masonry was left unfinished. Its rough surface, on the northwest corner of the building, serves as a memorial to the dead.

– July 29 –

1890   Auvers-sur-Oise, near Paris. Artist Vincent van Gogh, 37 and mentally disturbed, hid behind a manure pile and shot himself. He managed to walk back to the asylum where he had been staying. He died there, attended by his loving brother, Theo. His last words were, "I want to be going." Turning to art at 27 after failing as an art dealer's apprentice and as an evangelist, van Gogh sold only one of his hundreds of paintings while he lived. His last painting is titled *Wheatfield With Crows*. He finished it just before shooting himself. The crows wheeling above the golden wheat display a horrible menace.

Some think van Gogh's insanity was the result of his habit of eating his paints, which contained toxic chemicals. In 1990, Dr. I. Kaufman Arenberg proposed that van Gogh suffered from Ménière's disease, a painful inner-ear infection. It causes symptoms similar to those exhibited by van Gogh, including vertigo, vomiting, noise in the ear, and hallucinations. Attacks can last for days. The disease was discovered by a French doctor named Ménière in 1861, but few in van Gogh's time knew of the illness.

1988   Muncie, Indiana. Vance F. Martin, 25, went to a fast-food restaurant. He used the drive-through, but the restaurant employees couldn't understand him when he gave his order. He repeated it over and over—and they still couldn't understand him. They suggested he pull up to the pickup window and place his order there, but Martin had grown furious. He left the restaurant at high speed and struck a concrete median that launched his car into the air for forty feet. He crashed into a large rock, hit a utility pole, then flipped over. Martin died of massive head injuries.

– July 30 –

1975   Detroit. Teamsters Union boss Jimmy Hoffa, 62, disappeared. It is suspected that underworld bosses killed him because he was planning to retake control of his mob-influenced union and thereby disturb the status quo. An informant said Hoffa had been "ground up in little pieces, shipped to Florida and thrown into the swamp." Recently, it was claimed that Hoffa was buried by a goalpost in Giants Stadium. Hoffa said: "I may have my faults, but being wrong ain't one of them." He also said that only liars and cheats needed bodyguards.

1984   Scotland. A commuter express train running from Edinburgh to Glasgow hit a cow and derailed. Forty were injured, and fourteen died.

– July 31 –

1784   Paris. French writer Denis Diderot's wife warned him against eating an apricot. "How in the devil can it hurt me?" he countered. Diderot, 70, choked to death on it. Diderot once said, "All children are essentially criminal."

1875   Carter's Station, Tennessee. Andrew Johnson, 66, seventeenth U.S. president, died after suffering two strokes. Johnson was a tailor. While president, he made his own clothing. As vice president, he became president when Abraham Lincoln was killed. He continued Lincoln's moderate approach to Reconstruction, which offended those who wanted the South to be treated as a conquered land. They tried to circumvent him by ruling through his cabinet; in particular, through Secretary of War Edwin Stanton. Congress sought to protect Stanton by making it illegal for the president to discharge one of his own cabinet. When Johnson dumped Stanton, Congress began impeachment proceedings. His impeachment was defeated by a single vote. Nevertheless, Johnson was ruined politically. He left office in 1869 and retired to private life. He once said, "When I die, I desire no better winding sheet than the Stars and Stripes, and no softer pillow than the Constitution." That was how he was buried.

– August 1 –

1903   Calloway Hotel, Terry, South Dakota. Martha Jane Canary, 51, known as "Calamity Jane" after her reputation as a jinx, died of pneumonia. She went west with her parents in the 1860s, but both parents died during the trip. Poverty forced her to become a prostitute (one of her places of employment was the cowboy-catering "Hogg Farm" close to Fort Laramie). Affecting male dress, a six-gun, and a tough image that included drinking and swearing, she still managed to make a living, which tells us something about the desperate needs of frontiersmen. After the death of Wild Bill Hickok, she mourned him as if she had been his sweetheart and toured as such for years, but there is little evidence that she was anything more than a casual acquaintance. Jane demonstrated bravery and compassion when, during a smallpox epidemic in Deadwood, South Dakota, in 1878, she nursed the sick and bought drugs with her own money. Her legend spread across the nation via penny novels. Her last words were, "It is the twenty-seventh anniversary of Bill's death. Bury me next to Bill." She was. Although she died penniless, her funeral was genteel. The undertaker was one of the men she'd saved during the epidemic. He donated his services and the pine box.

As the 8/2/1876 entry shows, Jane actually didn't die on the anniversary of Hickok's murder. The prospector who was nursing her by feeding her spoonfuls of whiskey knew that Jane wouldn't last till the anniversary. So, to please her, when she asked what day it was, he lied.

1977   Encino, California. Francis Gary Powers, 46, who had been shot down while flying a U-2 plane over Russia in 1960, was killed when the helicopter he flew as a traffic reporter for KNBC crashed.

– August 2 –

1876   Mann's Saloon Number 10, Deadwood, Dakota Territory. After dining on the house specialty of beans and whiskey, gunfighter James Butler "Wild Bill" Hickok, 39, was shot in the back of the head while playing poker. His hand—ace of clubs, ace of spades, eight of clubs, eight of spades, and jack of diamonds—has since been called the "dead man's hand." The previous day, Hickok had played cards with his killer and had given him money for dinner after cleaning him out. Hickok was buried in a nearby graveyard, then three years later reburied in Mount Moriah Cemetery in Deadwood.

Hickok was born in Illinois, where his large upper lip and long nose earned him the mocking nickname "Duck Bill." Service under General Custer fighting Indians and as the sheriff of the wide-open cowtown of Abilene, Kansas, plus a moustache to hide the lip changed all that. Eastern magazines began to trumpet his exploits. This helped cause Hickok's death, for his murderer, Jack McCall, was seeking a reputation as a fierce gunfighter.

McCall was tried before a miners' court, which, upon hearing of an impending Indian attack, acquitted him. McCall had said that the reason he shot Hickok from behind was because he didn't want to commit suicide by confronting Hickok eye-to-eye. Later, a second trial was held. The first court was ruled invalid, and McCall was convicted of murder. He was hanged on March 1, 1877.

1923   San Francisco. Warren G. Harding, 57, twenty-ninth U.S.
       president, died of heart trouble, bronchopneumonia, and/or
       spoiled crab meat. His wife had been reading him an article
       from the *Saturday Evening Post* called "A Calm Review of a
       Calm Man," which praised Harding's administration. His last
       words were, "That's good. Read some more." Rumor says he
       was poisoned by his wife because of his infidelities. This story
       gained credence when it was discovered that he hadn't eaten
       any crab meat and when his wife refused to allow an autopsy
       (she died just over a year later). The publication of *The
       President's Daughter* by Nan Britton after Harding's death
       seemed to confirm his infidelity. Britton claimed she had
       borne Harding a child conceived on a couch in Harding's
       Senate office the year of his nomination. Britton said the
       Harding family had refused child support, thereby necessitat-
       ing the tell-all book.
            Harding had been nominated as a compromise candidate.
       He never thought he would reach so high. He said, "I am not
       fit for this office and never should have been here." Neverthe-
       less, Harding was popular with his political friends. Perhaps
       this was because of his agreeable manner. His father had told
       him "If you were a girl, Warren, you'd be in the family way all
       the time. You can't say no." H. L. Mencken hated Harding's
       manner of speaking. He said, "It reminds me of a string of
       wet sponges; it reminds me of tattered washing on the line; it
       reminds me of stale bean soup, of college yells, of dogs
       barking idiotically through endless nights. It is so bad that a
       sort of grandeur creeps into it." An example of Hardingese is:
       "Progression is not proclamation nor palaver. It is not pretense
       nor play on prejudice. It is not personal pronouns, nor
       perennial pronouncement. It is not the perturbation of a
       people passion-wrought, nor a promise proposed."

– *August 3* –

1886   Sioux City, Iowa. George C. Haddock was a fanatical
       antialcohol crusader and, as was his custom, was destroying a
       saloon. John Arensdorf, the owner and a brewer, didn't like

this and shot Haddock to death. The jury acquitted Arensdorf. Following the trial, the drinks were on the house.

1966   Hollywood. Comic Lenny Bruce, 41, died of morphine poisoning. He had struggled with drug abuse for years. One of his jokes: "My mother-in-law broke up my marriage. One day my wife came home early from work and found us in bed together."

– August 4 –

1873   Near Copenhagen. Hans Christian Andersen, 70, died of liver cancer while taking a midday nap. His last words were, "Don't ask me how I am, I understand nothing more." He was terrified of being buried alive and asked friends to cut one of his veins before putting him in a coffin. When ill, he would occasionally leave a note by his bed reading, "I only seem dead." He carried a rope in his luggage so that in case of fire he could escape out a window. Although Andersen visited brothels, he died a virgin. He just talked pleasantly with the girls.

1892   Fall River, Massachusetts. Andrew Borden, 70, and his wife, Abby Gray Borden, 65, were horribly murdered with a hatchet. Their daughter Lisbeth was tried for the murders but was acquitted. The all-male jury couldn't believe that such a respectable young woman could be guilty of such violence. Lizzie lived quietly with her sister until June 1, 1927, when, at nearly 67, she died. As requested in her will, she was buried secretly at night. Her will also gave $30,000 to a society to prevent cruelty to animals. Her grave is in Fall River's Oakdale Cemetery near the graves of her murdered father and stepmother. The crime was never solved. Children still learn the little ditty memorializing the incident.

One of the reasons Borden wasn't convicted was that her clothing bore no bloodstains, and the grisly ax murders must have produced much blood. A modern writer has suggested that the reason Borden's clothing was unstained was that she performed the killings in the nude. It would have been easy to quickly wash and dress again.

– *August 5* –

1962   Hollywood. 3:40 A.M. Marilyn Monroe, 36, was found in her
bed naked, dead of a drug overdose. Monroe once said, "Yes,
there was something special about me, and I knew what it
was. I was the kind of girl they found dead in a hall bedroom
with an empty bottle of sleeping pills in her hand."

Monroe's ex-husband Joe DiMaggio planned the funeral.
He barred the press and most Hollywood-associated people,
blaming them for Monroe's death. For years after the funeral,
DiMaggio had Monroe's tomb decorated with a single red
rose. He discontinued the practice when he discovered that
souvenir-hungry fans were routinely stealing them. Ironically,
the tomb is still so decorated, but now the rose-givers are
generous fans.

According to Hollywood historian James Bacon, Monroe
was involved with both John and Robert Kennedy. These
relationships had soured. Some believe she was killed because
she was about to go public in retaliation. Robert Kennedy was
reported to be in town to see her at the time of her death, then
to have rented a helicopter to hastily retreat to San Francisco,
where he claimed to have spent the day with family friends.
One associate claimed Monroe had speculated about replacing
Jacqueline Kennedy as First Lady. Yet Monroe had always
been discreet about her romances, and the press had always
protected the Kennedys from the consequences of their sexual
entanglements. There is little reason to think they wouldn't
have done so again.

Others suggested that career problems led her to suicide.
She had been fired from the film *Something's Got to Give*. Her
chronic lateness, which she blamed on illness and the studio
blamed on Monroe's temperament, caused friction. When
Monroe flew to Madison Square Garden to sing a sexy
"Happy Birthday" for John Kennedy's birthday (she had to be
sewn into her tight gown), studio officials claimed that she
had left without permission. They kicked her off the picture
and filed a $500,000 suit against her for breach of contract.
Dean Martin, her leading man in the film, had costar
approval in his contract. He refused to work with anyone else,
so Monroe was rehired—with a raise. The publicity from the

sultry birthday serenade, the firing/rehiring, and especially
the worldwide headlines that followed the filming of a nude
scene that highlighted the movie (she was the first major star
to do one) suggested that the film would make a fortune.
Monroe had little reason to be disappointed by the state of her
career.

Still others say Monroe was depressed over personal
problems. She was unmarried, childless, and growing older.
But a look at footage from her last film shows she had lost
weight and actually appeared younger than in earlier films. It
seems hard to believe that she lacked prospects for marriage,
and she had many friends.

Much has been made of Marilyn's vulnerability and
Hollywood's exploitation of her, but Monroe grew up in
Hollywood and was aware of its traps and stratagems. For
example, Monroe knew that the wiggle in her walk was
popular with male fans, so to emphasize it, she had a quarter-
inch cut off the right heel of her shoes. It's hard to imagine
such a self-aware star killing herself and, despite many
questions, no "smoking gun" has been discovered indicating
murder. The fatal drugs were probably a simple mistake, since
they induce forgetfulness, which can result in accidental
overdose. Monroe, who used large dosages daily, probably had
just grown too casual with their usage.

Monroe once said, "Hollywood's a place where they'll pay
you a thousand dollars for a kiss, and fifty cents for your
soul." And on another occasion, while entertaining 10,000
marines at Camp Pendleton, she wryly said, "I don't know
why you guys are so excited about sweater girls. Take away
their sweaters and what have they got?"

– August 6 –

1800   Lincoln, Maine. A tombstone reads:
                   Sacred to the memory of
                           Jared Bates
                 who died Aug. the 6th 1800.
                  His widow, aged 24, lives at 7 Elm
                  Street, has every qualification for a
                good wife, and yearns to be comforted.

1890 Auburn Prison, New York. William Kemmler became the
      first man in America to be executed by electrocution.
          In a *Daily News Magazine* article marking the centennial of
      the execution, Edison archivist Leonard DeGraaf described
      the story behind the execution. In 1886, members of the New
      York legislature witnessed the botched hanging of an over-
      weight criminal. A mistake in matching the length of the rope
      to the man's weight caused the prisoner's head to be torn off.
      The shocked legislators set up a commission to devise a more
      humane form of execution. The commission chose electricity.
          The legislature passed the necessary laws but didn't specify
      whether AC or DC current should be used. Electricity was
      just being introduced to the public. Thomas Edison was
      promoting his direct current, or DC, system, while his rival
      George Westinghouse was promoting his alternating current,
      or AC, system. Edison saw an opportunity to stigmatize AC
      current as deadly.
          Edison set to devising an electrocution apparatus. He and
      his staff conducted animal tests to determine the ideal voltage.
      When the ASPCA refused to provide dogs, Edison paid
      children to supply them. Fifty dogs, ten calves, and two horses
      died in the tests. The scientists even tested milder currents
      upon themselves. Finally, they completed a lethal device.
          Westinghouse didn't take this passively. He insisted AC
      was safe. Edison's assistant Harold P. Brown challenged
      Westinghouse to a duel. He would wire himself to a supply of
      DC current if Westinghouse would wire himself to the same
      voltage of AC. They would both take a five-second charge,
      then up the voltage, and take another charge. The first to
      unplug himself would lose. Westinghouse sensibly refused.
          Now that Edison had a device, he needed to name it.
      "Ampermort," "dynamort," and "electromort" were consid-
      ered. Edison's attorney suggested that like the guillotine, the
      device should be named after its "creator," the inventer of AC
      current, Westinghouse. A criminal would then be "West-
      inghoused" to death. Ultimately, the device was simply named
      the "electric chair," although convicts playfully nicknamed it
      "Old Sparky."
          William Kemmler was chosen as the first victim. He had
      killed his mistress, Tillie Zeigler, with a hatchet in a jealous
      fit. Kemmler's lawyers unsuccessfully tried to prove that the
      device was cruel and unusual punishment, and on this date,

Kemmler sat in the chair saying, "I believe I am going to a good place, and I am ready to go." He tried to calm the nervous warden strapping him into the chair. Kemmler wanted no mistakes. The warden signaled the executioner to throw the switch by saying, "Goodbye, William." One thousand to 1,500 volts ran through the chair for seventeen seconds. Kemmler was pronounced dead, and the warden began to unstrap him. But Kemmler moved. The aghast warden restrapped him and ordered a seventy-second blast. Blood vessels in Kemmler's face ruptured, flames darted from his back, and smoke filled the room. Now quite completely dead, Kemmler's body was locked in a sitting posture. Although Kemmler was undoubtedly unconscious after the first blast, the clumsiness of the execution caused widespread revulsion.

1945   Hiroshima was destroyd by an atomic bomb. Seventy-eight thousand died. There is evidence that American prisoners of war were being held there. One was reputedly lynched by Japanese survivors. Sixty to eighty Allied POWs are thought to have died in the Nagasaki attack on August eighth. Thirty thousand Japanese were killed. It isn't widely known, but Japan had its own atomic bomb project. Wartime shortages had slowed its progress.

– August 7 –

1957   North Hollywood, California. Comic actor Oliver Hardy, 65, died of the effects of a paralytic stroke. Hardy came from Harlem, Georgia, the son of a prominent lawyer and politician who died when Hardy was a baby. Hardy had planned a law career, but in 1910, after unsuccessful stays at the Georgia Military Academy, the Atlanta Conservatory of Music, and the University of Georgia, Hardy decided to open a movie house. After three years of watching others perform, Hardy decided he could do it, too. He went to Jacksonville, Florida, where there was a small film business. His first roles were playing villains in one-reel comedies. He then went to Hollywood to work for Hal Roach. Stan Laurel was already working for Roach, but the two weren't teamed for a decade. When they were, they became stars, making over 100 films.

Of Hardy's death, Laurel remarked, "What's there to say? It's shocking of course. Ollie was like a brother. That's the end of the history of Laurel and Hardy."

– *August 8* –

1988   Cedar City, Utah. Owen Marc Gregerson, 18, was the son of a dentist. On this date Gregerson, Shawn Williams, 19, Christine Cherie Miller, 20, and Margaret J. Probert, 20, sneaked into the elder Gregerson's office. They crowded into a closet, where a tank of nitrous oxide, better known as "laughing gas," was stored, and began sniffing the gas. They probably had a good time, but we'll never know how good because during their revels they passed out, the gas filled the closet, and all four were asphyxiated.

– *August 9* –

1944   France. French pilot and author Antoine de Saint-Exupéry was lost while on a combat mission in his 43rd year. He wrote *The Little Prince*.

1969   Beverly Hills. Members of Charles Manson's "family" slaughtered actress Sharon Tate, and four of her friends. The house where the murders were committed was rented. Reportedly, it was a former resident, whom Manson felt had slighted him in a recording deal, who was the target for death. He wasn't there, so the killers butchered those who were. Gary Menna, of Hollywood's Grave Line Tours, claims that after the killings, the owner received thirty-five offers to buy the house, and that the owner sent a bill to the victim's parents for cleaning up the mess.

– *August 10* –

1945   Baltimore. Rocket pioneer Robert H. Goddard, 62, died of throat cancer. He published a paper in 1919 called "A Method of Reaching Extreme Altitudes" in which he predicted that one day rockets would reach the moon and beyond. Few took him seriously. Goddard received more than 200 patents, but it was Nazi Germany that first put his work to practical use—destroying Allied cities. In 1920, the *New York Times* scathingly observed of Goddard, "He seems only to lack the knowledge ladled out daily in high schools." When NASA landed a man on the moon in 1969, the *Times* issued an apology.

Goddard once said, "There can be no thought of finishing, for aiming at the stars, both literally and figuratively, is the work of generations, but no matter how much progress one makes there is always the thrill of just beginning."

1969   Los Angeles. Leno, 44, and Rosemary La Bianca, 38, were murdered by the Manson "family." Charles "Tex" Watson, a former high school football star, was the primary killer in this and the Tate killings (see 8/9/1969). He received a long prison sentence, but through visitation privileges, he married and fathered three children. He claims a conversion to fundamentalist Christianity. This so moved Susan Laberge, the La Biancas' daughter, that she supported Watson at a 1990 parole hearing. Laberge, a born-again Christian, claimed that Watson's conversion was evidence of his reformation. Nevertheless, Watson wasn't paroled, in part because of the countertestimony of Sharon Tate's mother.

– August 11 –

1975   Washington, D. C. General Anthony C. McAuliffe, 77, died of leukemia. He was buried at Arlington National Cemetery. At the Battle of the Bulge, McAuliffe and his men were surrounded at Bastogne by Germans, who demanded surrender or they would destroy the town, killing every soldier and civilian in it. McAuliffe wrote "Nuts!" on their message (this is the official quote—many believe his actual reply was saltier). McAuliffe's reply became famous and helped urge on relief efforts while stiffening resistance. It also caused GIs to nickname Bastogne "Nutsville." McAuliffe and his men held out, but McAuliffe was haunted by his reply for years. He once was invited to dinner by an elderly Southern lady. He enjoyed the evening very much because no one brought up the quote. As he was bidding his host good night, she took his hand, smiled, and said, "Thank you and good night, General McNut."

— August 12 —

1822   North Cray Place, Kent, England. The second Marquis of Londonderry, 53, better known as Viscount Castlereagh, was the British foreign minister. He suffered from gout and mental problems. Among other recommendations, his doctor prohibited him from eating hot buttered toast. One morning, his servant brought some of the forbidden food to him by mistake. Lord Castlereagh gave in to temptation and ate the toast. His biographer Benjamin Haydon described the results: "His brain filled with more blood, and he became insane!" Lord Castlereagh cut his own throat with a penknife. A few years later, Haydon also killed himself. This time buttered toast wasn't involved.

1944   England. Joseph P. Kennedy, Jr., son of Joseph Kennedy and brother of John, Robert, and Teddy, died at 29. His father wanted him to become president and thought that a distinguished military record would help. Joe joined the Army Air Corps, flew bombing runs in Europe, then volunteered for a secret mission. The military had fitted a bomber with an autopilot and crammed it with explosives. It would automatically fly to its target and crash into the ground. Because the autopilot couldn't perform a takeoff, a pilot was needed to get the plane into the air. The pilot would then parachute out. Joe signed up. The takeoff went fine, but before he could bail out, the plane exploded. No one knows why. Parts of the aircraft are still being found by local farmers. Joe Senior turned his ambitious attentions to his next son, John.

— August 13 —

1903   Liverpool. Friends of elderly rent collector William Shortis and his 224-pound wife, Emily Ann, became worried when they failed to hear from the couple for several days. On this date, with a policeman, they broke into the Shortises' house. They found Shortis badly injured. He had been helping his wife upstairs when she fell backward. Mrs. Shortis had died at once from a head injury, but her husband had remained trapped under her large corpse at the foot of the stairs for three days, too injured to push her off. Help arrived too late. Mr. Shortis died.

1910   London. Nursing pioneer Florence Nightingale died of heart failure in her home. She had spent three years nursing during the Crimean War and was largely responsible for the improvement in hospital nursing that followed.

Back in England, at the age of 37, she felt ill and thought her life "hung by a thread." She took to her bed to await death. She had palpitations, headaches, shortness of breath, and sundry pains. Her illness worsened when unwelcome visitors arrived or when anyone objected to her views. More likely, she was a tyrannical hypochondriac with no real physical illness until the last years of her life. Her "poor health" served as a club to pummel others into obedience. She died at 90, after spending fifty-three years in bed. Perhaps she would attribute her longevity to all that bed rest. On her deathbed, she refused burial in Westminster Abbey and asked to be buried in the nearest cemetery, attended by just two mourners. She was buried where she desired, but far more mourners turned out.

– August 14 –

1951   Beverly Hills. Newspaper publisher William Randolph Hearst, 88, died of heart disease. Orson Wells's movie *Citizen Kane* (1941) was virtually a parody of Hearst's life. Hearst was deeply offended, especially, it is rumored, by the use of the word "Rosebud." Supposedly, "rosebud" was his pet name for a part of the anatomy of his mistress, Marion Davies. Kane's mistress was a drunken, no-talent singer. Davies had a drinking problem, which she battled with Hearst's help, and while many thought her a passable actress, her career wasn't successful, despite Hearst's backing. Yet, unlike Kane's mistress, Davies was loyal to Hearst. When reverses caused him to be short of funds (he spent $500,000,000 during his life),

Davies lent him a million. She had invested earlier gifts from him in real estate.

As a young student at Harvard, Hearst was expelled after sending his professors chamberpots personalized with their photographs and names.

– August 15 –

1927 New York City. Businessman Elbert Henry Gary founded U.S. Steel (Gary, Indiana, was named in his honor). However, by April of 1927, Gary was 80 and frail. At a board meeting, he put his feet up on the table, leaning his chair back. He fell over. The fall injured his back, aggravating a heart condition that killed him on this date.

1935 Point Barrow, Alaska. Will Rogers, 55, was killed in a plane crash. His pilot was the famous aviator Wiley Post. They were traveling through northern Canada and Alaska. Although Post lost his way in a storm, he managed to land on Walakpa Lagoon. Post asked some Eskimos who lived near there how far they were from Barrow, Post's destination. Because Barrow was only ten minutes away, Post and Rogers climbed back into their aircraft and took off. Post banked toward Barrow; then his engine stopped. The plane crashed and exploded. One of the party that removed the bodies later said that the plane's gas tanks were empty. Charles Lindbergh arranged for the remains to be brought home.

Will Rogers said, in reference to the depression, "Stupidity got us into this mess—why can't it get us out?"

– August 16 –

1949 Atlanta. Margaret Mitchell, 49, author of *Gone With the Wind*, died of skull and pelvic fractures after being hit by a taxicab on the eleventh. The cabdriver was convicted of manslaughter. Mitchell had predicted years earlier that she would die in a car crash. Mitchell's book, the bestselling novel of all time, sold 22 million copies. She won a Pulitzer Prize for it in 1937. Adjusting for inflation, the movie based on it is the top moneymaking film ever. Ninety percent of the American public has seen the film at least once.

Mitchell had been a newspaperwoman, but a broken ankle forced her to adopt a more sedentary life. She spent the next ten years writing *Gone With the Wind*. After giving the manuscript to an editor, she had second thoughts and telegraphed him, asking him to return it, but the editor was already hooked by the story. Mitchell originally gave her heroine Scarlett a different name—Pansy.

1956   Los Angeles. Actor Bela Lugosi (born Bela Lugosi Blasko), 73, died of a coronary occlusion. He was holding a script called *The Final Curtain* when he died. Lugosi's wife remarked, "Three nights before he died, he was sitting on the edge of the bed. I asked him if he were still afraid to die. He told me that he was. I did my best to comfort him, but you might as well save your breath with people like that. They're still going to be afraid of death."

Lugosi is best known for the horror film *Dracula* (1931). He made many such films, but the genre faded and with it his fortunes. The abuse of morphine sped his decline. His last role was in what has been called the worst movie of all time, *Plan Nine From Outer Space*. He died before filming finished, and a stand-in completed his scenes. The replacement, who was markedly taller than Lugosi, wore a cape that he held over his face as he stalked from scene to scene.

Lugosi was buried wearing evening dress and his Count Dracula cape. The sight of him laid out in the funeral home in that outfit must have sent a shiver down the spine of everyone who viewed it. At least one person was terrified. A woman brought her son to the chapel, saying, "I'll show you that he is dead. He won't come back any more to frighten you. Because he was just a man like your father. Go ahead and touch him." The boy just ran.

1977   Baptist Memorial Hospital, Memphis. Elvis Aron Presley, 42, was pronounced dead on arrival of a heart attack later blamed on drug abuse. He was found in his bathroom at his estate, Graceland. Ten different drugs, all prescribed by his obliging doctor, were in his blood. One of his associates observed, "One moment he would be sitting at the table, piddling with his mashed potatoes. The next, he would be head down in the slop." None of his entourage would risk offending him by telling him to stop.

In 1990, writer Albert Goldman wrote that Elvis had killed himself to avoid the shame of being publicly labeled a junkie. He cited the testimony of Elvis's half-brother David Stanley, who was one of the first to see Elvis dead. Stanley said, "He was too intelligent to overdose. He knew the PDR— *Physicians' Desk Reference* [of drug effects]—inside and out."

Elvis was buried in a cream suit, pale blue shirt with diamond cuff links, and silver tie with diamond stickpin. A white hearse delivered his 900-pound copper coffin to a local cemetery. On the twenty-ninth, four men were arrested lurking about the cemetery. They were planning to steal Elvis's body and ransom it. Presley was moved to the grounds of Graceland, where he could be guarded. Seven hundred thousand visitors view his grave there each year. Their admission fees, plus recording royalties and merchandising of Elvis's likeness, bring his estate $15 million annually. His estate was worth $4.9 million at the time of his death and is estimated as approaching $100 million today. When his daughter Lisa Marie becomes 30, she will inherit it.

– August 17 –

1896   Near the Crystal Palace, London. Mrs. Bridget Driscoll panicked during a demonstration of an automobile and fell. The auto crushed her skull, and she became the first motor vehicle fatality.

1987   Spandau Prison, West Berlin. Rudolf Hess was one of Hitler's pals till 1941, when he parachuted into Scotland. He was trying to arrange a truce whereby Britain would retain her empire and Germany would keep Europe. This would free Germany to turn on Russia. Hess was being pushed out of Hitler's favor by rivals, and a diplomatic coup would have impressed Hitler. Reportedly, Hess had high-placed friends in Britain who, he was certain, would help him. In 1991, the *New York Times* obtained Soviet KGB files (including reports from British traitor Kim Philby) that indicate that British intelligence wrote Hess using the duke of Hamilton's name, without the duke's knowledge, promising a peace conference. They hoped to make mischief in Hitler's inner circle. They did. Hitler was furious, but Hess would never see Hitler

again. He spent forty-six years in prison for war crimes.
Efforts were made to arrange his freedom, but the Russians
always objected. Eventually, he was the lone occupant of
Spandau Prison. It took over $1,000,000 a year to keep him
there.

On this date, while Hess was walking in the exercise area,
his guard was inattentive. Hess disappeared into a garden
shed, where the guard later found him dead. The verdict was
suicide by self-strangulation with an electrical cord. There
were objections. Hess was an arthritic 93-year-old who could
neither form a fist nor raise his hands above his shoulders.
The British prison commandant (command rotated among
the Allied powers) burned the cord and the shed. An autopsy
revealed bruises that suggested Hess had been murdered. It
was speculated that the British government, thinking Hess
would be released because of his age, murdered him to
prevent his revealing the names of his friends in Britain. But
there was more mystery. A doctor announced that his
examination of Hess proved that the prisoner was an imposter.
He didn't bear the scars Hess had received in battle during
World War I. Photographs revealed that the plane Hess had
flown to Scotland bore different markings from the plane he
left Germany in. If Hess wasn't Hess, who was he, and for
whom did he work? Why didn't he talk? The British
government has released some of its Hess files but reclassified
others. They won't be made public till 2016.

Hess was buried in Bavaria. His family believed he
genuinely wanted to make peace. His tombstone bears: "It
was worth the risk."

– August 18 –

1503 Rome. Pope Alexander VI, 72, accidentally poisoned himself
and died. The poison was meant for one of his guests, but he
took it by mistake.

Alexander's corrupt eleven-year reign helped produce the
Protestant Reformation. A member of the notorious Borgia
family, he spared no effort advancing his family's fortunes. He
sired scores of illegitimate children, but his favorites were
Cesare, Giovanni, and Lucrezia. Using murder, intrigue,

strategic marriage, and war, Alexander managed to dominate much of Italy. When he needed money, he sold a cardinalship or an indulgence absolving a sinner of a sin either past or planned. On one occasion he sold for 24,000 gold pieces permission for a nobleman to sleep with his own sister.

Alexander himself was accused of incest with his daughter. He kept dozens of courtesans in the Vatican, staging elaborate orgies there. He even had a portrait of his favorite mistress in the guise of the Virgin Mary hung over his bed. Many believed that Alexander had sold his soul to the devil.

When Alexander died, his domain fell apart. Mobs looted his palace, preventing his burial. By the time he was placed in a coffin, he had swollen with putrefaction and had to be pounded into place.

1850 Paris. Writer Honoré de Balzac, 51, died after drinking too much coffee. He was in debt, fat, short, and a poor dresser, and publicly picked his nose. He still had great success with women.

On his deathbed, Balzac called for his favorite doctor—a fictional character he had created—saying, "If Blanchon were here, he would save me." His real doctors had applied a hundred leeches to Balzac to reduce his dropsical swelling induced by the coffee. Fatal gangrene resulted.

Balzac once said, "Men are so made that they can resist sound argument, and yet yield to a glance."

– August 19 –

1977 Los Angeles. Comic actor Julius Henry "Groucho" Marx, 86, died of pneumonia. He had been suffering from hip problems and a respiratory ailment for months.

The Marx Brothers comedy team was formed by the boys' mother, who saw the success of an uncle in vaudeville and decided her boys could do as well. They started touring the nation as a singing group, but in 1914, in Nacogdoches, Texas, they lost their audience when a mule ran away. Incensed that the locals found this animal Houdini more entertaining than they, they lashed out with wisecracks when the audience returned for the rest of their show. They yelled "Nacogdoches—full of roaches" and called the Texans "damn

Yankees." Instead of being insulted, the audience loved it. The Marx Brothers incorporated more and more humor into their act till it replaced their singing.

Their comic mayhem was carefully rehearsed. The boys would experiment with jokes, adding successful ones and cutting groaners. The result was the appearance of spontaneity in a carefully crafted act.

W. C. Fields said of the Marx Brothers, "Never saw so much nepotism or such hilarious laughter in one act in my life. The only act I could never follow. In Columbus I told the manager I broke my wrist and quit."

– August 20 –

1988   Donington Park Race Track, Donington, England. A heavy metal rock band was playing a concert. The crowd of 100,000 punk fans "slam-danced" to the music. Slam dancing consists of jumping up and down and throwing oneself upon other dancers. The result of this peculiar pastime—two were killed and two badly injured when they fell under the feet of other merrymakers.

1989   Near the Kora National Reserve, Kenya. Conservationist George Adamson, 83, was shot to death by Somali bandits. The bandits had robbed and beaten Adamson's assistants. Adamson, with three other assistants, drove to the rescue. He aimed his car at the bandits and attempted to run them down, but their gunfire killed him and two of the assistants. It was a bold act, but it should be noted that the assistants begged Adamson not to drive into the bandits. It was rather high-handed of him to "volunteer" their participation.

Adamson became famous after he and his wife reared three motherless lion cubs in 1956. His wife, Joy Adamson, wrote the book *Born Free* about their attempt to release the grown cubs. Joy Adamson was killed on Janurary 3, 1980, in a wage dispute with a native worker.

– August 21 –

1614   Hungary. Countess Elizabeth Bathory had been strange since childhood, but became a menace in her fifties. It was then that she put into practice a theory she had developed. She believed that if she bathed in the blood of young women she would gain eternal youth. To this end, she persuaded three of her servants to help her lure young women to her castle, where they were murdered and their blood drained into a large tub wherein the countess splashed about. Eventually, one girl escaped and returned with the authorities. The three servants were hanged, but since the countess was the cousin of the prime minister, she was walled alive into her bedchamber. A small hole allowed food and water to be passed inside. She died there, insane (or maybe just insaner), three years later on this date.

– *August 22* –

1751 Tring, England. Thomas Colley was hanged for his part in the murder of Ruth Osborne, a woman of 70. The murder occurred after a fellow named Butterfield claimed Osborne had cursed him when he refused to give her some milk. Butterfield suffered financially and became ill. A "white witch" summoned to thwart the curse set six men with pitchforks on a twenty-four-hour guard around Butterfield's house to discourage evil forces. Butterfield didn't improve, and the guards were expensive, so he arranged for town criers in all the surrounding villages to announce a public "ducking."

The notion behind ducking was that a witch would float, as the water would reject an unnatural creature, while an innocent soul would sink. Absolute proof of innocence was usually sought, causing hapless victims to drown under repeated, scrupulous testing. To this end, an angry mob of 5,000 assembled. The parish overseer, unaided by local clergymen, hid the woman and her husband, but the mob smashed the workhouse and threatened to burn down the village if the couple weren't produced. The overseer submitted, and the couple was dragged off to a pond, where both were ducked in the water till the old woman drowned. Her gasping husband was tied to the corpse and left by the pond, where he soon died.

The authorities were alarmed, especially since similar incidents had recently taken place. An inquest was held. The jury was made up of gentlemen, as locals of lesser station sided with witch-killers. Thomas Colley was convicted of being the mob's ringleader. The authorities organized an impressive military hanging by the pond to make the power of the state over the mob explicit. After the execution, Colley was hanged from a gibbet there to serve as a reminder to the locals to lay off witch-hunting. But Colley retained the favor of the mob. Few showed up at the execution, and nearly everyone avoided the gibbet till long after Colley's corpse was reduced to bones. They thought it unfair to persecute such a civic-minded fellow for the sake of an old witch.

– August 23 –

A.D. 79   Mount Vesuvius buried Pompeii and Herculaneum, killing 20,000. The Roman writer Pliny the Elder died in his 56th year when he sought to study the eruption scientifically. He was the author of a thirty-seven-volume natural history, and when his daughter saw the smoke of Vesuvius, he took ship for the area. He secured a house by the volcano, dictated observations, bathed, and ate supper. The ground and the house began to shake, so, tying a pillow to his head to shield it from falling pumice, Pliny fled, along with his servants. Waves kept them from escaping by ship, and the heat became intense. The plump Pliny lay down by a stream to cool himself and was killed by poisonous fumes that had collected in the low spot.

1926   New York City. Silent film star Rodolfo Alfonzo Rafaelo Pierre Filibert Guglielmi di Valentina d'Antonguolla, better known as Rudolph Valentino, died at 30. His last words were reported as, "Don't pull down the blinds! I feel fine. I want the sunlight to greet me." On August 14, he had collapsed in his suite at the Hotel Ambassador from abdominal pain. He refused to go the hospital, but when he developed a high fever, he was taken to New York's Polyclinic Hospital. He was operated on for a perforated gastric ulcer, and during the operation, it was discovered that his appendix had ruptured. In those days there were no antibiotics, so when infection rapidly spread through him, there was little hope. On this date, at 12:10 P.M., he died. Many women who had never seen more of him than a flickering black-and-white image killed themselves in grief. An English actress took poison, a New York housewife shot herself, and in Japan, two women jumped into a volcano.

When Valentino's body was displayed by the funeral home in New York City, a riot erupted. A second riot occurred when the funeral train passed through Chicago. The Hollywood funeral was marked by a one-hour shutdown by the community's movie studios. To this day, a mysterious "Lady in Black" visits Valentino's grave on the anniversary of his death to place flowers by his marker. Many women claimed to be the unknown lady and romantic rumors abound, but the most plausible claim was advanced by a bit actress many years later. She had once been ill and fearful of dying. Valentino had cheered her through her sickness, and she was showing gratitude for his kindness.

Just days before his death, Valentino had been assailed by the *Chicago Tribune* as the inspiration for "pink powder puff" homosexuals. The screen lover, known for his dramatic roles, threatened a duel, but the fact that both of his two wives were lesbians raised suspicions. During their divorce, the first accused him of hitting her and of lack of sexual attentions. During divorce proceedings, his second wife claimed that their marriage was unconsummated. The charges embittered Valentino, who asked his doctors as he was stoically dying in severe pain, "And now, do I act like a pink powder puff?"

– August 24 –

1770 London. To avoid starving to death, writer Thomas Chatterton, 17, ate arsenic. He became a symbol of the Romantic movement.

1970 University of Wisconsin Army Math Research Center, Madison. Members of the peace movement, protesting the killing in Vietnam, detonated a bomb, killing 33-year-old researcher Robert Fassnacht.

– August 25 –

1900 Weimar. Philosopher Friedrich Nietzsche died at 55. He is best remembered for his *Thus Spake Zarathustra*. His notion of an individualistic "superman" was exploited by the Nazis, although Nietzsche was opposed to anti-Semitism. He was a close friend of Richard Wagner for years, but eventually Nietzsche found Wagner's bigotry insufferable and ended the friendship. Nietzsche had had debilitating headaches since his twenties, and in 1889, while in Turin, Italy, he suffered a breakdown. When he saw a horse being beaten, he flung his arms around its neck and couldn't stop crying. He spent the next eleven years in an asylum and then under his family's care. His illness was probably caused by syphilis contracted as a young man.

Nietzsche once said, "A casual stroll through the lunatic asylum shows that faith does not prove anything." Leo Tolstoy said, "Nietzsche was stupid and abnormal."

– August 26 –

1974   Kipahulu, Maui, Hawaii. Aviator Charles Augustus Lindbergh, 72, died of lymphatic cancer, with his family at his side. In 1927 he made the first solo nonstop transatlantic flight. For this he was awarded the Congressional Medal of Honor. His fame brought him wealth. The wealth brought criminal interest, and Lindbergh's son was kidnapped and murdered (see 3/1/1932). Lindbergh was a prominent spokesman for U.S. isolationism, which brought him much negative criticism. When war came, he volunteered for combat service, but President Roosevelt, still angered by Lindbergh's antiwar views, rejected his request. Despite this, Lindbergh worked as a consultant to industry and the government and flew fifty missions in the Pacific, testing military aircraft. Because Lindbergh's politics had aroused resentment, his activities were little known. Years later, he received the Pulitzer Prize for his book *The Spirit of St. Louis.*

Lindbergh was ill for some time before his death. When he knew he was dying, he flew to his vacation cottage in Hawaii to spend his last days planning his funeral. According to his wishes, he was buried just three hours after he died, wearing his work clothes in a coffin made by Hawaiian cowboys.

1978   Phoenix. Despondent over the death by cancer of his wife, the great screen lover Charles Boyer, 80, killed himself with an overdose of Seconal. Boyer had had a crush on his teacher when he was a 13-year-old boy in France. He had managed to give her a kiss, but the startled woman responded by laughing. Boyer, whom female fans swooned over and whom male fans desperately tried to emulate, claimed that after that encounter, he never kissed a woman without expecting laughter.

– August 27 –

1908 Folsom, New Mexico. The Dry Cimarron flooded. Sarah J. Rooke, a telephone operator, stayed by her switchboard warning telephone customers that the flood was coming. She saved others but died herself.

1967 London. Record producer Brian Epstein, 33, whose best clients were the Beatles, killed himself with sleeping pills. When Epstein was first promoting the group, he offered singer Little Richard 50 percent of the group's profits for a small investment. Little Richard saw no future for the Beatles and turned it down.

– August 28 –

1951 Hollywood. Actor Robert Walker, 32, had been married to Jennifer Jones, but the marriage didn't last. After the divorce, Walker suffered several nervous breakdowns. He married Barbara Ford, daughter of director John Ford, but in just six weeks they were divorced. Walker drank heavily. Following an arrest for drunk driving, he suffered another breakdown, which led to a year in a mental institution. Walker recovered and returned to the screen to perform brilliantly in Alfred Hitchcock's *Strangers on a Train* (1951), wherein he played an unbalanced strangler. Walker was working on the film *My Son John* (1952) when, while experiencing a severe emotional episode, he begged his psychiatrist to sedate him. When the psychiatrist injected a sedative, Walker immediately went into respiratory failure and died.

1971 San Juan, Puerto Rico. Nathan F. Leopold, 66, died of a heart attack. In 1924, with Richard Loeb, he murdered Bobbie

Franks. Loeb died in prison, but Leopold was paroled in 1958 (see 5/21/1924). Leopold took a job as a mathematics teacher and hospital technician for $10 a month, but he was haunted by his past action, claiming it was always in his thoughts. He said, upon his parole, "I am a broken old man. I want a chance to find redemption for myself and to help others."

– August 29 –

A.D.   Machaerus. John the Baptist was beheaded. He was about 33.
29   Recently, a group of archaeologists claim to have found his tomb in a Coptic Christian church in Egypt. The severed skull is said to be entombed with the rest of his bones.

1877   Salt Lake City. Mormon leader Brigham Young, 76, died of what was probably appendicitis. His last words were, "Joseph! Joseph! Joseph!" He was calling for Joseph Smith, the long-deceased founder of Mormonism. In his will, Young laid out detailed funeral directions. He wanted a redwood coffin large enough "to have the appearance that if I wanted to turn a little to the right or left I should have plenty of room to do so." Young left twenty-nine widows.

– August 30 –

30   Alexandria. Egyptian queen Cleopatra, 39, killed herself using
B.C.   an asp. Her last words, when presented with the snake, are recorded as, "So here it is!"

Cleopatra, with her paramour Mark Antony, had led a failed rebellion against Rome, or, more precisely, against Rome's first emperor, Octavian. Some historians believe Cleopatra planned to seduce Octavian and tricked the defeated Antony into killing himself by sending him the false news that she had already killed herself. However, when the uncharmed Octavian's plans to carry Cleopatra back to Rome in a cage were made plain to her, the proud queen chose death, sending Octavian a message requesting that she be buried by Antony's side. Plutarch wrote that although Octavian sent soldiers to prevent her suicide, they arrived too late, discovering her body laid out upon golden cloth with one of her handmaidens nearby, dying of self-administered poison. When the guard asked the dying handmaiden, "Was this well done by your lady?" the woman replied, "Exceedingly well, as became a descendant of a long line of kings." Octavian buried her with Antony and contented himself with carrying a statue of Cleopatra back to Rome. The grave site has been lost beneath the modern city of Alexandria.

Although she followed most Egyptian royal traditions, Cleopatra was actually of Greek extraction, the descendant of one of Alexander the Great's generals (Alexander had conquered Egypt centuries earlier). As was the Egyptian custom, Cleopatra had married her brother, Ptolemy. Only another member of the Pharaoh's house was thought suitable for marriage with a Pharaoh. Cleopatra was the product of six generations of such marriage.

1968   Encino, California. Actor William Talman, 51, who played the ever-defeated defense attorney Hamilton Burger (Ham Burger!) on the TV show "Perry Mason," died of lung cancer. When he knew he was dying, he made a powerful antismoking commercial warning others.

– August 31 –

1888   Whitechapel, London. Jack the Ripper killed the first of five prostitutes. He was never found, but speculation has named several suspects. A number of doctors have been suggested, as well as several known sexual sadists. Sir Arthur Conan Doyle suggested that "Jack" was a woman, probably an insane midwife. A modern writer has nominated Edward, the duke of Clarence, Queen Victoria's grandson and the direct heir to the throne of England. Edward had a wild lifestyle and had contracted venereal disease. He died insane of its effects in 1892. One of the more likely suspects was Dr. Thomas Cream, an abortionist who had committed second-degree murder in Illinois and been released from Joliet Prison as rehabilitated. The time he spent in prison was his alibi for the crimes, but it is claimed that Cream had a double and that in those days before fingerprints were recorded, the two used each others' prison terms as mutual alibis. Cream had once used a prison term in Australia as an alibi for bigamy. In time, he was convicted and hanged for poisoning several prostitutes in London in 1891. It is reported that as the gallows were sprung, the executioner heard Cream shout, "I am Jack—"

1969   Newton, Iowa. Heavyweight boxing champ Rocky Marciano, 46, died in a single-engine airplane crash. Marciano was rushing home to attend a birthday party being held in his honor.

1986   Much Hatham, Hertfordshire, England. British abstract sculptor Henry Moore died at 88. No cause was announced, but he had been suffering from arthritis and diabetes. He was well known for his large, lumpy statues of women who often sported holes in their anatomy. His works were commissioned for parks around the world. One commission for an English village requested that should Moore see fit to put a hole in its statue, he should make sure that the hole was large enough to keep schoolboys from getting their heads stuck.

– September 1 –

1715   Versailles. Louis XIV of France died at 76 of gangrene. His last words: "Did you think I should live forever? I thought dying was harder." He reigned 72 years (the longest of any French monarch), increasing the grandeur of France, but also helping create the conditions that led to the French Revolution.

Louis was fond of gigantic meals, and after his death an autopsy discovered that his stomach was twice normal size. Although he was considered the most elegant man in Europe, Louis bathed only once a year. It was the custom at Louis's palace at Versailles to scratch on doors instead of knocking. This was considered more refined, and courtiers grew the nail on the left little finger long for that purpose. Prestige in the court was acknowledged by the height of the chair one was assigned—the taller the chair, the more important the person. Only the king and his queen were allowed chairs with arm rests.

During the French Revolution, Louis's tomb was broken into and his heart removed. It passed through various hands until the Very Reverend William Buckland, dean of Westminster, England, purchased the heart and ate it.

1914   Cincinnati Zoo. The last passenger pigeon, "Martha," died at 29. In 1880, two billion flew American skies, but overhunting wiped them out. Some hunters actually used cannon to kill them by the score.

1969   Washington, D.C. Journalist Drew Pearson, 71, died of heart disease. He had been warned not to exert himself following a heart attack in August, but while touring one of his farms, he spotted a poacher running across a field. Pearson's outrage induced another heart attack. His associate Jack Anderson inherited Pearson's column.

Pearson became a Washington columnist during the Hoover administration. One day he and Robert S. Allen, another reporter, decided to publish an anonymous book titled *The Washington Merry-Go-Round*, containing the dirt their editors wouldn't print. It became a sensation. When their identities were revealed, they began writing a successful column by the same name. Allen eventually left the column, but Pearson kept at it for over thirty-five years, becoming extremely influential and making numerous enemies.

Franklin Roosevelt called him "a chronic liar." Senator Kenneth McKellar spent over an hour describing exactly what kind of liar. In part, McKellar called him "a revolving, constitutional, unmitigated, infamous liar." Eleanor Patterson, his onetime mother-in-law and former publisher, called him "one of the weirdest specimens of humanity since Nemo, the Turtle Boy." Douglas MacArthur sued him. Harry Truman called him an "SOB." Senator Joseph McCarthy managed to do what many dreamed of—according to Pearson, McCarthy cornered him and kneed him in the groin. Pearson said, "I suppose I've got more enemies per square inch on Capitol Hill than anyplace else in the world." Before becoming a journalist, Pearson had hoped for a career as a diplomat.

Pearson kept a herd of 200 cows. Called a muckraker, he sold their manure under the brand name "Drew Pearson's Best Manure."

– September 2 –

459   Mount Telanissae, Cilicia (near Syria). St. Simeon the Stylite died in his 69th year. He had spent twenty-seven years dressed

in animal skins atop a pillar. Charitable folks brought him food, which he hauled up. Kings, clergy, and ordinary people came to seek his wisdom.

1964   Nashville. Sergeant Alvin Cullum York, 76, died of an acute internal infection following a decade of illness. A series of strokes had left him blind and paralyzed. York was drafted during World War I. He tried twice to be excused on the basis of his religion, but wasn't released from the service. He still planned to refuse to kill, but an officer spoke to him of the necessity of fighting a just war. After meditating two days in the mountains near his home, York decided to fight.

In France, after his company was nearly wiped out, Corporal York single-handedly killed 25 and captured 132 members of a German machine-gun battalion. York had only his rifle and the ability to imitate turkey mating calls. His gobbling caused curious Germans to reveal themselves. He said, "Every time one of them raised his head, I jes teched him off." His efficiency panicked other Germans into surrendering. York had only six men to manage his many prisoners, so he lined up the prisoners with his men behind them. The prisoners, facing forward, had no idea how many doughboys were guarding them. As they marched back, other Germans, thinking their whole unit was surrounded, surrendered and joined the parade.

York was promoted to sergeant and awarded the Medal of Honor. He was given a hero's welcome when he returned to the United States. When York visited the New York Stock Exchange, traders abandoned business to carry him around the trading floor on their shoulders. Congress gave him a standing ovation. Tennessee gave him a 396-acre farm. He was offered dozens of lucrative speaking engagements but refused them, saying, "This uniform ain't for sale." When he married his sweetheart, Gracie Williams, they were offered a honeymoon in Salt Lake City—hardly a Sodom or a Gomorrah. They refused. He said it was "merely a vainglorious call of the world and the devil."

York spent the rest of his life a farmer, excepting a short period during which he helped establish a trade school. In 1941, a movie starring Gary Cooper related his exploits. York was paid quite a bit. The IRS claimed he owed it $172,000, but York claimed he had given most of the money to the trade school. The legal battle lasted ten years. The IRS settled for

$25,000, but York couldn't pay. Speaker of the House Sam Rayburn raised the money. One of the Du Ponts set up a modest trust to support the aging veteran.

In World War II, York served on a draft board that drafted two of his five sons. Fortunately, both survived the war. York didn't like the scale of destruction atomic bombs could produce, but he favored their use if a war with Russia occurred, saying, "If they can't find anyone else to push the button, I will."

– September 3 –

1658   Whitehall. The leader of the English parlimentary forces and lord protector of England, Oliver Cromwell, died at about 55 of what the *Dictionary of National Biography* records as "a bastard tertian ague." It was the anniversary of his two greatest victories, Dunbar and Worcester. Cromwell's last words, upon being offered food: "It is not my design to drink or sleep; but my design is to make what haste I can to be gone."

Following the Restoration, Cromwell's body was dug up by order of Charles II. It was beheaded, and the desiccated head was stuck on a pike and carried through London while citizens pelted it with refuse. The skull was displayed on the pike atop Westminster Hall. Reportedly, it stayed there for twenty-five years till a storm dropped it in front of a sentry, who kept it as a souvenir. Still well preserved, it passed through various hands over the years. One eighteenth-century owner carried it with him to parties. Eventually, Cromwell's alma mater, Sidney Sussex College in Cambridge, purchased it and secretly buried it. Only a select few members of the college's staff know where.

1991   La Quinta, California. Film director Frank Capra, 94, died in his sleep of natural causes. Capra made warm, folksy films, such as *It's a Wonderful Life* (1946). That film bombed on its first outing. Postwar film-goers wanted more realistic fare. Reviewers labeled it "Capra-corn." As the years passed, the film languished, unremembered. When it came time to renew the copyright, Capra neglected to do so, and it was this error that brought the film new life. Television stations, anxious for holiday fare, no longer had to pay royalties to broadcast it. *It's a Wonderful Life* was soon being shown on every channel, and modern viewers were captivated by its message—that one good man can make a difference. The film is now celebrated as one of America's great works of art.

– September 4 –

1965   Labarene, Gabon. Nobel Prize winner Dr. Albert Schweitzer, 90, died of circulatory problems. Despite Schweitzer's humanitarian reputation, journalist John Gunther called Schweitzer "dictatorial, irascible, and somewhat vain." These traits helped Schweitzer succeed in building his hospital in a forbidding area and treating thousands of Africans. Part of his success was due to his running the hospital on African rather than European lines. He built a medical missionary station that seemed like a native village. Families were encouraged to stay with the patients, animals wandered about, and buildings were in native style.

Schweitzer developed an ethical system he called "Reverence for Life," which held all life sacred. This caused him to delay the construction of buildings when an anthill might be disturbed and to refrain from teaching his pet parrot to speak, as it would be demeaning for the bird.

– September 5 –

1930   Leavenworth. Carl Panzram, robber and confessed killer of twenty-one, had been sentenced to death for the murder of a civilian prison laundry foreman. The Society for the Abolishment of Capital Punishment took up his cause with letters and petitions. Panzram, however, was angry. He wrote the society: "I look forward to [the hanging] as real pleasure and a big relief...I will dance out of my dungeon...I wish you all had one neck and that I had my hands on it...the only way to reform people is to kill 'em." On this date, he went to the hangman happily.

1932   Benedict Canyon, Los Angeles. The nude body of Paul Bern, 42, assistant to MGM's Irving Thalberg, was found shot through the head lying before a full-length mirror in his mansion by his butler. Bern, known as a sympathetic intellectual, married sex goddess Jean Harlow on July 2, 1932. Supposedly he wasn't well endowed, and it is rumored that he unsuccessfully substituted an artificial phallus for his own on their wedding night. Whatever the cause, Harlow fled Bern's house that night after receiving a severe beating. This abuse may have caused her death (see 6/7/1937).

Bern left a note, which MGM boss Louis B. Mayer tried to hide from the police. It read:

> Dearest Dear
> Unfortunately this is the only way to make good the frightful wrong I have done you, and to wipe out my abject humiliation. I love you.
> Paul
> You understand that last night was only a comedy.

A second explanation of the incident suggests that Bern was murdered by a previous wife whom he hadn't divorced before marrying Harlow. This woman killed herself shortly after Bern died.

— September 6 —

1901 Pan-American Exposition, Buffalo. Polish immigrant Leon Czolgosz had had a hard time in America, so he bound a gun to his hand with a bandage, attended a reception, stepped forward to shake hands, and shot twenty-fifth U.S. president William McKinley, 58, twice, yelling, "I done my duty." When guards jumped Czolgosz, punching him in the face, McKinley remarked, "Be easy with him, boys."

One of the bullets grazed McKinley's ribs, deflected by a coat button. The second cut through his stomach. The doctors couldn't find it when they operated. Afraid that they might do more damage searching, they stitched him up. On exhibit at the exposition was a new invention, the X-ray machine. Had his doctors been just a little more up-to-date, they could have wheeled it in and found the bullet in minutes. McKinley lingered for eight days, his pancreas destroyed and his wound gangrenous. He died on the fourteenth. His last words were, "We are all going...We are all going...Oh, dear." He was buried in Canton, Ohio. Czolgosz was electrocuted for the murder.

Robert Todd Lincoln was present at the shooting. He was also present at the assassination of President Garfield and was at the side of his father, Abraham Lincoln, when he died. After McKinley's death, Robert swore never to attend another state occasion.

When McKinley began his campaign for president, his wife was ill with phlebitis, epilepsy, and depression following the infant deaths of her two daughters. He decided to stay home to care for her and conducted his entire successful campaign from his front porch. At the time, it was common to hide people who were afflicted with epilepsy. McKinley would have none of this and brought his First Lady to state dinners. She remained an invalid during his brief presidency, rising from her wheelchair only when McKinley was brought, wounded, to the White House. She rose to help nurse him, but to no avail. She died six years later.

McKinley's mother, Nancy Allison McKinley, was a devout Methodist who hoped her son would join the clergy and rise to a high clerical position. She lived to see him go from small-town lawyer to Ohio's governor to U.S. president, yet on her son's inauguration eve, family friends claimed they overheard McKinley's brother Abner consoling her, saying, "But, Mother, this is better than a bishopric.

1991 St. Louis. Robert Gremmelsbacher, 31, saw two teenage boys vandalizing a cardboard sign that advertised a church-sponsored fish fry. He tried to stop them. One of the boys pulled a gun and shot Gremmelsbacher to death.

– September 7 –

1969 Near the Dead Sea, Israel. The body of theologian Bishop James Pike, 56, was found at the foot of a cliff in the desert. Pike and his 31-year-old wife had left Bethlehem by car on September 1 to visit the Dead Sea. When their car got stuck, they tried to walk back. Not having brought any water, they soon collapsed. Pike's wife roused herself and went for help. She found it ten hours later, but when a rescue party returned for Pike, he was gone. He wandered in the desert wasteland, apparently finding water but unable to reach safety. It seems he fell while trying to climb the cliff. Authorities believe he had been dead for three or four days.

– September 8 –

1900 Galveston. A hurricane devastated the city, killing 6,000 (a fourth of the population). Looters pillaged homes, stores, and the dead even before the hurricane passed. It required two army regiments (about 2,000 men) to reestablish order. Their major said, "Shoot them in their tracks, boys! We want no prisoners!" and, on another occasion, "Plant 'em!" Over 500 looters were shot. One looter was discovered with twenty-three human fingers in his pockets. Each finger bore a ring. Rather than tug them off, he had resorted to the quicker procedure of removing the entire finger.

1935 Louisiana Capitol Building, Baton Rouge. Senator Huey "Kingfish" Long, 42, was shot. He died two days later. The attacker was presumed to be Dr. Carl A. Weiss—Long had insulted a family member—but recent investigations indicate that Long may have been shot by his own guards when they put sixty-one bullets into Weiss. Weiss may have only struck Long with his fist. In 1992, forensic scientist James Starrs of George Washington University exhumed the body of Weiss. He determined that Long's guards hadn't accurately reported the incident. They claimed Weiss was crouching as he rushed in to shoot Long, but Starrs found cotton fibers on two bullets in Weiss's skull. Starrs thinks Weiss was holding his arms up defensively and that the bullets passed through his shirt sleeves. Starrs has also determined that the bullet purported to have killed Long doesn't match Weiss's gun.

Long, the virtual dictator of Louisiana, whose vote-buying public works programs nearly bankrupted the state and who kept a private army of goons to thwart opposition, died thirty hours after the shooting. His last words: "Why would anyone want to shoot me?" He was buried in an opulent tomb near the capitol, and many still swear he was a wonderful fellow. Others think he was the closest thing to Adolf Hitler that America ever produced.

– September 9 –

1087   Rouen, France. William the Conqueror, 59, was conquered by
       Death. William had been traveling on doctor's orders to a
       French "spa," where he hoped to lose weight and improve his
       health. He had suffered his entire life from terrible weight
       problems (he was tauntingly accused of being pregnant).
       William ruled part of France at the time and, during his
       health trip, paused to lead a punitive attack against the French
       at Mantes. The town was captured, and while William rode
       about the burned wreckage, his horse trod on a hot coal. The
       animal reared, forcing the saddle pommel deep into William's
       ample stomach so forcefully that William's bowels were
       ruptured. Peritonitis set in. He lingered in agony for five
       weeks before he fell into a coma and died.
           The noblemen in his party quickly left to protect their
       holdings, fearing possible unrest following the king's death.
       When priests arrived to administer last rites, they discovered
       that servants had looted the chamber, stealing William's
       possessions and even the jewelry from his body.
           The funeral was a disaster. William's body, bloated by
       putrefaction gases and ripened by a hot day, burst when
       attendant bishops tried to forcefully close the coffin lid.
       Horrid fluids leaked from the coffin, and the dreadful odor
       drove mourners from the church. The coffin was interred at
       St. Stephen's Church in Caen, but in 1562, a Huguenot mob
       dug up William's skeleton and scattered it about the church's
       courtyard. Later, the bones were cast in with other unknown
       remains.
           By one account, William was the illegitimate son of Duke
       Robert of Normandy and a commoner, Herleve Fulbert.
       Legend purports that Robert spotted Herleve while she was
       washing laundry in a brook. He swept her up on his horse and
       rode off to his castle, where William was duly conceived.
       Herleve dreamed that night that a giant tree was growing out
       of her body and that the branches of this tree extended not
       only over Normandy but also over England.

1901   The estate Malromé. Henri de Toulouse-Lautrec died in his
       mother's arms at nearly 37 of a probable stroke. His health
       had been weakened by alcoholism, syphilis, and emotional
       problems. He was buried near the gates of the family estate of

Malromé but was later moved to the village churchyard of Verdelais.

Toulouse-Lautrec reputedly admired women with well-formed nostrils, since, as he was dwarfed by leg problems, nostrils were the first thing he saw when looking up at a woman's face.

1917   Laishev, Kazan, Russia. Two hundred Bolsheviks, seeking to disrupt the democratic government of Alexander Kerensky, set fire to the town but found a wine cellar they enjoyed so well that all 200 were killed by their own spreading blaze.

1920   Ritz Hotel, Paris, France. Silent movie actress Olive Thomas, 21, began as a Ziegfeld showgirl and model for Alberto Vargas, then became a success in Hollywood, where she was known as America's "kid sister" for her wholesome roles. She married the "Ideal American Boy," Jack Pickford, brother to "America's Sweetheart," Mary Pickford. They were called "the Ideal Couple." This ended on this date, when Thomas was found by a valet lying naked on her sable opera cape. She was in a stupor induced by overindulgence in champagne and cocaine after a wild evening at the Dead Rat Cafe in Montmartre. She was hurried to the American Hospital, where she managed to say, just before entering a fatal coma, "Well, Doc, this is what Paris did for me."

An investigation of a prominent Hollywood dope dealer, a Captain Spaulding of the U.S. Army, revealed that Thomas was one of his steady customers. Captain Spaulding was immortalized by Groucho Marx's satiric theme song, "Hooray for Captain Spaulding, the African explorer."

– September 10 –

1947   Clifton, Maine. Melvin Jellison, 100, Union veteran of the Civil War, died of natural causes. He had been a dutiful soldier and once, on guard duty, refused to let pass a man in civilian dress who didn't know the password. That man was Abraham Lincoln.

1965   Philadelphia. Black evangelist Father Divine died at his chateau at about 88 of lung congestion caused by arteriosclerosis and diabetes. Father Divine claimed to have been "combusted" fully grown in a puff of smoke at the corner of

Seventh Avenue and 134th Street in Harlem in 1900. A more mundane account has him born George Baker in 1877. He began preaching a "Live Ever, Die Never" form of Christianity in Georgia, wherein he proclaimed himself God and claimed his followers wouldn't die while in his care. He insured that this prophecy would come true by turning out into the street any follower who was deathly ill. Officials arrested him as a public nuisance, booking him as "John Doe, alias God." When they gave him the choice of leaving Georgia or going to an asylum, Divine moved to New York City, where he began a cult that called on members to live viceless lives and to give Father Divine all their money. He called his followers "angels" and had them live in celibate communes called "heavens." He acquired farms and hotels and a Rolls-Royce to tour them.

– September 11 –

1971   Moscow. Deposed premier of the Soviet Union Nikita S. Khrushchev, 77, died in his sleep of a heart attack in the Kremlin hospital. Heart problems had bothered him for years. News of his death wasn't released for several hours. Once, Khrushchev was giving a speech condemning the terrors of Stalin. Abruptly, a voice yelled out, "You were one of his colleagues, why didn't you stop him?" Silence followed. Khrushchev bellowed, "Who said that?" There was more silence. "Now you know why," Khrushchev said.

Dr. Henry Kissinger once asked Chou En-Lai what might have happened if Khrushchev had been assassinated instead of John Kennedy. Chou reflected, then offered: "I don't believe Mr. Onassis would have married Mrs. Khrushchev."

1971   Beverly Hills. Sardinian-born film actress Pier Angeli had starred in *Teresa* (1951), *Somebody Up There Likes Me* (1956), and *The Silver Chalice* (1954). The latter two were opposite Paul Newman. Her private life was less successful. She fell in love with actor James Dean, but her disapproving mother insisted Angeli marry singer Vic Damone. In true James Dean–style, Dean sat on his motorcycle across from the church during the wedding service, forlornly revving its engine. The marriage was unhappy, and Pier took Dean's death hard (see 9/30/1955). She wrote, "I'm so afraid to get old—for me, being 40 is the beginning of old age...Love is now behind me, love died in a Porsche." On this date, she managed to avoid old age. She killed herself at age 39 with barbiturates.

– September 12 –

1687 Duxbury, Massachusetts. John Alden died at about 88 of natural causes. He was the last of the *Mayflower* pilgrims. Alden had married Priscilla Mullins. They had eleven children and thousands of modern Americans can trace themselves to John and Priscilla.

1944 South Pacific. The U.S.S. *Sealion* torpedoed the Japanese freighter *Enoura Maru*. The freighter was carrying Allied POWs, and 1,000 were killed. As the Japanese Empire shrank, the Japanese brought POWs back to Japan. Some similar incidents were:

October 24, 1944. U.S.S. *Shark* sank *Arisan Maru*, killing 1,785 POWs.

December 15, 1944. Allied aircraft sank *Oryoku Maru*, killing 900 POWs.

September 7, 1944. U.S.S. *Barb* sank *Shinyo Maru*, killing 668 POWs.

The Allied forces couldn't have known about the POWs, some of whom probably welcomed death. After surviving Corregidor, the Bataan Death March, forced labor in Southeast Asia (some had worked on the River Kwai bridge), starvation, and torture, the POWs were driven to physical and mental exhaustion. The Japanese usually locked them below decks without food, water, sanitary facilities, or medical attention. Some went mad and killed themselves. Others were driven by thirst to vampirism, killing their fellows so as to drink their blood. One prisoner survived an Allied submarine attack because a lock was broken by the explosion of the torpedo. There were no boats and no land in sight, but he decided to do his best. He dove over the side and was gamely doing a smooth Australian crawl when the sub surfaced and picked him up. Nearly all the others died.

1953   Beverly Hills. Actor Lewis Stone, 73, became angry when a bunch of boys threw rocks at his house. Stone, best known for his role as Judge Hardy in the Andy Hardy films, chased them away, but the exertion triggered a fatal heart attack.

– September 13 –

1899   Seventh-fourth Street and Central Park West, New York City. Henry Bliss, 68, became the first recorded auto death in the United States when he was hit by a car.

1916   Erwin, Tennessee. Five thousand watched as "Mary," a circus elephant, was lynched for murdering three men. A steel cable and a railroad derrick were used. It took three attempts.

1986   Goiania, Brazil. Roberto Santos Alves, 17, found a 300-pound lead capsule in an abandoned building. With his friend Vagner Mota, he carried it to Mota's backyard. When they opened it with sledgehammers, they discovered a handful of beautiful blue powder that sparkled and glowed in the dark. Maria Vadia Mota later said, "Everyone who saw it had to touch it." Some rubbed it on themselves. One tasted it. Two hundred and forty-nine people eventually had some contact with the powder, which turned out to be cesium 137, a radioactive material used in cancer treatment. One hundred and twenty-one were hospitalized. One lost his forearm. Four died, including a 6-year-old girl. The bodies are buried inside two feet of concrete, as they will remain radioactive for two centuries. The abandoned building had been a clinic, and the four doctors who owned it had simply left the capsule behind. Roberto and Vagner survived.

– September 14 –

1836   Staten Island. Aaron Burr, 80, third U.S. vice president and killer of Alexander Hamilton, died broke. He had suffered several strokes and was paralyzed at the time. Burr was active in the Revolution and in politics afterward. He was chosen the Jeffersonian candidate for vice president, but when it came time to count the electoral votes for president, it seemed he would beat out Jefferson for the presidency. There were rumors that Burr was soliciting the votes of electors from the opposition party. The Jeffersonians prevailed and a constitutional crisis was avoided, but Burr was an outcast.

After leaving office, he attempted to set up an empire comprised of Mexico and parts of the western United States. He was caught and tried for treason, but as he had taken no overt action, he was acquitted. He fled to Europe, where he tried to get foreign backing for his imperial plans and attempted to stir up war between the United States and Britain. When these efforts failed and he discovered that it was safe to return to New York City, Burr went home to work as a lawyer. He had always enjoyed great success with women, and in his last days, he persuaded Eliza Jumel, a widow in her fifties, to marry him. He wanted her money. She soon left him, and on the date of Burr's death, she divorced Burr.

1852　Walmer Castle, Kent, England. Sir Arthur Wellesley, duke of Wellington and defeater of Napoleon at Waterloo, died at 83. He ate a late, heavy meal on the thirteenth, had a fit that night, and died on this date. Many women threw themselves at the famous duke. One, a young French actress named Mademoiselle George, claimed to have slept with both Wellington and Napoleon. She said the duke was the better of the two. She wrote her memoirs and sent blackmail notes to every man mentioned therein. For 500 pounds, she promised to delete a victim's name. Wellington's reply: "Publish and be damned!"

The dead from the Battle of Waterloo were the resource for a ghoulish industry. Dentures, called "Waterloo teeth," were made from teeth extracted from the corpses. The dentures were popular because the teeth were from young, healthy men. It was, in those days, a military requirement that soldiers have strong teeth—to chew hardtack and to tear open cartridges to load their muskets.

1927　Nice, France. Dancer Isadora Duncan, 49, died when her red silk scarf became entangled in a wire wheel of a 1927 Bugatti roadster she was test-driving. It was a cold evening, and Duncan refused the car salesman's jacket and a friend's cloak in favor of the scarf. The scarf snapped tight and broke her neck, hauling her completely out of the car. Her last words just before she started away were, "Adieu, my friends, I go on to glory." Duncan was cremated, and her ashes are beside the ashes of her two children in Paris's Père Lachaise Cemetery.

Duncan had lost Deirdre, 5, and Patrick, 3, in another freak auto accident. They were left in the backseat of a car near the river Seine in Paris by her chauffeur when the car stalled. He went to crank the engine, only to discover when it restarted that he had left it in reverse. The car backed into the river, drowning both children.

– September 15 –

1935   The Nuremberg Laws that made anti-Semitism the official policy of the German government were adopted on this date. These laws deprived Jews of citizenship and established criteria for Aryan purity. Also on this date, the swastika was adopted as the German national emblem. It was already a widely used symbol. The Navajo Indians, for example, used it in their weaving as a sign for the sun. Sales of blankets with this design declined dramatically after 1935.

1963   Sixteenth Street Baptist Church, Birmingham, Alabama. Four schoolgirls were killed during Sunday services by a bomb.

– September 16 –

1859   Near San Francisco, California. California Senator David Broderick, was active in the antislavery argument. While at dinner in a hotel, he announced that pro-slavery California Supreme Court Chief Justice David Terry was a crook. When Terry heard of this, he resigned his office and challenged Broderick to a duel. Broderick agreed. Their first meeting was thwarted by police, but at their second meeting, on a beach by the Pacific, the duel took place. Broderick accidentally fired his pistol into the sand near Terry's feet. Terry calmly aimed at the now-defenseless Broderick and shot him square in the chest. Broderick died on this date after three days of agony.

1920   Corner of Broad and Wall streets, New York City. A wagon loaded with dynamite and scrap iron exploded, killing thirty-eight and injuring hundreds. One victim was Thomas Watson, a sailor who had served on the U.S.S. *Maine* who had just avoided that explosion by a transfer. This time, he wound up with a steel plate in his skull. Years later, it began to affect his behavior. He started keeping a loaded gun under his pillow and exhibiting paranoia. His family was forced to have him committed but were fearful of how he would react when the ambulance arrived. The attendant knew his business, however: He saluted and told the sailor that the navy needed him to return to duty. Watson dutifully packed his duffel bag and went. He spent the rest of his life in an asylum. The anarchist bomber who ruined so many lives was never caught.

– September 17 –

1876   Northfield, Minnesota. Hollywood often portrayed settlers as the cowardly prey of outlaws, but this was hardly the case. All knew how to use firearms, and many had seen combat during the Civil War or in Indian fighting. The successes of outlaws were due to surprise and to the miles of rugged terrain they could hide in. When prepared, the citizenry weren't easily abused. This was the case when the James gang and assorted other bandits tried to rob the Northfield First National Bank. The town had been warned. Their ambush and pursuing posse destroyed the gang.

1908   Fort Meyer, Virginia. Orville and Wilbur Wright were demonstrating their airplane for U.S. Army brass and a crowd of 2,000. Lieutenant Thomas Selfridge, 26, of the Signal Corps volunteered to go up with Orville in the contraption as a passenger. All went well as they made three circuits of the parade ground; then the propeller snapped. The machine fell 180 feet. Wright fractured his thigh, hips, and ribs, but Selfridge fractured his skull and became the first person killed in an airplane crash. Selfridge Air National Guard Base at Mount Clemens, Michigan, is named after him.

– September 18 –

1705   Pirates took control of New York City for a day before British artillery forced them out.

1932   Hollywood. British actress Peg Entwistle, 24, had been a
       Broadway success, so she went to Hollywood. Her first film
       was a flop, and she couldn't find work. Despondent, she
       climbed the fifty-foot "H" in the famous HOLLYWOOD sign
       and jumped. She didn't know that in her mail was an offer for
       an excellent stage role playing a girl who commits suicide.

1970   London. Rocker Jimi Hendrix, 27, took too many sleeping
       pills and suffocated on his own vomit. When rock singer Janis
       Joplin, also 27, heard of his death, she complained, "Goddam-
       mit! He beat me to it." She died of a drug overdose on
       October 4, 1970, less than three weeks later.

– September 19 –

1881   Elberon, New Jersey. On July 2, 1881, at the Baltimore and
       Potomac Station in Washington, D.C., James Abram Garfield,
       49, twentieth U.S. president, was shot by Charles Guiteau.
       Guiteau was a vain man, who became convinced that God
       wanted him to kill Garfield after he failed to obtain a
       diplomatic post for which he was entirely unqualified.
       Guiteau chose a pretty, bone-handled pistol for the job
       because he thought it would look nice in a museum case. He
       visited Washington's jail to check its accommodations, which
       he deemed "excellent." He practiced firing from the bank of
       the Potomac, a few hundred yards from the White House,
       then stalked the president, getting within close range three
       times. The first time the First Lady was with Garfield, so
       Guiteau, perhaps not wanting the bad press of shooting
       Garfield in front of her, didn't fire. The second time Guiteau
       thought the weather too hot for the exertion. The third time
       he fired, hitting Garfield twice, in the shoulder and in the
       lower back. He immediately threw the gun down and
       surrendered to a policeman, lest he be shot himself. Guiteau
       announced, "I did it and want to be arrested. I am a Stalwart
       [an anti-Garfield faction], and Arthur [vice president and a
       Stalwart] is president. Take me to the police station." He was
       insistent on the last point. He wanted to be safely jailed before
       a mob could lynch him.
           A doctor tried to assure the president that he would
       recover. Garfield, a Civil War veteran, said calmly, "I am a
       dead man." Although the shoulder wound wasn't serious, the

wound in his lower back was. The doctors couldn't find the bullet and continually probed for it with their unsterile fingers, enlarging the bullet hole to a twenty-inch oozing gash. The first doctor tore a hole that later doctors thought the bullet hole. An army doctor stuck his finger clear in to the ribs. A navy doctor actually poked a hole in Garfield's liver. They believed the bullet was low in the president's abdomen. An operation to remove it was deemed impossible. In the days before antibiotics, abdominal surgery was likely to be fatal. To ease Garfield's discomfort, navy engineers rigged one of the first air conditioners to cool the summery White House. A trip to the seaside was arranged via a specially laid railroad track. Garfield welcomed the new environment but soon became delirious and, after eighty days of suffering, died on this date. His last words were, "The people my trust."

Garfield's autopsy showed the bullet wasn't where his doctors had supposed. It could have been removed. This raised great controversy. Congress was so outraged that it paid only $10,000 of the $85,000 doctor's bill. The assassin Guiteau claimed that the doctors, and not he, killed the president. Nevertheless, he was convicted and executed (see 6/30/1882).

1902   Birmingham, Alabama. Two thousand black churchgoers jammed the Shiloh Baptist Church to listen to Booker T. Washington give a speech. After his speech, an argument broke out over a seat. The word "fight" was yelled, but the crowd heard "fire" and panic ensued. The entrance was soon blocked by a ten-foot-high pile of bodies. Washington and church officials tried to stop the panic but failed, and 115 were trampled to death or suffocated.

– September 20 –

1950   Salt Lake City. Mabel Young Sanborn, 87, the last of Brigham Young's fifty-six children, died of natural causes. She was his fifty-fourth child.

1973   Near Natchitoches Municipal Airport, Louisiana. Musician Jim Croce, 30, was killed in an air crash. His first album had sold a million copies. Croce's hits included "Bad, Bad Leroy Brown," "Operator," and "You Don't Mess Around with Jim." His tunes still earn $3 million to $4 million each year.

– September 21 –

19
B.C.
Brundisium. The Roman poet Virgil died at about 50. He had been touring Greece, researching locations for a revised version of his *Aeneid*, when he got wet and caught a fatal chill. According to Suetonius, Virgil once held a funeral on his villa's grounds for a fly, with pallbearers, eulogies, and a grave for the insect. Graveyards were tax-exempt in Rome, and by conducting the burial service, Virgil made his home a burial ground and avoided taxes.

1327
Parliament, London. The death of Edward II (in his 43rd year) was announced. He had been deposed in favor of his son, Edward III, who was under the control of Edward II's wife and her lover. Edward II's homosexual affairs and interest in the peasantry had touched off revolts by the nobility. He was imprisoned in filthy conditions meant to induce death by disease. When this failed, fearing attempts to restore him to the throne, his captors murdered him by forcing a red-hot spit into his anus. It is thought that this was done so that there would be no indication of foul play. At the time, killing a king was considered the most horrible crime possible, other than killing a pope.

– September 22 –

1692
Salem, Massachusetts. Seven witches were hanged, the last executed in the American colonies (contrary to myth, witches weren't burned in America). In total, nineteen were hanged, three died in jail, and one was pressed to death under heavy rocks. Four of the dead were men. All who were killed refused to confess, even though they might have been spared death by confessing. Two hundred and fifty were arrested but not killed.

Today, Salem is a blue-collar town of 38,000 souls. A local modern witch claims there are 2,000 witches in the area, although she says these are all followers of a positively oriented earth religion. A cartoon witch decorates the city's newspaper and police cruisers. City officials are planning a 300-year anniversary commemoration of the witch trials that will include televised reenactments. They stress that it will be a

commemoration of the courage of those who refused to
confess in the face of hysterical innuendos and vicious
suspicion.

1927   Los Angeles. The famous Jack Dempsey–Gene Tunney fight
so excited a listening fan that he accidentally stabbed himself
to death with an icepick while cheering.

– September 23 –

1939   London. Father of psychoanalysis Dr. Sigmund Freud, 83,
died of cancer. Freud was a chain smoker and cocaine addict.
Indeed, his praise for the then-new drug caused it to be
sampled by thousands. He gave up cocaine but refused to stop
smoking, even when a painful swelling appeared in his mouth
in 1917. Malignant jaw cancer was diagnosed in 1923. He
underwent surgery that year, but the surgeon was clumsy.
Freud nearly bled to death, and the scar twisted his mouth
into a knot. Within months, another operation removed his
right jaw, part of his tongue, and a portion of his palate. He
underwent 31 operations to remove tumors and to adjust a
prosthesis that replaced much of his mouth. He still smoked
twenty cigars daily, even though he could barely insert them
in his shrunken mouth. He claimed they allowed him to work
hard and be creative. He refused painkilling drugs, believing
they dulled his mind.

Unable to eat, Freud shrank into a skeleton. Cancer
appeared in his cheek. Radium treatments, a last resort,
worsened the cancerous ulcer, which grew so odorous that
even Freud's dog left his side. Finally, Freud said to his doctor,
"My dear Schur, you remember our first talk. You promised
me you would assist me when I could no longer carry on. It is
strictly torture now. It no longer makes any sense. Tell Anna
[Freud's daughter] about our talk." Schur administered a fatal
dose of morphine. Freud fell into a deep sleep. On this date,
two days later, while still asleep, he expired. His body was
cremated. A favorite Grecian urn became his final abode.

Freud, a Jew, died in exile. In 1938, he fled Austria after
Princess Marie Bonaparte of Greece paid a ransom of 20,000
pounds to Nazi officials.

Onetime friend Carl Jung said of Freud, "Sexuality evidently meant more to Freud than to other people." Vladimir Nabokov said, "I think he's crude, I think he's medieval, and I don't want an elderly gentleman from Vienna with an umbrella inflicting his dreams upon me." Historian Charles Panati has written, "Whereas other psychiatrists observed that the penis is attached to the man, Freud discovered that the man is attached to the penis." Poet Anna de Noailles gave a quite French evaluation of Freud: "Surely he never wrote his 'sexy' books. What a terrible man. I am sure he has never been unfaithful to his wife. It's quite abnormal and scandalous."

Freud, who found sexual origins for most actions, was celibate for the last forty years of his life. The astute explorer of the mind never took rail trips alone—he couldn't figure out train schedules. He was also not the life-of-the-party type. Of one social engagement, he said, "I fit in no better than the cholera would have." Maybe this was because of the way he viewed people: "I have found little that is good about human beings. In my experience most of them are trash."

In 1991, a paper was presented by several physicians at the American Association for the Advancement of Science. It revealed that Freud's "talking cure" of psychoanalysis was based on poorly conducted research. Freud used only six case histories for his central work. Of these, one patient ran out on him in disgust, two weren't treated by Freud personally, one got little therapy, and of the remaining two, whom Freud claimed to have cured, one said Freud's account was untrue. Morris Eagle, a Toronto psychologist, observed that psychoanalysis has never been subject to the scientific tests that other medical practices have faced. He said such proof was necessary, or "it [psychoanalysis] will go the way of the dinosaur."

– September 24 –

1984   Escondido, California. Actor Neil Hamilton, 85, died of complications related to asthma. Hamilton had been a star in silent films but is best remembered as the police commissioner in the 1960s TV show "Batman."

1985   Bronxville, New York. Actor/director Paul Mann, 71, died of a stroke. He was famous for his acting workshop (his students included Faye Dunaway and Sidney Poitier), but a conviction for sexually abusing eight female students in 1984 clouded his reputation.

– September 25 –

1980   London. Actor Peter Sellers, 54, died of a heart attack. Sellers is best remembered as the bumbling Inspector Clouseau in the Pink Panther movie series. In 1966, he was made a Commander of the Order of the British Empire. Sellers had been ill for some time, and it is suggested by some that his involvement with a "psychic surgeon" helped cause his death by leading him to avoid standard medical attention.

Sellers said of himself, "If you ask me to play myself, I will not know what to do. I do not know who or what I am."

1988   Plains, Georgia. William Alton "Billy" Carter III, brother to President Jimmy Carter, died at 51. Billy was noted for his coarse behavior, beer drinking, anti-Semitic remarks, employment as an agent for the Libyan government, and troubles with the IRS. Through it all, Billy smiled and joked, but in later years, he admitted to being an alcoholic. He successfully battled this but was struck down by pancreatic cancer, which, after a long battle, proved fatal. His father and an older sister had both died of the same disease.

– September 26 –

1820   St. Charles County, Missouri. Frontiersman Daniel Boone had suffered a stroke in 1818 and was in poor health. On September 23, he aggravated a fever with acute indigestion from eating too many yams—his favorite food. Boone died after spending three days in bed. Twenty-five years later, the bodies of Boone and his wife were moved to Frankfort, Kentucky.

In 1816, Boone traveled far into hostile Indian territory in what is now Nebraska. He followed the Platte River all the way to the Rocky Mountains, crossed Wyoming, and headed into Yellowstone. He eluded Indians and made it through winter. When he returned to his starting place, Fort Osage in Missouri, he had traveled over 2,000 miles. Boone died in his eighty-sixth year and was 82 when he started the journey.

Boone was a great woodsman and fierce Indian fighter who understood Indian culture far better than most whites. He lived with the Indians and was adopted by the Shawnee chief Blackfish. Nevertheless, his daughter was kidnapped by Shawnees (he stole her back) and two of his sons were killed by Indians. Israel Boone was shot in an ambush (and died in the elder Boone's arms) when a militia commander ignored Boone's advice. James Boone was captured by Shawnees and tortured to death. John Bakeless, a Boone expert, observed that Boone couldn't talk about their deaths without tears thirty years later.

Boone didn't like coonskin caps. He thought them uncivilized. He did most of his traveling without a compass, prompting a writer to ask him if he ever got lost. Boone replied, "No, I can't say as ever I was lost, but I was bewildered once for three days."

1937 Clarksdale, Mississippi. Blues singer Bessie Smith, 43, died following a car accident. Contrary to legend, which says she was refused entry to a white hospital, she was treated on the scene by a white doctor and then rushed to the nearest hospital, the black Afro-American Hospital.

– September 27 –

1944 Oakland, California. Evangelist Aimee Semple McPherson, 53, died of an overdose of barbiturates. Her mother, Minnie Kennedy McPherson, had been a Salvation Army worker in Canada. She prayed God to grant her a lady preacher in the family, and God obliged. Aimee, guided by her mother, went from tent revivals to her own Los Angeles tabernacle, which was topped by a rotating neon crucifix. She also had a nationally heard radio show. Minnie handled the cash, while Aimee drew the largest flock ever assembled.

In 1926, Aimee disappeared while swimming off Venice, California. A search was mounted, and two of her followers died in the effort. Five weeks later, Aimee appeared in Mexico, claiming to have been kidnapped. It was soon discovered that she had actually been vacationing with a lover in Carmel, California. The newspapers went wild, and they went even wilder when Minnie showed up at a hospital with a smashed nose. She said Aimee had punched her and threatened her life. Aimee said Minnie had gotten the injury by throwing herself to the floor in a tantrum. Mother and daughter didn't reconcile.

The scandal slowed Aimee down a bit, but she continued preaching until her death. She also continued having affairs, including, allegedly, one with Milton Berle.

1965   Los Angeles. Silent screen actress Clara Bow, 60, died of a heart attack while watching television with her nurse. Bow was the classic Roaring Twenties flapper and was known as the "It" girl because she had it—sex appeal. She was brought up in a Brooklyn tenement, where her mother prostituted herself for food and rent money. Bow and her father sent a picture of Bow to a magazine beauty contest in 1924. When her mother found out, she tried to murder Bow with a kitchen knife so that Bow would never prostitute herself before Hollywood cameras. Bow escaped by hiding in the bathroom. Her photo won the contest, and she was soon earning $7,500 a week in Hollywood.

Bow led a wild life, and her lovers are said to have included Gilbert Roland, Gary Cooper, John Gilbert, Eddie Cantor, Bela Lugosi, and the University of Southern California football team (one player was John Wayne). Despondent over her infidelity, one lover slashed his wrists and let the blood dramatically fall on a picture of Bow. Fortunately, he was saved. Bow said, "Jesus Christ, he's got to be kidding. Men don't slash their wrists, they use a gun!" Scandal eventually ruined Bow's career. She spent the last half of her life dealing with a series of emotional breakdowns.

– September 28 –

1902   Paris. French writer Emile Zola, 62, died of carbon monoxide poisoning from a faulty stove. He and his wife had retired for the night but woke at 3:00 A.M., violently ill. Zola tried to open a window, but collapsed. The gas was denser near the floor, so while Zola's wife survived the incident, Zola died. His last words were, "I feel sick. My head is splitting. No, don't you see the dog is sick too. We are both ill. It must be something we have eaten. It will pass away. Let us not bother them."

1964 Hollywood. Arthur (formerly Adolph) "Harpo" Marx, 75, died following heart surgery. Although he played a mute, Harpo was in reality very loquacious and was a member of the famous group of wits called the Algonquin Round Table. Harpo and his wife loved children. They adopted several, and Harpo enjoyed coming home to a smiling face in each window.

1978 The Vatican. After serving only thirty-four days, Pope John Paul I, 65, died. His rise to the papacy was unexpected, and he didn't feel qualified. It is said that he prayed daily that he would die so that he could escape his duties. His abrupt death caused unsavory speculation, including a charge that he had been poisoned. An investigation showed this to be unlikely. It reported that the pope had suffered pain three times just before he died. He didn't receive medical care because he hadn't yet chosen an official physician. A Church official found him sprawled on the floor in his rooms, dead of a massive seizure. The body was supposedly placed in bed, posed with reading glasses and papers, to suggest a more serene demise. It was in this position that a nun discovered the pope when she came to wake him.

– September 29 –

1988 New York City. Cartoonist Charles Addams, 76, noted for his macabre creation "The Addams Family," suffered a heart attack while in his car. He died shortly afterward. His wife Marilyn observed, "He's always been a car buff, so it was a nice way to go." The couple had been married in 1980 in a pet cemetery. She said Addams thought it would be a "cheerful" spot.

– September 30 –

1955 Highway 41, near Paso Robles, California. Actor James Dean, 24, died when he crashed his Porsche Spyder at 85 m.p.h. Dean's passenger and the driver of the car Dean struck received minor injuries. After learning of his death, some fans committed suicide. Other fans maintain that Dean wasn't killed but was disfigured and is hiding from the public. Dean's last words concerned the other car, which, oblivious to him, started to turn across Dean's path, "That guy's got to stop. He'll see us." Dean's Porsche was gray, it was twilight, and Dean didn't have his lights on.

Two hours before the crash, Dean received a ticket for speeding. A few days earlier, he filmed a public service TV commercial with Gig Young promoting safe driving. In it, he advised careful driving because "the life you save may be mine." Six months earlier, Dean posed for *Life* magazine lying in a coffin (the magazine never ran the morbid picture).

Dean was reputed to be involved in sadomasochistic activities in East Hollywood. It is said that he encouraged others to use his chest for an ashtray, and the autopsy mentioned a "constellation of keratoid scars." Dean also claimed to have beaten the Korean War draft by pretending to be gay. He supposedly told Hedda Hopper, "I kissed the medic." Whether these claims were true or not, Dean was notorious for his difficult, moody behavior.

Only one of Dean's movies was released while he was alive, *Rebel Without a Cause* (1955). He beat out Paul Newman for the role. Newman made *The Silver Chalice* (1954) instead—a movie Newman hated so much that he took out a full-page ad apologizing years later when the movie was shown on television. Dean's two other films were *East of Eden* (1955) and *Giant* (1956). Both were classics. Dean received just $20,000 for *Giant*. Since his death, licensing fees for his image on mugs, T-shirts, posters, etc. have earned $2 million to $3 million a year.

– October 1 –

1909   Los Angeles. The *Los Angeles Times* was a nonunion paper, and in an attempt to force unionization, the presses were bombed by labor agitators. Twenty-one workers burned to death. Two unionists were caught and sentenced to long prison terms.

– October 2 –

1985   Plymouth, Michigan. High school administrator Leonard Tyburski, 45, reported his wife, Dorothy, missing. Mr. Tyburski expressed great concern and helped police in their search. Police questioned him, but when he passed a lie detector test they turned their attention elsewhere. After a year, they closed the case without having found Mrs. Tyburski.

    One of the couple's daughters, Kelly Tyburski, 20, became a student at Michigan State University. She was troubled by nightmares wherein her mother was "in a place where she couldn't move, either tied up or locked up." She recalled that the key to the family freezer in the basement had been lost after her mother's disappearance. On a visit home, three-and-a-half years after her mother had gone missing, Kelly pried open the freezer. She found more than frozen peas. Inside was the battered, frozen body of her mother. Leonard Tyburski confessed to murder, saying he kept the body because he loved his wife and wanted her nearby.

– October 3 –

1226 Assisi. St. Francis of Assisi had been a wealthy medieval "playboy" but abandoned his wealth to become a monk. He inspired a revival of charitable poverty in the clergy, which had become avaricious and luxurious. In 1224, he was living in a crude mountain cell when stigmata—wounds similar to Christ's—appeared on his body. St. Francis self-consciously hid the wounds by keeping his hands inside his habit and by wearing stockings and shoes instead of his normal sandals. His health was seriously affected by the stigmata. Church officials ordered him to visit the pope's physicians, but they couldn't help him. When they told him this, he said, "Welcome, Sister Death!" He weakened and, nearly blind, died on this date at 44. He had asked to be buried in a criminal's cemetery, but his followers buried him in a churchyard, then secretly moved him to a basilica built by one of his followers. The grave remained a secret till 1818.

St. Francis spent many years living in a cave and was said to get along famously with animals. Perhaps this was because he smelled like one. He preached that dirtiness was saintly and didn't bathe. This belief wasn't unique. St. Jerome discouraged his followers from bathing, St. Catherine of Siena gave up bathing, and St. Agnes is said never to have bathed at all.

1656 Duxbury, Massachusetts. Pilgrim Miles Standish, 72, died of natural causes. There is little evidence to back the story that he had John Alden act as intermediary in the pursuit of Priscilla Mullins's hand only to have Mullins fall for Alden, but it has influenced the popular image of Standish. We think of him as too inept to "speak for himself." In reality, he was charged with the protecting of the precarious colony with just a handful of soldiers. He learned the language of the Indians and, despite a few problem years, produced nearly fifty years of peace that led to the English domination of North America.

– October 4 –

1969   West Hollywood, California. Diane Linkletter, 20, youngest daughter of Art Linkletter, had been experimenting for some time with LSD. On this date, after arguing with her boyfriend, she took a substantial dose. She became suicidal, calling her brother Robert, who would himself die tragically in a car accident in 1980, and telling him she planned to kill herself. Before Robert could get to her, Diane jumped from the kitchen window of her sixth-floor apartment. Her boyfriend snatched for the belt loops of her dress, but Diane fell to her death. Her father blamed the incident on drugs. He insisted that the details be made public, saying, "I want the parents and I want their kids to read about this and be shocked, be frightened by what can happen."

1989   Maidstone, Kent, England. Graham Chapman, 48, one of the founders of the Monty Python comedy team, died of cancer. In November of 1988, his dentist had noticed a growth on Chapman's tonsils. It proved cancerous. It was removed, but in July of 1989, tests showed that Chapman was also suffering from cancer of the spine. Confined to a wheelchair, Chapman blamed smoking for his disease. Eventually, he suffered a massive hemorrhage and was rushed to a hospital. At the time of his death, fellow Pythons Michael Palin and John Cleese were at Chapman's bedside. They were companionably joking and talking over the old days.

– October 5 –

1813   Near the Thames River, Ontario. Shawnee Indian chief Tecumseh, 45, was killed. Tecumseh sought to establish an Indian nation in the upper Midwest, and the British, wishing to thwart American expansion they deemed a threat to Canada, supplied him with weapons. When the War of 1812 broke out, Tecumseh joined his forces with the British. William Henry Harrison (later, ninth U.S. president) defeated them at the Battle of Tippecanoe and at the Battle of the Thames. Colonel Richard M. Johnson (later U.S. vice president under Van Buren) killed Tecumseh in hand-to-hand combat.

Tecumseh was a powerful orator and is credited with limiting the Indian custom of torturing prisoners. Before him, it was standard practice in many tribes to torment and then burn to death captives in elaborate, hideous rituals. After his death, the old ways returned.

Following the battle, Tecumseh was buried by his followers in an unmarked grave. In 1941, a skeleton thought to be his was unearthed. It was reburied under a cairn by the St. Clair River on the Walpole Island Indian Reserve in Ontario.

– October 6 –

1989   Paris. Film star Bette Davis, 81, died of cancer. She had appeared in over eighty films, was nominated for ten Academy Awards, and won two Best Actress Oscars for the films *Dangerous* (1935) and *Jezebel* (1939). Davis gave the award its nickname when she remarked of the bald figurine, "He looks just like my ex-husband Oscar."

Davis wasn't always well liked by her coworkers—most notably, Joan Crawford, with whom she warred for years. Their quarrels were both professional and personal and ranged from who had the best lines in *Whatever Happened to Baby Jane?* (1962), to a Pepsi machine brought onto the set by Crawford, a Pepsi Cola Company board member (Davis countered with a Coke machine), to Crawford's husband Franchot Tone, whom it was rumored that Davis courted. So public became their battles that when a lamp fell during the shooting of *The Corn Is Green* (1945), clipping Davis, a cameraman is said to have looked up and called, "Is that you up there, Joan?"

– October 7 –

1849   Baltimore. Writer Edgar Allan Poe died at 40. He invented
the detective story with "The Murders in the Rue Morgue"
and is remembered for his poem "The Raven" and for his
story "The Fall of the House of Usher."

Unconscious and beaten, Poe was found sprawled over
some barrels dressed in someone else's clothing. He'd been
drunk five days on liquor supplied by political hacks in return
for his voting multiple times. Unrecognized, Poe was delivered to Baltimore's Washington Hospital, a charitable institution, where he raved at the walls. When a woman attempted
to calm him by reading Scripture, Poe exploded, crying, "The
best thing my friend could do would be to blow out my brains
with a pistol." He grew increasingly incoherent over the next
four days, then abruptly grew quiet. He said, "Lord, help my
poor soul," then died.

Poe was buried in Baltimore's Westminster Presbyterian
Cemetery, which he had often frequented in search of
inspiration. Since Poe died a pauper, his doctor paid for the
burial, and the doctor's wife sewed the shroud. Only four
people attended the service. A tombstone wasn't provided for
years, and then it took four attempts. Train wreck, bankruptcy, and earthquake disposed of the first three markers.
The one that was finally delivered bears a raven and reads:
"Quoth the Raven, Nevermore." His grave is beside that of his
wife, Virginia, who died at 25 of tuberculosis (Poe's cousin,
Virginia was 13 when she married Poe). Since 1949, a man
dressed in black has placed roses and a bottle of cognac on
Poe's grave on the anniversary of his death.

Some believe Poe may have died from a brain tumor or a
diabetic coma. Others suspect that he was hypersensitive to
alcohol. This dangerous problem causes violent mood swings
and bizarre behavior.

Poe attended West Point, but was court-martialed for
neglect and disobedience. He missed parades, skipped classes,
and refused to attend chapel. Reportedly, the act that got him
kicked out occurred when Poe took the parade dress instructions, which called for wearing "white belts and gloves, under
arms," literally. Poe showed up on the parade ground wearing

the belt and gloves and shouldering his rifle. Aside from these
military accoutrements, Poe was naked.

1916   Atlanta. Cumberland University lost to Georgia Tech in
college football's most lopsided game: 222 to 0.

– October 8 –

1869   Concord, New Hampshire. Franklin Pierce, 64, fourteenth
U.S. president, died of stomach inflammation. He was buried
in Concord's Old North Cemetery. Some historians claim he
died of alcoholism compounded by tuberculosis.

Pierce had had three children with his wife, Jane Appleton
Pierce. The first died in infancy, the second at four, and the
third at 11 in a horrid train accident in front of his parents.
The last death so upset his wife that she spent the rest of her
life in mourning. She didn't even attend Pierce's inaugural
ball and wore black throughout Pierce's stay in the White
House. Living as a recluse, she spent her days writing notes to
her dead son and managed to persuade her husband that the
boy's grisly death was God's price for Pierce's becoming
president. She died of tuberculosis two years before Pierce
died.

1871   Chicago. A fire destroyed a third of the city. The flames were
spread by high winds through the city's wooden buildings,
which had been dried into tinder by drought. The fire killed
300, burned 17,450 buildings, and caused $196 million in
damages. Three hundred thousand were left homeless. Several looters were shot and one was stoned to death when they
were discovered setting new fires so they could continue
looting. Legend blames Mrs. O'Leary's cow for the blaze,
saying the surly bovine kicked when being milked, knocking
over a lantern into a pile of hay.

1871   Peshtigo, Wisconsin. A fire destroyed most of the city, killed
1,500, and burned 1.28 million acres of timber. A drought had
dried the surrounding forest, but loggers, railroad workers,
and farmers continued their practice of casually burning
debris. These small fires combined into a firestorm, which
struck the town just after an evening church service. First,
white ash fell like snow, then suffocating smoke filled the

streets, and flames driven by fierce winds fell from the sky. Terrified citizens ran as wooden sidewalks and houses blazed. Three hundred died crossing a wooden bridge. It collapsed, trapping people between its timbers, then burned. A tornado of fire smashed buildings, hurling deadly debris. Citizens who hid in wells were smothered. Some who sought safety in the Peshtigo River were burned about their heads. Still others were trampled by stampeding cattle. The blaze was the most deadly fire on the North American continent, but the simultaneous fire in Chicago caused this far worse disaster to be virtually ignored.

– October 9 –

1930   San Quentin. William Kogut avoided execution for murder by committing suicide. Prison officials are careful to remove the materials of self-destruction from cells, but Kogut knew his chemistry. He scraped the red spots off a deck of cards (at that time made of explosive material), compacted them in a pipe bed leg, and placed the pipe on the cell's radiator, where he held it in place with his head. When it warmed sufficiently, it blew his head off.

– October 10 –

1980   Film actor William "Billy" Thomas, 49, died of a heart attack. He had starred in eighty-nine *Our Gang* films as Buckwheat. He first appeared in that series at age three in 1934 and continued till 1944. Years later, Eddie Murphy pretended to be the adult Buckwheat and sang pop songs in Thomas's unique vocal style. In October 1990, another impersonation was done by a Tempe, Arizona, grocery bagger. He convinced ABC's magazine show "20/20" that he was Buckwheat and that he'd just been lying low for years. It broadcast a segment depicting the bogus Buckwheat's modest lifestyle. Thomas's son and family soon set the record straight.

1985   Los Angeles. Actor/director Orson Welles, 70, was found dead of an apparent heart attack in his home by his chauffeur.

He was a great success when he was young. Herman J. Mankiewicz observed of the talented, self-involved Welles, "There, but for the grace of God, goes God." Welles's success faded quickly (in part due to overcritical critics), and Welles's career eroded into commercial voice-overs. Welles once said, "I hate television. I hate it as much as peanuts. But I can't stop eating peanuts."

– October 11 –

1809   An inn by the Natchez Trace, near Nashville. Explorer Meriwether Lewis died at 35. With William Clark, he had led the famous Lewis and Clark expedition to explore the West. The circumstances of Lewis's death are unclear. He may have been murdered, but according to one account he committed suicide by shooting himself twice, in the side and in the head. The head wound exposed his brain, but he lingered for hours, begging someone to finish the job. His last words, spoken as the sun was rising, were, "I am no coward, but I am so strong. It is so hard to die."

1961   Hollywood. Chico (Leonard) Marx, 74, the eldest of the Marx Brothers, died of heart problems. The brothers were as wild offscreen as on. Once, when MGM producer Irving Thalberg kept them waiting in his office, they grew impatient. They sent out for a bag of potatoes, and when Thalberg came by, an hour late, he found the brothers squatting around his fireplace naked, roasting potatoes. Thalberg apologized and sent for butter.

Chico loved to gamble, talk, and chase women. Groucho said of him, "If there was no action around, he would play solitaire—and bet against himself," and "There were three things that Chico was always on—a phone, a horse, or a broad."

1991   Los Angeles. Comedian Redd Foxx, 68, died of a heart attack while rehearsing for his TV series "The Royal Family." Foxx is remembered for his earlier TV series "Sanford and Son," which ran from 1972 to 1977. A recurring joke on that show was Foxx clutching his chest at a moment of shock and claiming that "the big one" had come.

– October 12 –

1870   Lexington, Virginia. In September, Robert E. Lee suffered an attack of what was probably angina. He died of its effects on this date at 63. A flood in the region had destroyed all but one coffin—a child's coffin. The short Confederate general was buried in it in uniform but without boots, so that he might fit. Lee's last words were, "Strike the tent!" Lee, who fought to destroy the United States, was the son of "Lighthorse Harry" Lee, George Washington's foremost cavalry commander. Lee's wife was the great-granddaughter of George Washington.

Lee, who won many startling victories, has a reputation for being a nonbloodthirsty man. Yet, as historian Alan Nolan has recently reminded us, Lee's victories were all won at a higher proportional rate of casualties than he inflicted, and no army on either side suffered higher casualties than his Army of Northern Virginia.

– October 13 –

1966   Beverly Hills. Actor Clifton Webb died in his home of a heart attack. He gave his age as 69, but records indicate he was at least 72. He is remembered for his films *Laura* (1944), and *Sitting Pretty* (1948), and as Mr. Belvedere in that film series. It is said that the last role wasn't acting, as Webb personified all of Mr. Belvedere's qualities. Webb's career, which included both Broadway and Hollywood, began at age six. His every professional act was guided by his mother, Mabelle Hollenbeck Webb. An unsuccessful actress and a single parent, she devoted her life to her son. The pair were so close that Cole Porter mentioned their inseparability in a song. Mabelle participated in all of Clifton's social activities, living with him till her death in her nineties in 1960. Her last words were, "How is Clifton? Has he had his luncheon?"

Clifton mourned her for years. Friend Noel Coward grew impatient. Once, when conversing with Webb long-distance, he snapped, "Unless you stop crying I shall reverse the charges." He said it worked. Coward also observed, "It must be tough to be orphaned at 71!"

– October 14 –

1959   Vancouver. Actor Errol Flynn, 50, died of a heart attack
        Doctors said he had the body of a man in his seventies. He
        was buried at Los Angeles's Forest Lawn Cemetery. Above his
        grave is a bronze statue of a nymph.
            Flynn was Australian and spent his childhood in Tasmania.
        An ancestor had been one of the H.M.S. *Bounty* mutineers,
        and when a silent movie telling that story was made on
        location in the 1920s, Flynn was cast in a small role. It was
        years before Flynn made another film. In the meantime, he
        prospected for gold, worked as a health official, ran a coconut
        plantation complete with native-girl "wife," was ambushed by
        headhunters and then tried for the murder of one of their
        number, lived as a gigolo, stole a woman's diamonds, joined
        and deserted a Hong Kong regiment, was fleeced by an
        Eurasian con-woman, was stabbed nearly to death by a Hindu
        cabdriver he refused to tip, bummed his way across the
        Australian outback, and labored on a sheep ranch, where he
        castrated sheep. Eventually he got a job in a children's play in
        London. After a series of stage roles, he was spotted by a
        Hollywood talent scout. He became a superstar in films such
        as *Captain Blood* (1935) and *They Died With Their Boots On*
        (1941). His fame only increased when he was charged and then
        cleared of statutory rape. Characteristically, he met a girl
        during the trial and wound up married to her.
            During World War II, Flynn was criticized for making war
        films while avoiding military service. Recently opened FBI
        files suggest that Flynn and another actor paid a doctor $5000
        to find "spots" on X rays of their lungs and thereby get them
        classed 4-F. In Flynn's defense, he may have had his own
        medical reasons for avoiding the draft. He was undoubtedly
        an alcoholic, and his sexual activities may have affected his
        health. A 4-F classification on those grounds would have been
        a disaster for his career. Perhaps he preferred a false "spot"
        over more embarrassing truths. A recent book has suggested
        that Flynn was a Nazi spy and that he stole secrets about the
        defenses at Pearl Harbor while making a movie there just
        before the war. There is little reason to believe Flynn was pro-
        German. At that time, nearly any prominent person could be
        linked with some Nazi, somewhere.

After the war, Flynn had a falling out with his studio. He tried to make his own films but was swindled. His business manager died of cancer, and it was discovered that he had stolen millions for a final spree. The manager had also neglected to pay Flynn's taxes, and Flynn owed Uncle Sam millions. He squeaked through by selling a number of paintings he had collected. He made a critical comeback playing John Barrymore in a film. It was the kind of dramatic role he had always sought, but it didn't revive his career. His last film was the dreadful *Cuban Rebel Girls* (1959), wherein, playing himself, he battled side-by-side with some of Castro's girl guerrillas against Batista.

Flynn wrote his autobiography, *My Wicked, Wicked Ways*, shortly before he died. Despite his finances, his sagging career, his divorces, and his health, he remained optimistic. In the final pages, he recalled a fan in a wheelchair who thanked the surprised Flynn for the escape his films had given her. He decided that perhaps the years of make-believe weren't wasted. He finished his book with: "The second half-century looms up, but I don't feel the night coming on."

1977   Madrid. Actor/singer Harry Lillis "Bing" Crosby, 73, died of a heart attack after playing golf. He remarked before dying, "That was a great game of golf, fellers." Crosby had a fifty-year career, making numerous films and selling over 300 million records, including the most successful single ever, "White Christmas." He once suggested as his own epitaph, "He was an average guy who could carry a tune." Some time after his death, Crosby's son Gary wrote an unflattering book about his father that caused Bob Hope to say, "It's not even safe to die anymore."

As a schoolboy, Crosby loved a comic strip called "The Bingville Bugle." His friends nicknamed him "Bing" from this.

– October 15 –

1917   Vincennes, France. Mata Hari, 41, whose nude dancing pleased many men but whose spying for Germany probably killed far more, was executed. There were thirteen French soldiers in the firing squad, but there were only four bullet wounds in her body. No one claimed Hari's body. It was sent to a medical school for dissection. Hari left three sealed letters—one for her daughter when she turned twenty-one, and two for lovers. Of the last two, she warned, "Don't mix up the addresses. That would be fatal."

1946   Nürenberg. Nazi war criminal Reichsmarshal Hermann Goering, 53, killed himself in prison with cyanide hours before he was due to be hanged. Goering, a fighter pilot in World War I, became the head of the Luftwaffe and deputy to Hitler. He fancied himself a connoisseur and looted the museums of conquered nations of $200 million worth of art for his private collection. A drug abuser, he affected effeminate mannerisms, including makeup and a pink full-dress uniform. Goering was certain the Allies would need him to rule Germany and was surprised at his death sentence. He also thought that someday, every home in Germany would have a statue of him.

– October 16 –

1793   Paris. French Queen Marie Antoinette, 37, was guillotined. During her trial, her son, the dauphin, was forced by beatings, terror, and brandy to make vile sexual accusations against her. Dressed in a morning gown with a muslin fichu and a white cap to hide her hair, which had been cropped short by her jailors, she behaved bravely till she was upon the scaffold. She began to weep. Concerned that the crowd would enjoy her discomfort, she quickly went to the block. In her haste, she trod upon her executioner's toe. Her last words were to him: "Monsieur, I beg your pardon." Afterward, her clothing was stripped from her body. No one knows what became of her son.

– October 17 –

1814   London. A large beer tank burst and the resulting flood killed nine.

1849   Paris. Polish composer Frédéric Chopin, 39, died of tuberculosis. He had suffered from the disease for years, and his companion, George Sand, was forced to great extremes to care for him. In 1838, they traveled to Majorca for a possible cure, but wherever they went, they encountered fear of the contagious disease. They wound up living in an abandoned monastery, which, while it provided romantic inspiration, further weakened him. When Chopin wished to return home, the only vessel that would take him was a ship carrying pigs. Chopin's last words were to his doctor, who was trying to take his pulse, "It is not worth the trouble—soon you'll be rid of me." Too weak to continue speaking, he then wrote: "The earth is suffocating...Swear to make them cut me open, so that I won't be buried alive."

Composer Robert Schumann didn't care for Chopin's work. He said, "Nobody can call that music."

– October 18 –

1931   West Orange, New Jersey. Inventor Thomas Alva Edison died at 84. His last words were, "It's very beautiful over there." As he was looking out a window at the time, it is unclear whether he meant the view through the window or the afterlife.

Edison had suffered for years from Bright's disease, a kidney ailment, which flared up in October of 1929 following a dinner celebrating his invention of the light bulb fifty years earlier. Henry Ford hosted the affair, and President Herbert Hoover had just finished a speech when Edison collapsed from renal failure. He grew worse over the next two years. Doctors could do little, so Edison treated himself. On October 15, he fell into a coma. On the seventeenth, he roused long enough to utter his cryptic last words. On this date, at 3:24 A.M., he quietly died of uremic poisoning.

Among Edison's many inventions were wax paper, the mimeograph, the phonograph, the vacuum tube, the motion-picture camera, the dictating machine, and the electric rail car.

Edison once said, "When down in the mouth, remember Jonah. He came out all right."

1984   Beverly Hills. Actor Jon-Erik Hexum, 26, was removed from life-support machines after being declared brain-dead. He was the costar of the successful TV show "Cover Up." On October 12, while between scenes on the set, he decided to play Russian roulette with a pistol loaded with blanks. He thought a blank could cause no harm, but the blast a mere inch from his head severely injured him. His last words were to crew members: "Let's see if I get myself with this one." He did. Recently, a tabloid whirlwind blew up when it was discovered that Hexum's heart had been transplanted into the body of a Las Vegas escort service owner.

– October 19 –

1216   Newark, Nottinghamshire, England. King John "Lackland," 48, scourge of Robin Hood and signer of the Magna Carta, died of overconsuming unripe peaches and beer, which probably induced dysentery. Shakespeare and folklore say the cause was poison squeezed from a toad by a monk, but English toads have no such venom. John's final illness was possibly hastened by the loss of his treasury, which was accompanying him on packhorses, in a quicksand-guarded stream. Part of the evil-monk tale was the notion that the monks who tended the king in his illness knew the secret of the location of the lost treasury. They supposedly killed him to keep it. If so, they underestimated the difficulties involved in removing the gold from the stream. It was never recovered.

1745   Dublin. Paralyzed and declared of unsound mind, Jonathan Swift died at 77. His last words were, "I am dying like a poisoned rat in a hole. I am what I am! I am what I am!"

In *Gulliver's Travels*, Swift described the two moons of Mars, giving their size and rotation speed. Neither was discovered till more than 100 years later. Once Swift grew annoyed with John Partridge, a popular astrologer. To squash Partridge, Swift invented his own astrologer, Isaac Bickerstaff. He wrote an almanac of predictions under the name of the fictional Bickerstaff. One of the predictions was that Partridge would die on March 29, 1708. On March 30, Swift published a description of how Bickerstaff's prediction had come true. Partridge had great trouble persuading the public that he was actually still alive. The publisher Richard Steele so liked the jest that he made Bickerstaff the editor of his magazine *The Tatler*.

Swift wrote, "When men grow virtuous in their old age, they only make a sacrifice to God of the devil's leavings."

1978 New York City. Actor Gig Young, 64, shot himself and his 31-year-old wife of three weeks (she was his fifth wife). There was no sign of a struggle, so police theorized a suicide pact. Biographer George Eells has said that a drinking problem led to Young's suicide. Young had played a professor who was immune to alcohol in the movie *Teacher's Pet* (1958), which also starred Doris Day and Clark Gable. Young had once said, "You can't tell about people from their outside. They've spent a lifetime covering up their fears."

– October 20 –

1890 Trieste, Austria-Hungary. Victorian explorer Sir Richard Burton, 69, died after having trouble breathing. His last words were to his wife, "I am dying; I am dead." His devout Catholic wife summoned a priest and insisted that Burton was still alive so that the priest would adminster last rites.

Burton, the first Christian to enter Mecca, nearly found the source of the Nile, fought Indians with Kit Carson, befriended Brigham Young, and was one of the first white men to go up the Amazon. He knew twenty languages and translated many Arabic works (including *The Arabian Nights*). He studied the sex lives of the natives wherever he went, collecting a library of anthropological information. After he died, his wife burned much of it. She thought it pornographic.

1964 New York City. Herbert Hoover, 90, thirty-first U.S. president, was suffering internal bleeding. Transfusions proved ineffectual. After falling into a coma, he died, surrounded by his sons.

Hoover was a Stanford-trained engineer (Jimmy Carter was the only other engineer president). He worked in China, and by the time he was forty, he had built an international engineering company and become a self-made millionaire. Following World War I, Hoover organized the American Relief Committee, which saved thousands of starving Europeans. It was a difficult task, given the many governments involved and the antagonisms left over from the war. Hoover managed brilliantly. This led to his election to the presidency in 1928. His successes ended with the Great Depression in 1929. Many chose him as a scapegoat. His reluctance to enact emergency measures was widely derided. Hobo shantytowns became "Hoovervilles." He was badly defeated by Franklin Roosevelt, but despite Roosevelt's many programs, only World War II would kill the Depression.

Hoover, a fiscal conservative, observed, "Blessed are the young, for they shall inherit the national debt."

– October 21 –

1969   St. Petersburg, Florida. Beat writer Jack Kerouac, 47, died from abdominal bleeding induced by drinking. He is remembered for his book *On the Road*, which inspired a generation to cast off convention. Ironically, Kerouac never learned to drive a car.

Truman Capote said of Kerouac's work, "That's not writing, that's typing."

1985   San Francisco. Supervisor Dan White killed Mayor George Moskone and gay City Supervisor Harvey Milk in November 1978. Using the "Twinkie defense," which claimed junk food had diminished his mental capacity, White was convicted of just voluntary manslaughter. He was paroled in January 1984 after serving five years. On this date, White, 39, ran a hose from his car's exhaust pipe to its interior and killed himself with carbon monoxide.

– October 22 –

1934   A cornfield near East Liverpool, Ohio. Bank robber and murderer Chester Arthur "Pretty Boy" Floyd, 33, was shot and killed by FBI agents. His last words: "Who the hell tipped you off? I'm Floyd all right. You got me this time." Reportedly, Floyd had sensed his impending doom. Shortly before his death, he selected a gravesite beside his father (killed in a feud and avenged by Floyd) and told his mother, "I expect to go down with lead." The funeral was a circus, with spectators, reporters, and newsreel cameramen coming by the thousands.

Beefy farmboy Floyd got his nickname in 1929 when he entered a Kansas City whorehouse. The madam had said, "I want you for myself, pretty boy."

– October 23 –

1939   Altadena, California. Western author Zane Grey, 64, died of a heart attack. He was christened "Pearl" but used his mother's family name for obvious reasons. He wrote fifty-four novels and sold 15 million copies. Before his success, he worked as a dentist, enduring many rejections by publishers. One wrote: "You've wasted enough of our time with your junk. Why don't you go back to filling teeth? You can't write, you never could write, and you never will be able to write."

1983   New Hope, Pennsylvania. Newswoman Jessica Savitch, 35, drowned. She and a friend were leaving a restaurant parking lot on a dark night when they turned the wrong way and their car plunged into a canal.

– October 24 –

1601   Near Prague. Danish astronomer Tycho Brahe, who extended the work of Copernicus, was aristocratic in manner and temperament. This caused him to fight a duel while a student over a difference concerning mathematics. In that duel, he lost the tip of his nose. Thereafter, he wore a silver nosepiece to hide its absence.

His aristocratic attitude also led to his death at 54 on this date. He had a sickly bladder and failed to relieve himself before a banquet, where he drank a great deal. It would have been ill-mannered to leave the table, so Brahe remained. His bladder burst. He died after eleven days of suffering.

1944   South Pacific. After sinking twenty-four Japanese ships, the submarine U.S.S. *Tang* sank itself. A defective torpedo circled back and hit her. Nearly all hands were lost. The submarine U.S.S. *Tullibee* is also thought to have sunk itself in a similar manner. All but one crewman died. There is only one report of a U.S. sub torpedoing an Allied surface vessel during World War II: The U.S.S. *Guardfish* sank the U.S.S. *Extractor*, a salvage ship. Six were killed.

1969   Examination of the 3,000-year-old mummy of King Tut-ankhamen of Egypt showed that the boy pharaoh was killed by a blow to the head. He was murdered.

1983   San Diego. Louise Ramos, 64, was arrested for shoplifting. She demanded to be set free, swearing that she would hold her breath "until I turn blue." She did turn blue. Then she turned gray. She died.

– October 25 –

1921   New York City. William Barclay "Bat" Masterson died at 67. He didn't die in some lurid shoot-out or frenzied Indian attack. The hero of the Wild West had become a sportswriter for the *San Francisco Morning Telegraph* and was found slumped over his desk in a newsroom, dead from a heart attack. President Teddy Roosevelt had offered to make him the U.S. Marshal of Arizona, but Masterson declined, saying that he didn't want to be forced to kill all the young gunmen who might seek to gain a reputation by killing him.

1944   South Pacific. The U. S. escort carrier *St. Lo* was struck by the first Japanese kamikaze attack. During the war, 1,228 kamikazes attacked Allied ships, sinking 34 and damaging 288. Officials downplayed the damage, but if the attacks had started earlier, Japan might have won the war.

     At the critical Battle of Midway, American aviators attacked the Japanese when it was nearly certain death to do so. They suffered losses of nearly 90 percent, but were instrumental in winning the battle. An admiring Japanese officer called the doomed Americans "samurai." It is ironic that these American "suicide" pilots were ultimately more effective than the Japanese kamikazes.

– October 26 –

1881   Tombstone, Arizona. Three were killed in a shoot-out at the O. K. Corral between the Earp brothers and the Clanton gang. The Earps won. Ike Clanton's last words were, "God, God, won't somebody give me some more cartridges for a last shot...?" Morgan Earp also died there. He had resisted his brother's views on the lack of an afterlife, but his last words were, "I guess you were right, Wyatt, I can't see a damn thing."

One hundred and three years later, as reported by the Associated Press, two angry Cleveland men staged a similar shoot-out in an apartment building hallway using antique pistols. The two men fired twelve shots at each other at nearly nose-to-nose range. Neither combatant was injured. Perhaps this was because one gunman was 76 and the other was 77. In addition, one had glaucoma and the other had to support himself with a cane while blazing away.

1974   Lawrence, Massachusetts. Gas station attendant Joey Fournier, 17, was robbed of $276.37 by three men. Despite his begging for mercy, one of the thieves, William R. Horton, Jr., stabbed him nineteen times and left him in a garbage can, dead. Horton was convicted of armed robbery and first-degree murder. Governor Michael Dukakis had vetoed a death penalty bill, so Horton was sentenced to life in prison. In 1986, under a furlough program, he was on the streets. Massachusetts was the only state furloughing murderers sentenced to life without the possibility of parole. Horton kidnapped a Maryland couple, tortured the man, and raped the wife. They barely escaped before Horton could murder them. Horton was recaptured.

Outrage over the furlough program met with bureaucratic tut-tuts. They said that everyone knew that a life sentence never actually meant life, especially as Governor Dukakis had commuted twenty-eight life sentences. The furloughs would give criminals an opportunity to prove themselves reformed so they could then be released, and besides, Horton had been furloughed nine times without incident. The fact that furloughs endangered the public wasn't important. A bill to ban furloughs was vetoed by Dukakis, who refused to meet with the families of victims of furloughed criminals even while he was meeting with convicts. The victim families forced another ban bill through the legislature. Dukakis, with the 1988 presidential campaign to win, refrained from vetoing this one but expressed his intention to set up a new program to commute the sentences of first-degree murderers.

During the presidential primaries, supporters of Democrat Albert Gore aired a television commercial citing the furloughs as evidence of Dukakis's lack of concern for the victims of crime. During the general election, a group backing George Bush aired a similar commercial showing Horton's mug shot. The Bush campaign used a commercial showing criminals passing through a revolving door. Dukakis responded by charging Bush with racism.

1990   York, South Carolina. William Anthony Odom, 15, of Charlotte, North Carolina, was staging a haunted house in his grandmother's basement, complete with spider webs, plastic bats, and a dead pirate hanging in a cupboard. Odom played the pirate. He wore black trousers, a red shirt, a gold earring, and a three-foot nylon rope around his neck. For some unknown reason, the noose tightened, and when his friends opened the cupboard, they found him dead.

Just a week earlier, a 17-year-old died in a similar way in Lakewood, New Jersey. He was supposed to scare passengers on a hayride by posing as a hanged man on a roadside tree. He slipped and was found dead.

– October 27 –

1964   Palms, California. Actor Sammee Tong is remembered as houseboy Peter Tong on TV's "Bachelor Father." That show was canceled in 1961. Tong got a role on Mickey Rooney's comedy series "Mickey" in 1964, but soon after it went on the air, Tong grew depressed. He killed himself on this date at age 63.

1975   Danbury, Connecticut. Mystery writer Rex Stout, 88, died of natural causes. His fictional detective was the obese Nero Wolfe, who was assisted by the dapper Archie Goodwin. Despite his working only thirty-nine days a year, Stout wrote forty-six books featuring Wolfe. These were translated into twenty-two languages and sold over 45 million copies. Before becoming a writer, Stout had made $400,000 with a scheme for school banking that encouraged children to save. This fortune allowed Stout to develop his interest in writing.

– October 28 –

1704   High Laver, Essex, England. After years of poor health, philosopher John Locke, 72, died of natural causes while being read the Psalms. He once said something modern scientists, bureaucrats, and other jargon-slingers should remember: "There is no such way to gain admittance, or give defense, to strange and absurd doctrines, as to guard them round about with legions of obscure, doubtful, and undefined words: which yet make these retreats more like the dens of robbers, or holes of foxes, than fortresses of fair warriors."

1975   Chicago. "Ziggy," a bull elephant of about 58 years, died of age. Ziggy was named after Florenz Ziegfeld, who purchased the animal in the 1920s for his daughter. The elephant toured with a circus and then was sold to the Brookfield Zoo in Illinois. There, during mating season, Ziggy charged his trainer. The trainer was injured, and Ziggy was chained up in a dark cell. He remained there for thirty years. The injured trainer decided this was unjust and campaigned for Ziggy's relief. With the help of a fund financed by children and the Chicago Zoological Society, Ziggy was moved to a spacious, open-air compound in 1970.

– October 29 –

1618   The Tower of London. At the order of James I, Sir Walter Raleigh, who was about 64, was beheaded for leading an unsuccessful expedition to Guiana. His words upon examining the ax: "This is sharp medicine, but a sure remedy for all evils." His last words were to the executioner, "What dost thou fear? Strike, man, strike!" Two blows were required to sever Raleigh's head. His wife had the head preserved, keeping it by her for the rest of her life.

1877   Near Memphis. Confederate war hero Nathan Bedford Forrest, 56, died after wasting away to just 100 pounds. His illness had the symptoms of diarrhea but was probably a more serious intestinal problem. Jefferson Davis visited his bedside shortly before Forrest died. The bodies of Forrest and his wife are buried under a grand, equestrian statue of Forrest in Memphis's Forrest Park.

Forrest was an untrained but instinctive military genius, managing to routinely defeat larger Union forces. His prescription for military success: "Get there first with the most." He has been long held up as an example of the best the Confederacy could produce.

Forrest also serves as an example of the worst of the Confederacy. He commanded the forces that committed the infamous Fort Pillow massacre. That fort was held by Tennessee Unionists and black soldiers. The garrison put up a good fight but was overwhelmed. The Confederates were outraged to see black men in Union uniforms and refused their surrender. They shot them down, even bayoneting wounded men. Forrest was unapologetic. He wrote, "It is hoped that these facts will demonstrate to the Northern people that Negra soldiers cannot cope with Southerners."

Following the war, Forrest became Grand Wizard of the Invisible Empire—the Ku Klux Klan—when Robert E. Lee turned down the position.

1901   Auburn Prison. Leon Czolgosz, 28, was electrocuted for the assassination of President William McKinley (see 9/6/1901). Czolgosz had suffered a nervous breakdown three years before the killing and had become an anarchistic socialist so wild that even anarchists thought he was nuts. One anarchist newspaper warned other anarchists to avoid him because he was too dangerous.

Czolgosz said nothing during his trial, but before being electrocuted declaimed, "I killed the President because he was the enemy of the good people—the good working people." Czolgosz's brother demanded the body. He wanted to sell it to a crime museum for $5,000. Authorities instead gave the killer an unmarked grave, pouring acid over the body to destroy it lest vengeful citizens or entrepreneurs steal it.

1957   Hollywood. MGM moviemaker Louis B. Mayer, 72, died of leukemia. Mayer had been forced from his command of MGM, and his last words were, "Nothing matters."

Mayer introduced the studio system that turned out film stars like an assembly line. He made many famous films, but he turned down the biggest movie ever when Irving Thalberg persuaded him not to film *Gone With the Wind*. Thalberg said, "No Civil War picture has ever made a nickel." Mayer also lost out on an even greater movie enterprise. In 1928, MGM executives urged him to hire a young cartoonist called Walt Disney after they saw a preview of a Mickey Mouse cartoon. Mayer was unimpressed. He thought a mouse blown up to huge dimensions on a movie screen would terrorize pregnant women. Later, he would say, "The cinema has given precisely one great artist to the world: Greta Garbo—unless you also count that damn mouse."

– October 30 –

1941   The North Atlantic. The U. S. destroyer *Reuben James* was torpedoed and sunk by a German U-boat one month before Pearl Harbor. More than a hundred sailors were killed.

    Franklin Roosevelt had ordered U.S. Navy ships guarding convoys to Britain to harass German subs, hoping for an incident that would get America involved in World War II. When the unmarked *Reuben James* dropped depth charges, the Germans, thinking it was a British warship, fired back. Roosevelt used the sinking to justify further hostile acts against Germany, but it took Pearl Harbor to bring America into the war. This was also a goal of the British government. British naval authorities even considered having a British submarine disguised as a German vessel attack an American ship. Undoubtedly, America needed to become a combatant, but the means Roosevelt used were unsavory.

1983   Americus, Georgia. Lillian Carter, mother of President Jimmy Carter, died at 85. The hospital gave no cause other than declining health, but she had been treated for cancer at 81. Her outspokenness charmed the public till one of her "frank" statements expressed the hope that Teddy Kennedy wouldn't be assassinated, like his brothers, if he succeeded in defeating her boy for the Democratic presidential nomination. Miss Lillian once said, "Sometimes when I look at my children I say to myself, 'Lillian, you should have stayed a virgin.'"

– October 31 –

Halloween

1916   Texas. Charles Taze Russell, 64, publisher of the *Watchtower*, died of a heart attack on a train. He had traveled the world, preaching that Christ was about to return to earth. While dying, he pleaded to be wrapped in a Roman toga. His assistants obliged by winding him in Pullman sheets. Earlier in his career, Russell had predicted that 1874 would be the year of the Second Coming but that mankind would be unaware of the event. Russell's followers adopted the name "Jehovah's Witnesses."

1926   Detroit. Erich Weiss, better known as Harry Houdini, died at
       42. A college student confronted him after a performance and
       asked him if his claim to be able to take blows to the stomach
       without flinching was true. Houdini, who was sitting for a
       portrait and reading his mail, said yes, if he had time to
       prepare, but the student immediately hit him, four times, and
       would have continued hitting him if his companions hadn't
       pulled him back. Houdini assured his friends that he was all
       right. However, his appendix had burst. He insisted on
       completing that day's shows and performed the next night,
       but he collapsed afterward. His wife persuaded him to go to a
       hospital the next morning. His ruptured appendix was
       removed too late; peritonitis had set in.
           Death should have been in hours, but Houdini held out for
       days. His last words were to his brother Dash: "I am tired of
       fighting, Dash. I guess this thing is going to get me." He died
       on Halloween. He was buried in a coffin that he had used in
       his escape routines. Houdini, who had exposed many phony
       spiritualists, said that if it were possible to contact the living
       from beyond the grave, he would do so. His wife held a séance
       every Halloween for a decade, then stopped, saying, "Ten
       years is long enough to wait for any man."

1968   Hollywood. Silent film star Ramon Novarro, 69, was mur-
       dered by two young male street hustlers he had admitted to
       his home, perhaps for sexual purposes (his body was found
       nude). He was severely beaten and choked to death on his
       own blood. His two murderers were sentenced to life in
       prison.

1990   Indianapolis. "Amazing Joe" Burrus was seeking to outdo
       Houdini. Houdini had failed in attempting to perform a
       buried-coffin escape. Burrus had succeeded in a similar stunt
       but wanted a more spectacular triumph. On this date, while
       being videotaped by his family, Burrus had himself chained
       and padlocked, then buried in a clear plastic coffin, but this
       time, Burrus had concrete poured over the coffin. He had
       neglected to calculate the weight of the concrete, and the seven
       tons of material crushed his coffin, suffocating him. Burrus's
       wife recalled her husband had once quoted Houdini as saying,
       "It will be either fate or my foolishness that kills me."

EM

– November 1 –

1907　Pioneer of the Theater of the Absurd Alfred Jarry called for a toothpick on his deathbed. When one was produced, he smiled and died in his 34th year.

1981　Parma, Ohio. Ernest A. Pecek, 23, wanted a terrific costume for a Halloween party he was to attend on this date. He decided to be a vampire and thought a large knife in the chest, with suitable false blood splashed on his shirt front, would be perfect. He strapped a pine board to his chest and then stuck a double-edged dagger into the board. Pecek either hammered it in too far or slipped and fell, driving the blade too deep. Either way, the blade pierced the board and Pecek's chest, killing him.

– November 2 –

1950　Ayot St. Lawrence, Hertfordshire, England. Playwright George Bernard Shaw, 94, died of complications following a fall in his garden, which broke his thighbone, and an operation for kidney stones. He had remarked: "Sister, you're trying to keep me alive as an old curiosity, but I'm done, I'm finished, I'm going to die." His last words were to a visitor, "Well, it will be a new experience, anyway." Shaw directed that there be no religious funeral service and that no "cross or any other instrument of torture or symbol of blood sacrifice" be placed over his grave. He wanted his body cremated and the ashes spread over his garden. In memorial to him, theaters around the world were darkened.

English novelist Israel Zangwill didn't care for Shaw and said, "The way Bernard Shaw believes in himself is very refreshing in these atheistic days when so many people believe in no God at all." H. L. Mencken told Shaw, "The more I think you over, the more it comes home to me what an unmitigated Middle Victorian ass you are!" Shaw once sent Winston Churchill two tickets to the opening of one of his plays. With the tickets Shaw enclosed a note saying, "Bring a friend—if you have one." Churchill sent back a note expressing his regrets. He was engaged that evening but asked for tickets to the second night—"If there is one!"

1989   Kansas City, Missouri. John Gardner, 72, was returning to his nursing home after an excursion to purchase a cheeseburger and french fries when four young men shot him to death for his meal.

1991   Salt Lake City. Jerry Lee Robertson, 26, and his wife, Cassie J. Robertson, 20, were playing a game of Monopoly with their roommate Gerald B. Thomas, 56. An acrimonious argument broke out over the game's rules. Later, when Thomas fell asleep, the Robertsons beat him to death with a claw hammer.

– November 3 –

1926   Greenville, Ohio. Cowgirl sharpshooter Annie Oakley, 66, died of pernicious anemia. She had been paralyzed on one side of her body since a train accident in 1901. She had outlined her funeral in detail. She had a woman embalmer so as to keep her modesty, she was cremated, the ashes were placed in one of her trophy cups, and the service was held in secret one day prior to its announced date to keep the funeral private. Her husband died just weeks after her.

1954   Nice. French artist Henri Matisse, 84, died of a heart attack.

His painting, *Le Bateau*, was exhibited by The Museum of Modern Art for forty-seven years before it was noticed that the painting was upside down.

– November 4 –

1955 Near Phoenix, Arizona. Willie Bioff, 55, was killed when his truck blew up. He had made millions for the Chicago mob extorting money from the film industry through his control of film unions. He was exposed and turned state's evidence, sending many of his chums to jail (excluding Frank Nitti, who killed himself on 3/19/1943). He retired to a ranch with $3 million from his labors but never got to enjoy his money.

– November 5 –

1942 New York City. Theater legend George M. Cohan, 64, died of cancer. His last words were of concern for his wife: "Look after Agnes." He wrote hundreds of songs, including "Over There" and "It's a Grand Old Flag." Cohan actually *was* born on the Fourth of July, in 1878.

1989 Murfreesboro, Tennessee. In 1966, Green Beret Staff Sergeant Barry Sadler cowrote "The Ballad of the Green Berets" while recovering from a wound received during service as a medic in Vietnam. The song sold 9 million copies and was a number-one hit for five weeks. Sadler went on to write a number of adventure novels. He also helped build a trust fund for Vietnamese orphans. In the 1980s, Sadler became involved in the Contra movement in Nicaragua. He was reported to be training them in firearms and field medical care. In September 1988, while entering a taxi in Guatemala City, Sadler was shot in the head by an unknown attacker. After fourteen months of hospitalization, he died at 49 on this date.

– November 6 –

1893 St. Petersburg. Composer Pyotr Ilich Tchaikovsky, 53, died of cholera. The first time he conducted one of his pieces in public, he became so nervous that he thought his head was going to fall off.

A Russian scholar in 1978 claimed that Tchaikovsky didn't die of cholera. He said that a Russian nobleman had objected to a homosexual affair Tchaikovsky had had with the nobleman's nephew. A secret court of aristocrats sentenced Tchaikovsky to death by suicide or the affair would be revealed to the czar, ruining Tchaikovsky's career. The scholar said Tchaikovsky took arsenic, then drank contaminated water to cover the poison.

1991   Houston. Actress Gene Tierney, 70, died after a long battle with emphysema. Brooklyn-born Tierney appeared in many films, but is best remembered as the star of *Laura* (1944), a mystery wherein the detective falls in love with the portrait of the victim.

Tierney's own life undoubtedly inspired a mystery. In 1943, she contracted measles while pregnant. Her daughter was born retarded. Tierney suffered greatly, divorce followed, and, in the 1950s, she was treated for mental illness. Writer Agatha Christie used a similar situation as the basis for her murder mystery *The Mirror Crack'd*.

– November 7 –

1872   New York City. The *Mary Celeste* set sail for Italy. It was later found with all hands mysteriously missing. One theory suggests that the crew, smelling a leak in the ship's cargo of explosive alcohol, abandoned ship before a chance spark could set it afire. Once they were in their lifeboat, the wind carried the *Mary Celeste* away. The spark never occurred, and while the ship was found, the lifeboat was lost with the crew and passengers.

1938   Paris. The Nazis had driven the family of Herschel Grynszpan out of Germany and left them destitute. Grynszpan went to the German Embassy in Paris on this date and shot the first German official he saw, Ernst vom Rath. Rath died two days later, and the Nazis used his death to justify a giant attack on German Jews. Thirty thousand were arrested. One hundred and ninety-one synagogues and over 1,000 Jewish shops were burned. The mounds of broken glass from shop windows gave the night of terror its name—

Kristallnacht ("Crystal Night"). Ironically, Ernst vom Rath was an anti-Nazi being watched by the Gestapo.

1959   Newport Beach, California. Gruff actor Victor McLaglen, 72, died of a heart attack. McLaglen's films included *The Informer* (1935), *Klondike Annie* (1936), *Gunga Din* (1939), *Fort Apache* (1948), *She Wore A Yellow Ribbon* (1949), *Rio Grande* (1950), and *The Quiet Man* (1952). McLaglen played a drunkard in *The Informer*. To give the role authenticity, director John Ford made McLaglen stay drunk for much of the film. McLaglen nearly quit because of the hangovers, but won an Academy Award for Best Actor for his performance. His performances in military roles were given authenticity by his service in the British Army. In one silent military film, McLaglen argued with another soldier over a girl. They exchanged realistic soldierly dialogue. As the captions were tamer, no one thought there would be any problem—that is, until deaf members of the audience read the actors' lips.

1962   New York City. Eleanor Roosevelt, 78, FDR's First Lady, died from bone marrow tuberculosis. She was determined to die without drugs and firmly clenched her teeth to prevent hospital staff from forcing them on her. She should have resisted earlier. When she began bruising and bleeding at the slightest touch, her doctors diagnosed a fatal blood disease but chose to skip doing a painful open bone marrow biopsy. They prescribed prednisone to combat the blood disease. A side effect of prednisone is that it lowers the patient's resistance to infection. This helped her tuberculosis spread faster and caused her to die sooner. The skipped test would have revealed the erroneous diagnosis. The doctors succeeded in covering up their mistake till the 1980s.

Mrs. Roosevelt championed many liberal causes, such as the U.N. and labor unions. She said she would never under any condition cross a picket line. A less liberal pundit immediately called for volunteers to establish a permanent picket line around her home.

– November 8 –

1308   Cologne. Irish scholar John Duns Scotus, 42, died of apoplexy. He devised the doctrine of the Immaculate Conception and was considered a near equal of Thomas Aquinas, yet the term "dunce" comes from his name. His followers, who were called "Dunses," resisted the Renaissance, and their name became associated with obstinate stupidity. This date is celebrated as Dunce Day in recognition of dunces everywhere.

Some days after the internment, Scotus's subterranean vault was reopened. His body was found outside his coffin, his hands bloody. apparently, he hadn't been completely dead. He awoke in his coffin and escaped it, but couldn't claw through the vault's locked door.

1674   Chalfont St. Giles, Buckinghamshire, England. John Milton, 65, died of gout. He is best known for *Paradise Lost*, which relates the fall of Man from the Garden of Eden. His purpose was to "justify the ways of God to man." To this, the author A. E. Housman replied, "Malt does more than Milton can, / To justify God's ways to man." Milton was involved in the English Civil War on Parliament's side, serving as Cromwell's Latin Secretary of State. Since all diplomatic documents were done in Latin, it was a high post.

Milton was blind most of his adult life. He met and married his second and favorite wife when he was blind. She died in childbirth and in a sonnet he described a dream wherein he could see her.

1887   Glenwood Springs, Colorado. Dentist/gunman John Henry "Doc" Holliday, 35, died in a tuberculosis sanatorium. He had just had a glass of whiskey, and Doc's last words were, "I'll be damned!" Holliday had moved west after his doctor told him he would die within a year of tuberculosis. The climate was supposed to help his condition. Holliday had been a mild, even timid, man, but after a cowboy disputed his treatment, "Doc" shot him dead. His lifestyle changed, and he killed thirty men, becoming the friend of Marshal Wyatt Earp, alongside whom he fought at the O.K. Corral. Perhaps killing and liquor were good for him, for instead of one year, Holliday lived fourteen.

1978   Stockbridge, Massachusetts. Artist Norman Rockwell, 84, died after two years of ill health. His first illustration sales had been for the Boy Scouts of America, and local Scouts served as an honor guard for his funeral. He was buried in Stockbridge. Rockwell, who chronicled rural life, was raised at 103rd Street and Amsterdam Avenue in New York City.

Columnist Ellen Goodman has written, "He knew he didn't portray America. He portrayed Americana. His boys were all Tom Sawyers, his doctors made house calls, and his dogs were puppies." Rockwell did choose pleasant topics, but as a Vermonter who grew up during the late Rockwellian Age, I can vouch for the veracity of his images. We did run around barefoot and straw-hatted. Doctors did make house calls. And we owned puppies. I don't know what's sadder— the passing of that way of life, or the smug disbelief that it ever was even possible.

– November 9 –

1940   Heckfield, near Reading, Hampshire, England. Former Prime Minister Neville Chamberlain, 71, died after falling into a coma. He had undergone intestinal surgery and never fully recovered. His last words were, "Approaching dissolution brings relief." His ashes were interred in Westminster Abbey.

Chamberlain signed the Munich Pact with Hitler, which gave Czechoslovakia to Germany in return for Hitler's promise to grab nothing more. It convinced Hitler that the British would do nothing to stop him. Apologists for Chamberlain say that England needed the year between Munich and the outbreak of war to prepare. This neglects the preparations that Germany made during the same time.

1953   St. Vincent's Hospital, New York City. Welsh writer Dylan Thomas, 39, died of pneumonia and liver disease, following six days of coma induced by drinking eighteen straight whiskeys. Thomas had his first poem published when he was 12. Unfortunately, he had plagiarized it.

1965   The failure of a Canadian power plant near Niagara Falls produced the Great Blackout, which killed the lights over a large section of the Eastern Seaboard for over twelve hours, leaving 30 million people in the dark. Only one person died. A Florida tourist fell down an open elevator shaft while looking for the way out of his New York City hotel.

– November 10 –

1891   Marseilles. The French poet Arthur Rimbaud, 36, died of cancer. Raised in a poor, religious, rural home, he had run away to Paris at 16. He committed himself to a life of mysticism and sensation-seeking. He sought out perversity, hoping that the suffering that follows sin would yield transcendental insights. He traveled two years with the poet Paul Verlaine, who had left his wife for Rimbaud. They parted after Verlaine shot Rimbaud in the wrist. At 19, Rimbaud abandoned poetry forever. He became a trader in Africa till a tumor on his leg forced him to return to civilization. The tumor proved fatal.

– November 11 –

1938   North Brother Island, Hudson River, New York. Mary Mallon, 68, better known as "Typhoid Mary," died of a stroke while under detention. A carrier of that disease, she caused seven epidemics, killing at least 1,000; she saw no reason for her freedom being limited and protested her detention loudly. A domestic cook, she was ideally situated for spreading the disease. Health officials let her out of detention in 1910 when she promised to find other employment. She didn't keep her word and continued working as a cook until the epidemic of 1915 was traced to her. Redetained, she enjoyed expressing her defiance of the doctors and her anger at the public, who were scared stiff of her. As a carrier, she was immune to the illness.

– November 12 –

1912   Antarctica. The bodies of Robert Falcon Scott's expedition were found. They had attempted to be the first to reach the South Pole but when they arrived, they found they had been beaten. They died on the way home. The last entry in Scott's journal, dated March 29, 1912, read: "We are showing that Englishmen can still die with a bold spirit, fighting it out to the end...Had we lived, I should have had a tale to tell of the hardihood, endurance and courage of companions which would have stirred the heart of every Englishman. These rough notes and our dead bodies must tell the tale...It seems a pity but I do not think I can write more." Scott was 43. He took a movie camera with him, and today we can see his expedition marching through the snow.

– November 13 –

1868   Passy, near Paris. Opera composer Gioacchino Rossini, 76, died of an inflammation of the chest. He was buried in Florence. Rossini composed most of his work while drunk.

1983   Cumming, Georgia. Comic Junior Samples, 56, of TV's "Hee Haw," died of a heart attack.

– November 14 –

1831   Berlin. Philosopher Georg Wilhelm Friedrich Hegel, 61, died of cholera. He believed in a mind-ordered world and a dialectical progression toward ultimate knowledge. He explained this in such pedantic prose that while lots of folks think he was a great guy, many find him a grand example of old-style German scholarship wherein Herr Professor concocts an all-encompassing theory that completely explains everything, everywhere, forever. His last words were: "Only one man ever understood me...And he didn't understand me."

1915   Tuskegee, Alabama. Black educator/scientist Booker T. Washington, 59, who had been born a slave, died of a heart condition. His last words: "Take me home. I was born in the South, I have lived and labored in the South, and I wish to die and be buried in the South."

Newspaperman Jenkin Lloyd Jones tells a story of how he went to Tuskegee as a young reporter to interview Washington. He found Washington hoeing a vegetable bed. Jones expressed surprise that the agricultural scientist, who was famous for his work with peanuts and sweet potatoes, was doing such lowly work. Washington replied, "Civilization started with a hoe."

1927   The largest gasometer in the world was in the middle of Pittsburgh, Pennsylvania's industrial section. On this date, repairmen sought to find a leak in the huge device, which held 5 million cubic feet of natural gas. It was dark, so they lighted their way with a lantern, which had an open flame. The resulting explosion flattened a square mile, killing twenty-eight and injuring hundreds.

– November 15 –

1954   Van Nuys, California. Actor Lionel Barrymore, 76, died of a
        heart attack. Barrymore, like his sister, Ethel, and brother,
        John, was a theater star but is best remembered for his film
        roles, such as the crusty Dr. Gillespie in the *Dr. Kildaire* series.
        His finest performance was undoubtedly as a dying clerk
        learning to live, in the classic *Grand Hotel* (1932).
            Lionel proposed as his own epitaph: "Well, I've played
        everything but a harp."

1978   New York City. Anthropologist Margaret Mead, 76, died after
        a yearlong battle with cancer. Mead attained fame with her
        work *Coming of Age in Samoa* in 1928. She examined
        adolescence among the Samoans, comparing it to adolescence
        in Western societies. Her conclusion was that the easygoing
        Samoan approach was superior. Other anthropologists crit-
        icized her subjective studies, but Mead became an influential
        advocate of change in personal behavior and in the institutions
        of society. She was a sort of reverse missionary, carrying the
        message of the innocent, happy islander to the jaded, civilized
        neurotic.
            Years later, other anthropologists reexamined the same
        natives. The natives told them that they had had a lot of fun
        making up strange sexual customs for Mead. They said they
        tried to see how far they could stretch the truth before she
        would realize they were teasing her. Apparently, Mead never
        caught on. Still other anthropologists discovered that the
        portion of the Polynesian people who were most casual about
        sex were the plebeian class, while the ruling class were very
        puritanical. It appears that the rulers encouraged promiscuity
        to keep their subjects docile—too busy chasing grass skirts or
        being chased to wonder why they were subjects of often
        extremely brutal rulers. The ruling class, on the other hand,
        practiced strict sexual discipline to control royal lines and
        thereby maintain power.

– November 16 –

1532   Cajamarca, Peru. Dominican monk Vicente de Valverde
        accompanied the conquistador Pizarro on his expedition to
        Peru. On this date, a meeting between Valverde and the Inca
        king Atahualpa was arranged. The intent was to establish the

Incas as heretics and thereby fair game for conquest. Valverde handed the king a breviary. The king didn't recognize it and set it aside. This proved to the monk that the king was a heretic. He urged Pizarro to massacre the lot. Pizarro did. Seven thousand died. The Inca king was strangled, then burned at the stake. Valverde went on to become bishop of Cuzco. He was comfortable in this post, burning nearly every written record of the Inca culture, till 1541, when his patron Pizarro was killed by Spanish enemies. Valverde fled to Panama, but when his ship stopped at Puná Island off Ecuador, the local natives ate him.

1960   Presbyterian Hospital, Los Angeles. Two days after Clark Gable finished filming *The Misfits* with Marilyn Monroe, he suffered a heart attack. Monroe's eccentricities had caused filming to take months, and Gable had fought the boredom of the hot Nevada desert by doing most of his own stunts. Before his attack, Gable told his agent that he liked Monroe, but her unprofessional behavior had nearly given him a heart attack. On this date, while reading a magazine in his hospital bed, Gable died at 59 of a second heart attack.

Gable made sixty-one films in a thirty-year career. He was fastidious, shaving his armpits and chest and showering several times a day. Despite this, he loved the outdoors, fishing, and hunting. His endearing smile was artificial, as he wore false teeth. During World War II he enlisted in the Army Air Corps and was decorated for his service as a gunner on several bomber missions (see 1/16/1942). He chose an epitaph for himself, but it wasn't used. It was: "Back to the silents."

1981   Santa Monica, California. Actor William Holden, 63, was found dead in his apartment. He had been drinking heavily (his blood alcohol level was .22), when he tripped on a rug and struck his head against the edge of a table. He lay down on his bed and attempted to stop the flow of blood with tissues but soon passed out and bled to death. There is little doubt that if he had been more sober, he would have been able to get help. He had made over fifty films, including *Stalag 17* (1953) and *The Bridge on the River Kwai* (1957).

– November 17 –

1917   Near Meudor, France. Sculptor Auguste Rodin, 77, died. His most famous work, *The Thinker*, was a portrait of Dante. In his last years, Rodin was poor and forgotten by the public. He asked to be allowed to live in a small room in one of the museums that contained statues he had donated to France. He was refused, and while his statues were kept nice and warm, Rodin died of frostbite in a garret.

– November 18 –

1886   New York City. Chester A. Arthur, 57, twenty-first U.S. president, died of a cerebral hemorrhage. On the seventeenth, a servant brought his breakfast to his bedroom and discovered Arthur unable to speak. A doctor diagnosed a stroke. Arthur survived till the dawn of this date.

Arthur had been vice president and entered the presidency when James A. Garfield died of an assassin's bullet. Arthur wasn't widely admired. Woodrow Wilson described him as "a nonentity with side whiskers." Arthur claimed to have been born in Fairfield, Vermont, but some historians think he was actually born in Canada and was thereby illegally president. As president, Arthur auctioned off all the historic furniture in the White House, replacing it with Victorian monstrosities.

1978   Jonestown, Guyana. Nine hundred and twelve cult members of the People's Temple committed suicide by drinking Kool-Aid laced with cyanide. Representative Leo Ryan, 53, of California had visited the cult's plantation at the request of worried relatives of cult members. He had been favorably impressed by the visit, but offered to take any member who wished to leave with him. Several went, and to prevent exposure of the cult's bizarre lifestyle, desperate cultists ambushed the delegation, killing Ryan and four staff members. Cult leader Reverend Jim Jones saw his empire disappearing, so he ordered mass suicide. Two hundred and seventy-six of the dead were children, including thirty-six babies. The infants were killed by squirting the poison into their mouths with syringes and were the first to die. Next were the older children, then the adults, and finally the oldest members. This ordering was deliberate, as Jones thought that once the children were dead, their parents wouldn't resist. Jones was probably the last to die. He recorded a rambling socialist diatribe while directing the deaths, then, surrounded

by his dead followers, shot himself. The Kool-Aid's flavor was
grape.

– November 19 –

1703   Bastille, Paris. The mysterious "Man in the Iron Mask" died.
He had been imprisoned by Louis XIV for forty years with
his head locked in an iron helmet that hid his features. No one
knows who he was, but speculation has included the English
duke of Monmouth, a son of Oliver Cromwell, and the twin
brother of Louis XIV. One guess was Count Anthony
Matthioli, secretary of state to Charles III, duke of Mantua.
Supposedly, Louis bribed Matthioli to help him occupy Italy.
The count betrayed Louis, who, for revenge, kidnapped
Matthioli. Great secrecy—hence the mask—was necessary, as
other nations would have stopped diplomatic relations with
France if they had discovered Louis had arrested a diplomat.

1887   New York City. Poet Emma Lazarus, 38, died of cancer. A
Zionist and a crusader against anti-Semitism, she organized
relief efforts for refugees. She is best remembered, however,
for writing the poem "The New Colossus" in 1883 to raise
money for the Statue of Liberty. It is inscribed on the statue's
pedestal and in part reads, "Give me your tired, your poor,
your huddled masses yearning to breathe free..." The statue
wasn't originally meant for New York Harbor. It was planned
as a lighthouse for Alexandria, Egypt, to mark the entry to
the Suez Canal.

1961   Off the coast of Netherlands New Guinea. Michael Rock-
efeller, youngest son of millionaire Nelson Rockefeller (New
York governor and U. S. vice president), was reported missing.
It is suspected that headhunters killed him.

– November 20 –

1820   The Pacific. The *Essex*, a Nantucket whaling ship, was sunk
by a sperm whale. Only eight members of her crew were
rescued after spending ninety-six days at sea, during which
they were reduced to cannibalism. The incident is thought to
have inspired Herman Melville to write *Moby-Dick*.

1910   Russia. Writer Leo Tolstoy, 82, died of pneumonia. He got a
        chill while trying to run away from his turbulent wife, Sonya.
        His last words: "I don't understand what I'm supposed to do."
        In his fifties, Tolstoy underwent a religious conversion and
        sought to give away his wealth. Sonya didn't agree and kept
        control of him by threatening suicide. She did allow him to
        become a vegetarian. He once gave a dinner party where a
        woman said that she knew of his diet but that she preferred
        meat and asked him to serve her a chicken. Tolstoy tied a live
        chicken to her chair, saying, "My conscience forbids me to kill
        it so I'd be greatly obliged if you'd do it for me."

1986   Canton, Massachusetts. Rod Matthews, 13, wanted to find out
        what it would be like to kill someone. He found out by luring
        Shaun Ouillette, 14, into the woods and beating him to death
        with a ball bat. He tried to impress friends by telling them
        how he planned the murder and showing them the body.
        None of these friends informed authorities. Ouillete was
        missing for four weeks before police found him. In 1988,
        Matthews was convicted of second-degree murder. He was
        sentenced to life but could be paroled in fifteen years.
        Ouillette's mother was upset, "He planned this. Fifteen years.
        No, I'm sorry, that's wrong. Shaun is not coming home in
        fifteen years, is he? He's not ever coming home." Matthews's
        mother said, "It's terrible! A child shouldn't be persecuted and
        forced to go through something like this. God only knows
        how much worse it's going to make his condition." His
        attorney blamed society.

– November 21 –

1718   Near Ocracoke Island, North Carolina. Edward Teach,
        known as Blackbeard the pirate, was killed in a fierce fight.
        Teach was shot five times and slashed by cutlass twenty-five
        times, but the fatal blow came from behind. Someone nearly
        hacked off his head. After death, his head was completely
        severed and displayed on a pike on the bowsprit of the
        victorious Royal Navy cutter. Legend has it that his skull was
        turned into a punchbowl and that Teach's headless ghost
        wanders the Eastern Seaboard in search of it.

1963   Springfield, Missouri. Robert "Birdman of Alcatraz" Stroud, 73, died in his sleep in prison. He had spent fifty-four years behind bars—forty-two in solitary confinement.

Born in Seattle, Stroud ran away at 13. He hoboed his way to Alaska, where at 18, he lived with a dance-hall girl in her thirties. One day, he discovered the woman badly beaten. She blamed Charles Dahmer. Stroud hid by Dahmer's home and shot him down when he came by. Stroud turned himself in and pleaded guilty to manslaughter, expecting to be treated leniently because he was defending a woman. The judge gave him the maximum sentence of twelve years in a Washington prison. Bitter, Stroud became a troublemaker. When he stabbed an inmate, six months were added to his sentence, and he was moved to Leavenworth Federal Penitentiary. He was due to be released in 1916. On March 25, 1916, Stroud returned from a work detail to find a fruit basket on his bunk. His brother had visited, but prison authorities had sent him away because visiting hours had expired. Stroud was outraged that an exception hadn't been made. At mess, he complained to a neighbor. Guard Andrew Turner warned Stroud that talking was forbidden. The next day at mess, in front of 1,100 witnesses, Stroud stabbed Turner to death. Stroud was sentenced to be hanged, but his mother persuaded President Woodrow Wilson to commute the hanging to life in solitary confinement.

When a storm tossed an injured bird into his cell, Stroud nursed it to health and began studying birds. He collected over 300 birds and, despite only a third-grade education, became an expert on bird diseases, writing two books on the subject. Stroud also married, hoping this would aid in obtaining parole. However, his mother, outraged that Stroud was no longer dependent on her, announced that Stroud should never be paroled. He wasn't.

In *Birdman of Alcatraz* (1962), Stroud (played by Burt Lancaster) was an unjustly treated, stoic hero. Those who knew him thought otherwise. Stroud was called "surly," "morose," and a "psychopath." He enjoyed many privileges because of his celebrity. In 1942, three-and-a-half gallons of alcohol were found in his cell. He had distilled it from birdseed smuggled in by bird lovers in the bottom of bird cages. Prison authorities transferred him to Alcatraz. There, he wasn't permitted to have birds, but was given a job in a print shop. Stroud often walked around his cell naked and shaved every hair from his body. He spent his last years in a prison hospital.

1981 Ted Tolwinski, 26, and David Radnis, 28, watched *The Deerhunter* (1978) on WFLD-TV. In that film, a soldier in Vietnam becomes addicted to Russian roulette. The film inspired Tolwinski and Radnis to play a game of simultaneous Russian roulette. They sat at their kitchen table. Each placed a revolver loaded with one bullet to his temple, and began. They pulled the triggers in unison. Both guns clicked on the first pull. On the second pull, the results were different. Both guns fired, and both players were instantly killed—a draw.

Before the incident, psychologist Dr. Thomas Radecki, an expert on suicide, had asked the television station to edit out the Russian roulette scenes, citing twenty-eight shootings and twenty-five deaths by people who had watched the movie in other cities.

– November 22 –

1963 12:30 CST, Dallas. John Kennedy, thirty-fifth U.S. president, was assassinated. He was 46. Kennedy's last words: "My God, I've been hit."

Unscrupulous writers have sold countless books and movies describing assassination conspiracies. It has been variously claimed that the CIA, the FBI, the KGB, the Mafia, the Klan, Texas oil tycoons, the Rockefellers, Castro, anti-Castro Cubans, and Lyndon Johnson staged the killing. Some claim Kennedy never died, surviving as a vegetable in a secret nursing home.

The most unscrupulous conspiracy peddler is undoubtedly director Oliver Stone, whose $40 million film *JFK* (1991) distorted key events to foster Stone's "myth-making." Stone blames the air force, the army, the navy, a group of New Orleans homosexuals, the media, the CIA, the military-industrial complex, the nuclear industry, Cuban exiles, the Dallas police, the New Orleans police, and others for the killing. Their motive is supposed to be Kennedy's intent to pull out of Vietnam, to patch up relations with Castro, and to end the cold war, thereby denying the military-industrial complex profits. Never mind that the strongly anti-Communist Kennedy repeatedly called the country to "bear any burden" in the fight against Communism and that his closest associates thought we were in Vietnam to stay (only two antiwar senators and a single, wishful Kennedy aide have ever claimed otherwise), nor that Kennedy had authorized elaborate anti-Castro measures, nor that Kennedy had had little luck persuading the Russians to be peaceful. It is absurd to suppose that conspirators capable of the conspiracy would treasonably murder a president on such flimsy evidence of his intent.

Stone is a splendid example of the overindulged Hollywood boss. He's made successful big-buck films, so, by Hollywood logic, he must therefore be a genius, and his every delusion must be a new truth revealed. Actually, Stone feels no duty to the truth—only a fashionable hatred of "the Establishment" and an egotistical urge to impose his own prejudices on reality. Stone has even hinted that criticism of his film is motivated by the conspirators.

The truth is most certainly that Lee Harvey Oswald, a Communist ex-defector to Russia and Marine Corps marksman, firing from an ideal post, killed Kennedy all by himself. His first shot missed, the second passed through Kennedy's neck and into Texas Governor John Connally, and the third struck Kennedy's head, killing him. There was an eyewitness. Howard L. Brennan, from directly across the street, saw Oswald fire. On his deathbed, Brennan swore to his minister that there was no doubt in his mind that Oswald was the killer and that he would never forget the look on Oswald's face. In addition, there are many witnesses (including Oswald's wife and brother) to Oswald's character, motive, and presence at the Texas School Book Depository with a gun-shaped package. The weapon bore his fingerprints (he was photographed before the killing holding it), and the recovered bullets were matched to it. In his attempt to escape, Oswald killed one police officer and nearly killed a second, demonstrating his brutality and eagerness to flee.

Looking backward, one can concoct numerous chains of speculation, but they are all flawed. For example:

Ruby killed Oswald to prevent his talking.
If this is true, why wasn't Ruby killed for the same reason?

The FBI had been warned of an attack upon Kennedy and, after the assassination, upon Oswald.

The FBI receives many warnings about and threats against presidents. Nearly all of these are baseless. It is reasonable that the FBI would dismiss Oswald as insignificant when his main political activity consisted of handing out leaflets on street corners. The same is true of threats against Oswald. After his arrest, people worldwide wished for his death, but he was in the custody of the Dallas police. Seventy officers guarded him. Who could imagine that they would let bystanders get so close? It was later revealed that the police chief wanted the news cameras to see that Oswald hadn't been beaten. With hindsight, it all seems so inept, but ineptitude is hardly evidence of conspiracy. The FBI simply mishandled the threats and the Dallas police underestimated the danger to Oswald.

The Zapruder film shows Kennedy snapping backward after the fatal shot, proving that another gunman fired from in front of Kennedy.

Firearms expert Dr. John Latimore of Columbia University has shown that a man hit from Oswald's high position would move backward. When the skull shattered, debris was ejected forward, causing a corresponding movement backward.

The single bullet that passed through Kennedy's neck and into Connally pursued an erratic course, was largely unmarred, and couldn't have produced all the damage attributed to it, proving that more than three shots were fired and that more than one gunman must have been involved.

Careful examination of the victims' positions has indicated that the bullet's path does line up. The bullet hit no bones going through Kennedy but did lose velocity. A slow-moving bullet can cause incredible damage with little deformation.

A tape of police radio broadcasts shows that there were more shots fired than officially declared.

This tape has been discredited. Conversation that occurred after the shooting appears before the purported shots on the tape. In any case, it was never determined which microphone was responsible for the transmissions or where that microphone was located or if the sounds were shots.

Autopsy photographs show that Kennedy's skull wound was altered. A small hole is shown, but the Warren Commision describes a large hole.

The Zapruder film shows the president's scalp hanging after the fatal shot. In the autopsy photograph, someone, wishing to show the small entry wound, pulled the scalp back into position. Indeed, the hand holding the scalp down is visible in the photograph. If the scalp had been released, it would have revealed the cavity in the skull. The doctors who examined the wound in 1963 were recently shown all official photographs of the body as part of an excellent *Nova* television show. They declared that the photographs were entirely consistent with their memory of the body's state.

Oswald was mixed up with all sorts of cloak-and-dagger types, including anti-Castro fanatics. He must have been a CIA spy.

Oswald loved the furtive, self-dramatizing political fringe and sought out every opportunity to be around other oddballs. He may well have tried to pass himself off as anti-Castro in order to get information that he could pass on to the Cubans to prove to them that it was worth paying attention to him. Just because the CIA had connections to the anti-Castro underground doesn't mean the CIA had connections to everyone else who might have been involved with anti-Castroites. In any case, Oswald's connections are highly speculative. The few purported witnesses have minimal credibility.

Oswald was a simpleminded, nonviolent patsy, not even a good shot, and was hardly capable of killing a President.

Oswald had attempted to assassinate General Edwin Walker, a right-wing politican, on April 10, 1963, but his one shot missed. When he learned that Kennedy would pass his workplace, the School Book Depository, Oswald smuggled his rifle in, constructed a "nest" of boxes to hide himself from casual view, and waited. The window provided an excellent sniper post; his rifle had a telescopic sight. Only a little luck was needed to do the job with three shots. The ruthless killing of a Dallas police officer after the assassination clearly showed an impulsively violent personality. The officer who captured Oswald barely managed to get Oswald's gun away from him. Oswald had tried to sneak a shot into the man's stomach.

What was Oswald's motive?

Stone makes much of this question, implying that Oswald had nothing to gain and that only the mysterious conspirators benefited from Kennedy's death. This plays on the grief of Kennedy admirers and the insecurities of Americans in general. People don't want to believe that a single, evil man can change history. Yet at the same time they want to believe that a single, good man can. Unfortunately, we are daily confronted with terrible examples that fanatics can do terrible things for little or no sensible reason.

Like other presidential assassins, Oswald was a vain pseudointellectual seeking to make his mark in history. In modern times, such people seem to be everywhere, from Belfast to Peru to Berlin. They stalk movie stars. They plant bombs in pubs. They drive trucks loaded with explosives into embassys. They take and torment hostages. They construct camps to reeducate or to simply process people like cattle, killing millions. They command powerful nations and have plunged the world into war again and again. Why should we be surprised that an obscure, Marxist fanatic with a gun would want to kill a U.S. president noted for his anti-Communist beliefs?

Oswald's mother said of her son, "He was a lonely person. He trusted no one. He was too sick. It was the fantasy of a sick person, to get attention only for himself."

In summary, what Stone calls "the assassination community" has little interest in truth. First, there is no money to be made proving Oswald acted alone. Secondly, the Kennedy assassination conspiracy is an ever-flexible weapon that can injure any purported villain it is pointed at. Stone uses it to link John Kennedy's assassination, the killing of Robert Kennedy, the murder of Martin Luther King, the Vietnam War, the inflation caused by the Great Society, Watergate, the race riots, the alienation of the sixties generation, the drug problem, the Iran-Contra scandal, and nearly every bad thing that has happened since 1963 to an "invisible...unelected parallel covert government." Who are these evildoers? Stone says, "It's a moving, fluid thing, a series of forces at play. It's not necessarily individuals." Read: Anyone Stone doesn't like.

John Kennedy once said, "Forgive your enemies, but never forget their names."

1980   Hollywood. Actress Mae West, 87, died following a stroke.
        Her naughty ways and extravagant tastes entertained millions
        but didn't please all critics. Some thought her obscene, and
        one film critic called her "the greatest female impersonator of
        all time." Among her remarks: "Between two evils, I always
        pick the one I never tried before," "A hard man is good to
        find," and one that was cut from her film *Every Day's a
        Holiday* (1937), "I wouldn't let him touch me, even with a ten-
        foot pole."

– November 23 –

1849   Boston. Dr. John White Webster, 57, killed Dr. George
        Parkman, 59, a creditor, with a stick of firewood. He then
        dissected the body in his laboratory and burned the pieces.
        However, some of the remains were discovered by a janitor.
        Webster's trial was a sensation at the time, and many political,
        religious, and literary figures involved themselves. He tried to
        kill himself in jail with strychnine, but his stomach was
        nervous, and he threw up. Webster was hanged August 30,
        1850.
1983   San Francisco. Boss of the Condor Club, Jimmy "the Beard"
        Ferrozzo was crushed to death in his nightclub when a
        spangled piano rigged to rise above the stage pinned him to
        the ceiling. He and stripper Teresa Hill, 23, had been making
        love on the piano and had inadvertently triggered the piano
        lift's switch. The girl wasn't seriously injured despite being
        trapped under Ferrozzo's 204-pound corpse for hours. Police
        couldn't explain why Ferrozzo didn't jump off the piano,
        which rose slowly. Hill, who was nude, had been drinking and
        said she couldn't recall anything other than waking up under
        Ferrozzo's corpse.

– November 24 –

1494   Soothsayers claimed that the conjunction of Jupiter, Mars, and
        Saturn in the sign of the scorpion foretold the outbreak of a
        terrible disease. Perhaps they were right. Columbus had
        recently returned from the New World to Barcelona, and a

new disease broke out. It caused fetid ulcers, spots, ravaged flesh, and death. Those who survived were crippled in mind or body. In a few years, the disease was named "syphilis" and had spread throughout Europe. American Indian defenders have denied this west-to-east transmission, and certainly European diseases such as measles and smallpox killed over 90 percent of some tribes, but fossil analysis shows that syphilis in the New World dates far back into prehistoric times. Other research suggests that rheumatoid arthritis may also have originated in the New World.

1963 Dallas. Jack Ruby shot Lee Harvey Oswald, 24, on live television. Oswald, guarded by 70 policemen, was being transferred from a city jail to a county jail. He was rushed to Parkland Memorial Hospital, the hospital that had treated Kennedy. The same staff tried unsuccessfully to save the assassin's life. Dallas Detective James Leavelle was one of the two officers who flanked Oswald as he was shot. Leavelle has said, "Just prior to getting on the elevator [to take Oswald downstairs to be transferred], I said, 'Lee, if anybody shoots at you, I hope they're as good a shot as you are.' And he kind of laughed and he said, 'Oh, nobody's going to be shooting at me. You're just being overdramatic.'"

Oswald was buried in Rose Hill Cemetery. His family had prepurchased the plot so, under Texas law, cemetery officials, who didn't want the body, couldn't prevent the burial. Recently, the body was exhumed to verify Oswald's identity. A British writer had suggested that a Soviet agent had been substituted for Oswald during Oswald's stay in Russia. The body's teeth and a mastoid operation scar matched Oswald's pre-defection records.

Oswald's mother, Marguerite Oswald, gave an interview in 1973 to W. C. Martin for *Esquire*. She described herself as "a mother in history." She added, "My signature is worth something. If I am going to sign my name, I am going to get $100 for it to buy some groceries, I also refuse to let anyone record my voice or take my picture without paying." She said that everything in her house was a "historical item" and that she wouldn't part with anything without being paid. She said, "I would also like to sell the headstone from Lee's grave, but I hope it will go to a museum or library. They know they are not going to get it for nothing." She admitted that this might sound bad but claimed, "I am doing the best I can for myself and for my son. I think any man in America would be proud to have a mother like me."

1987   Pennsylvania Avenue and Fourteenth Street, Washington, D.C. Director and choreographer Bob Fosse, 60, collapsed before his hotel and died of a heart attack. His works included *Sweet Charity, The Pajama Game, Damn Yankees, Redhead, Pippin, Dancin', Cabaret, Lenny,* and *All That Jazz.* The last concerned a choreographer who works and plays himself to death. It was autobiographical. Fosse smoked up to six packs of Camels a day, labored long hours, and had three wives. At the time of his death he was opening a revival of *Sweet Charity* at the National Theater, just across the street from where he collapsed. While firemen tried to save his life on the sidewalk, ticketholders walked around the scene to attend his last production.

– November 25 –

1970   Tokyo. Yukio Mishima, 45, Japanese poet, backed by his private army, kidnapped a Japanese general. His purpose was to force a return to militarism, but when he addressed the general's troops, they jeered. Humiliated, he committed *seppuku*—ritual suicide by self-disemboweling.

The job was poorly done. Mishima had planned to pause after his first incision to write the character for "sword," using his own blood. However, the pain was more intense than he had imagined it would be, and he collapsed. Masakatsu Morita, his second-in-command and probable lover, attempted to behead Mishima, as a friend is supposed to do in this circumstance, but failed to sever Mishima's head in two tries. A second associate seized the sword and finished the job. Morita then stabbed himself, and the abler associate whacked off Morita's head.

Mishima's last words were before the laughing soldiers, "Long live the emperor!" and then to a comrade, "I don't think they even heard me." His body was cremated.

During World War II, Mishima feigned tuberculosis to avoid the draft. Later, he became a writer, actor, and bodybuilder. As an actor, he was most successful playing gangsters, but he also made a film depicting *seppuku* in loving detail. He termed it "the ultimate form of masturbation." Following his death, the film was destroyed by his widow.

Mishima loved Nō theater, the traditional theater of Japan, and romanced a number of Nō actresses. The Nō theater is all-male, and the "actresses" are female impersonators. Perhaps Mishima's sexual orientation had something to do with how women viewed him. A Japanese magazine poll revealed that 50 percent of its female readers would kill themselves before they would become his mistress.

– November 26 –

1989   Polo Grounds Housing Project, Harlem. Walter McMillan, 12, was found dead atop one of the building's elevators by housing authority police. They theorized that the boy was "elevator surfing." Children climb onto elevator cages and, while riding them up or down, jump onto neighboring cages, also in motion. Sometimes they let the cables carry them far into the air. McMillan was the eleventh New York youngster since 1984 to die in elevator falls, by cable entanglement, or by being crushed against elevator shaft roofs.

1990   Chicago. Prison authorities, impressed by Samuel Santiago's conduct while serving a three-year sentence for auto theft, released him under a program of high-tech house arrest. Santiago had an electronic bracelet attached to his ankle and a monitoring device placed in his home. If he moved more than 100 feet from the device, it would call the police. Santiago, 18, and his friend Federico Conde, 19, allegedly managed to triumph over technology on this date when they lured Rudy del Castillo to a passageway outside Santiago's home. They pretended to be selling cocaine, then surprised Castillo by robbing him of $1,300 and numerous gold chains. They finished by shooting Castillo to death.

Santiago ordered a pizza the next night and robbed the deliveryman of $70. He didn't shoot him, and the deliveryman called the police. They searched Santiago's home, finding enough evidence to arrest Santiago for murder and robbery.

– November 27 –

1953 Shelton Hotel, Boston. Nobel– and Pulitzer Prize–winning playwright Eugene O'Neill, 65, died of pneumonia. He is best remembered for his play *Long Day's Journey Into Night*. O'Neill had been unable to write for several years because of Parkinson's disease. One of his last acts was to tear up six unfinished plays. He didn't want anyone else to work on them. O'Neill's father was an actor, and the family traveled a great deal. Just before dying, O'Neill looked around him and said, "I knew it! I knew it! Born in a hotel room and God damn it, dying in a hotel room."

1988 Milan. Actor John Carradine, who had appeared in over 500 films, died at 82 of heart and kidney failure. Critic Pauline Kael described Carradine as having a face "like an African mask" and a "voice like molasses dripping."

Carradine's movies included the classics *Stagecoach* (1939), *Drums Along the Mohawk* (1939), *The Grapes of Wrath* (1940), and *The Ten Commandments* (1956). Yet by the end of his career, directors spurned him. Carradine carried on undiminished. His was often the only redeeming element in the grade-Z flicks he starred in, films such as *Sex Kittens Go to College* (1960), *Invasion of the Animal People* (1962), *Astro Zombies* (1968), and *Billy the Kid vs. Dracula* (1966). The last was a story of the Old West, wherein Dracula, one of the Undead and hence impervious to gunfire, becomes a master gunfighter in nocturnal shoot-outs.

– November 28 –

1981 The yacht *Splendor*, Catalina. Actress Natalie Wood (born Natasha Gurdin) was best known for *Miracle on 34th Street* (1947) and *Rebel Without a Cause* (1955). On this date, at 43, she fell into the sea while trying to climb into a dinghy. Her husband Robert Wagner and family friend Christopher Walken, aboard the yacht, were unaware of her plight, as a neighboring loud party covered her screams. Some of the partiers are said to have heard her cries and to have mockingly promised to come to her aid. She couldn't climb into the rubber dinghy, and currents carried her out to sea. A prominent pathologist reconstructed her last moments. She gamely kicked away, holding onto the dinghy, but she couldn't beat the current. Hypothermia caused her to pass out and drown just 200 yards from shore. The current, which had pulled her out, pushed the dinghy back onto the beach minutes later.

Wood once said, "I'm frightened to death of the water, and yet it seems I'm always required to go into it on every one of my pictures. I can swim a little bit, but I'm afraid of water that is dark." A less somber remark of hers was, "The only time a woman really succeeds in changing a man is when he's a baby."

– November 29 –

1939   Clayhidon, Devon, England. The day after celebrating his 36th birthday, "Puss," a tabby cat owned by Mrs. T. Holway, died. He holds the record for domestic feline longevity.

1984   Huntsville, Alabama. "Miss Baker," a fourteen-ounce spider monkey, died at 27 of kidney failure. She was America's first space traveler when, in 1959, she rode an intercontinental ballistic missile into space.

1986   Davenport, Iowa. Debonair movie actor Cary Grant died at 82. He was preparing to give a lecture titled "A Conversation With Cary Grant" for a fund-raising event when he suffered a severe stroke. He was rushed to a nearby hospital, where he died in its emergency room.

Born Archie Leach in Bristol, England, Grant came to America with a troupe of acrobats. He went into vaudeville and was eventually tapped to costar in a Mae West film. He went on to make seventy-two films in his thirty-year career.

Grant said of himself, "They all repeat the rumors that I'm a tightwad and that I'm homosexual. Now, I don't feel that either of those is an insult, but it's all nonsense. And it's only half-true. I am not gay, but I am tight with a dollar. And what's wrong with that? When I was married to Barbara

Hutton, my valet gave an interview saying I was so cheap I kept the buttons when I threw away my shirts. Well, I did, but it seemed a sensible thing to do."

– November 30 –

1900   Paris. Irish writer Oscar Wilde, 46, died in social exile and poverty. Wilde had attained success as a playwright, but his friendship with Lord Alfred Douglas ruined him. Douglas, called "Bosie," hated his father, the eccentric Eighth Marquis of Queensberry of boxing fame. The marquis responded to his son's affair with abusive letters, and, just four days after *The Importance of Being Earnest* opened in London, he sent his card to Wilde's club with "For Oscar Wilde posing as a somdomite [sic]" written upon it. Urged on by Bosie, Wilde sued Queensberry for criminal libel, confident that his peccadillos wouldn't be brought out in court. Indeed, for a time, Wilde's humorous remarks made fools of the opposing side. However, several boys testified that Wilde had had sexual relations with them, and Queensberry was acquitted. Wilde was soon charged with gross indecency. After two trials wherein Wilde's wit was again displayed, he was sent to prison for two years at hard labor. He spent them in solitary confinement. Although Wilde has often been held up as a victim of homophobia, today, some of his purported activities would be termed child abuse.

Prison broke Wilde. Bosie remained devoted, and they were reunited in self-exile in Italy and France upon Wilde's release. They didn't live happily ever after. Petty slights, money problems, ill health, and recriminations plagued them till Wilde's final illness three years later. In September 1900, an ear infection related to an injury Wilde received in prison flared up. In October, he was operated on, but the operation was a failure. Although the nature of his illness is disputed, most probably the infection and operation induced fatal cerebral meningitis. Penniless, Wilde called for champagne as he was dying, saying, "I am dying, as I have lived, beyond my means." He is also said to have remarked upon the poor quality of the wallpaper in his death room, saying, "This wallpaper is killing me; one of us has got to go." On this date, at 1:50 P.M., after being baptized a Roman Catholic, Wilde died. Following death, infection caused Wilde's body to burst, and this has led some medical historians to suggest neurosyphilis as the death cause. Wilde was buried at Père Lachaise Cemetery in Paris.

Wilde once said, "The brotherhood of man isn't a mere poet's dream: it is a most depressing and humiliating reality."

1979   Palm Springs, California. Comic Zeppo (Herbert) Marx, 78, died after a long illness. His doctors withheld the cause of death. He was the last survivor of the Marx Brothers. He served as straight man to their antics but grew tired of the role and became an agent.

– December 1 –

1842   U.S.S. *Somers*, homeward bound from West Africa. Midshipman Philip Spencer, son of Secretary of War John Caulfield Spencer became the only U.S. naval officer hanged for mutiny (two enlisted men were also hanged). He supposedly had plotted to turn his ship to piracy. A later court martial cleared him of the charge.

1973   Tel Aviv. First Prime Minister of Israel David Ben-Gurion, 87, died two weeks after suffering a brain hemorrhage. He was buried at a site he had chosen—a promontory overlooking the biblical wilderness of Zin near the Negev Desert. At his request, there was no eulogy. The Israeli government declared a national minute of silence, signaled by sirens. Because of the precarious state of life in Israel, it was necessary for the authorities to designate a steady siren wail as the signal for mourning and a warbling siren wail as a signal that Arabs were launching an attack.

– December 2 –

1814   Charenton Asylum, France. Marquis Donatien-Alphonse-François de Sade, 74, died of pulmonary congestion related to asthma. Famed for his pornographic writing and bizarre lifestyle, he spent a total of twenty-eight years in prison. The first time was for twelve and a half years, at the behest of his mother-in-law. The French Revolution freed him (one account says his shouting from his tower cell incited the storming of the Bastille), and he became a judge during the Reign of Terror. His mother-in-law appeared in the docket before him, but he was unable to bring himself to send her to the guillotine. He was attacked as a moderate and nearly faced the guillotine himself. He turned to the theater, but after writing a humorous pamphlet in 1801 about Napoleon and Josephine, he was committed to an insane asylum, where he staged plays using inmates as actors. In his will he requested that his coffin remain open forty-eight hours to avoid premature burial.

1859   Charleston, West Virginia. John Brown, 59, was hanged for leading a raid on the Harper's Ferry Arsenal. The U.S. troops that captured him were led by Robert E. Lee and included many who would make names for themselves in the Civil War. John Wilkes Booth attended the hanging. Brown's last words were, when asked upon the scaffold if he was tired, "No, but don't keep me waiting longer than necessary."

– December 3 –

1894   Apia, Samoa. Writer Robert Louis Stevenson, 44, best known for *Treasure Island*, died of apoplexy. He had spent his life as a near invalid after contracting tuberculosis from his mother when he was an infant. With his wife, he searched the world for a healthful climate, finally settling on the island of Samoa in the South Pacific. He remained ill but enjoyed the exotic location. On this date, he felt particularly well and, after a productive morning's writing, went downstairs to speak with his wife. She wasn't cheerful. She had a premonition of doom. Stevenson unsuccessfully tried to change the subject, then helped prepare a lunch of fruit salad. He was mixing mayonnaise when he shouted, clutching at his temples. It was a stroke. He asked his family, "Do I look strange?" then cried, "My head, my head!" collapsing. He lapsed into unconsciousness, dying that evening without a further word.

　　　　Stevenson was popular with the Samoans because of his

storytelling. They built a coffin of tropical hardwoods, rubbed his body with coconut oil, then laboriously carried it to the top of the island's 1,200-foot volcanic mountain, Mount Vaea. He was buried there, high above his chosen earthly paradise.

Treasure Island began when Stevenson drew a fanciful treasure map to entertain his stepson on a rainy day. The boy wanted stories to go with the map, and Stevenson obliged. He had so much fun that he decided to write a full-length book.

1988   Oakland, California. According to his passengers, Darryl Ray Poole, 19, wanted to make traffic speed up, so he shot Lawrence Ellingsen, 53, the driver of the car ahead of him, in the back of the head, killing him. Poole wanted to drive faster so that one of his three passengers could use a bathroom.

– December 4 –

1952   England. A killer smog killed 4,000 people. As many as 8,000 later died from its less-immediate effects.

1984   Peterborough, New Hampshire. Dr. John Rock died at 94 of a heart attack. He helped develop the birth control pill. Rock was a Roman Catholic and tried, unsuccessfully, to convince the Church that the pill conformed to its teachings, as it used natural hormones.

– December 5 –

1791   Vienna. Austrian composer Wolfgang Amadeus Mozart, 35, who sometimes composed while playing billiards, died of malnutrition, overwork, and kidney disease. He was composing a Requiem Mass and his last words were: "Did I not tell you that I was writing this for myself?" Mozart was deeply in debt and, unknown to his wife, his coffin was dumped in a pauper's grave.

1951   Greenville, South Carolina. Outfielder "Shoeless" Joe Jackson, 63, died of natural causes. He had been barred for life from baseball for complicity in the 1919 White Sox World Series bribery scheme known as the "Black Sox Scandal."

Jackson, an illiterate southern country boy, said he had refused to go along when his teammates connived with gamblers to throw the World Series to the Cincinnati Reds for $10,000 each (Jackson's salary was $6,000 a year). He said he tried to sit out the game, then to give back the money, then to tell Charles Comiskey, the team owner, of the plot, and finally, when Comiskey just kept him waiting in his outer office, Jackson claimed, he decided to play the best game he could. He made no errors and set a World Series record (till 1964) of twelve hits.

When the scandal broke, on the advice of Comiskey's lawyer, Jackson and the others confessed before a grand jury. Later, their testimony disappeared and they were acquited of criminal charges, but Baseball Commissioner Judge Kenesaw Mountain Landis ignored the acquittal and barred all the players from professional baseball for life.

Jackson, 31 and at his prime, played semi-pro in the South for ten years, managed for a few more, then opened a liquor store with his wife. The childless couple were popular with the local kids, whom they indulged. Jackson seldom talked of his fall, but, according to a 1989 *People* magazine article, on his deathbed, Jackson took his brother's hand and said, "I'm going to meet the greatest umpire of all—and he knows I'm innocent."

Jackson was nicknamed "Shoeless" because as a boy he had played ball in his stocking feet to avoid wearing out his only pair of shoes.

1983   Cartoonist Charles Schulz based his *Peanuts* character Charlie Brown on a close friend who was inept at sports and generally unlucky. He also used his friend's name. On this date, the original Charlie Brown died at 57.

– December 6 –

1889   New Orleans. Confederate President Jefferson Davis, 81, died after catching a severe cold, which was aggravated by a recurrence of malaria. His last words were in regard to a dose of medicine he was offered, "Please excuse me, I cannot take it." Davis's funeral was elaborate, and he was mourned throughout the South. His body, in Confederate uniform, was buried in Richmond, Virginia, in the same cemetery that holds U.S. Presidents Monroe and Tyler.

Years earlier, Texan Sam Houston, a Unionist, observed, "Yes, I know Mr. Davis. He is as ambitious as Lucifer, cold as a snake, and what he touches will not prosper." This was the case with Davis's Presidency. He was obsessed with detail and inadequate in grand strategy. Unlike Lincoln, who mobilized the North, Davis couldn't even get Southern states to share supplies.

During the war, while walking the streets of Richmond, Davis was approached by a ragged Rebel soldier who asked him if he were the Confederate president. Davis said yes, and the soldier exulted, "I knew it, I knew it—you look just like a goddamn postage stamp."

Davis spent two years in prison following the war but wasn't tried for treason because of a technicality. He refused amnesty, so when he died, he wasn't a citizen of the United States. A few years before his death, Davis toured the South to great applause. He gave speeches proclaiming the righteousness of the Confederate effort in such terms that the *New York Tribune* called him "an unrepentant old villain." Nonetheless, in the last speech of the tour he said, "The past is dead; let it bury its dead, its hopes and its aspirations. Before you lies…a future of expanding national glory, before which all the world shall stand amazed. Let me beseech you to lay aside all rancor, all bitter sectional feeling, and to take your places in the ranks of those who will bring about a consummation devoutly to be wished—a reunited country."

On this date in 1989, several hundred people, many in Confederate uniform, gathered in Montgomery, Alabama, to celebrate Davis's life. Actors reenacted Davis's swearing in, and there was a thunderous cannon salute. Spectators sang "Dixie," waving Confederate flags. A local professor of education claimed, "The ignorance is so pervasive about the war being over slavery. Out of the 50,000 Alabamians who died in the war, 90 percent owned no one," and "The majority of the people here today believe Jefferson Davis was right and I do, too." John Brown's body probably left off a-mouldering to spin awhile.

– December 7 –

1817   Bond Street, London. William Bligh, 64, captain of the
H.M.S. *Bounty,* and subject of history's most famous mutiny
died during a visit to his Bond Steet doctor. The cause was an
internal complaint that was most likely a malignant growth.
He was buried in St. Paul's churchyard, Lambeth.

Bligh was cast adrift with eighteen others in a small boat
following the mutiny. It was hardly an act of mercy. They
were in poorly explored waters, low on supplies, and the few
islands nearby were inhabited by hostile natives. Bligh managed to navigate nearly 4,000 miles of ocean to reach safety.
With a new ship, he went on to complete the *Bounty*'s mission
of gathering breadfruit plants. He also published his own
account of the mutiny in 1790.

Bligh's discipline wasn't excessive by the standards of the
time, but he did have a temper and was a martinet. After the
delights of Tahiti, his crew didn't respond well to his style of
command. Fletcher Christian, who had enjoyed the company
of a beautiful island princess, considered suicide before
turning to mutiny. Some of the crew remained on Tahiti,
where they were captured and returned to England. Three of
these were hanged. The mutineers aboard the *Bounty* established a colony on Pitcairn Island with a group of Tahitians.
They didn't live happily there. Ned Young, who helped
instigate the mutiny, talked the male Tahitians into murdering Christian and all the mutineers except himself and his
friend Jack Adams. Young then talked the female Tahitians
into killing the male Tahitians. Young died of cancer in 1793.
Adams organized the survivors into a community that still
exists.

Bligh was to experience another humiliation when, as
governor of New South Wales, Australia, he was caught up in
a rebellion and, after being dragged from under his bed, was
again nearly killed. After two years in jail, he returned to
England, where he was made a vice admiral and retired.

1941   The Japanese attacked Pearl Harbor, Hawaii. 2,403 Americans died and 1,178 were wounded. Before the war ended, 16
million Americans served in her armed forces. Over 405,000
died and over 671,000 were wounded.

The Japanese military had been trying to conquer China

for ten years, causing hundreds of thousands of deaths. In reaction to this and the Japanese alliance with Nazi Germany, the United States cut off sales of American oil and steel. The Japanese knew they couldn't continue their China war without these resources, so they decided to take them from other Asian nations. To prevent the United States from interfering, the Japanese decided to destroy U.S. naval power in the Pacific. Their sneak attack on Pearl Harbor directly triggered all the horrors of the Pacific War—including the atomic bombings of Japan.

At Pearl Harbor, many sailors were trapped below decks aboard partially submerged ships and signaled their plight to the outside world by hammering. With few exceptions, shipyard workers had to work on less damaged vessels so that they could leave the harbor before another attack could destroy them. The unanswered tapping stopped December 23.

In 1990, a Florida man, whose father had been killed at Pearl Harbor, purchased a Sony VCR. He consulted the manual and discovered that the example for how to set the VCR's clock used the date of December 7. Sony apologized.

– December 8 –

1859   Edinburgh, Scotland. Author Thomas De Quincey, 74, best known for *Confessions of an English Opium-Eater*, died of natural causes after thirty years in seclusion. He was a packrat and when his lodgings would become too jammed to live in, he would just lock the door and move to new lodgings, which he would soon fill up. According to the *Dictionary of National Biography*, De Quincey was an unusual father. "At home he was charming, though frequently alarming his children by setting fire to his hair during readings." De Quincey once said, "If once a man indulges himself in murder, very soon he comes to think little of robbing; and from robbing he next comes to drinking and Sabbath-breaking, and from that to incivility and procrastination."

1978   Jerusalem. Former Israeli Prime Minister (1967–74) Golda Meir, 80, died of a liver infection and jaundice following viral hepatitis. She had suffered from leukemia for twelve years.

She was born in Kiev in Russia. Her father brought the family to the United States to avoid pogroms. Meir lived in Milwaukee and Denver before going to Israel in 1921 as a Zionist. She was well known as a tough leader.

In 1973, Pope Paul VI invited her to the Vatican. There, Meir said to an associate, "Listen, what's going on here? Me, the daughter of Moshe Mabovitch the carpenter, going to meet the pope of the Catholics?" The associate replied, "Just a moment, Golda. Carpentry is a very respectable profession around here."

1980   New York City. John Lennon, 40, was shot in front of the Dakota Hotel. He and wife Yoko Ono were returning from an evening recording session. Lennon, long reclusive, was making a comeback with a new album. His killer, Mark David Chapman, fancied himself the hero of the novel *The Catcher in the Rye*, saving children from hypocrisy. Lennon was cremated, and two hearses were used to deliver his ashes to his wife Yoko Ono at the Dakota. The first was a decoy for the press and fans. The ashes were disguised as a Christmas gift to prevent their theft.

Chapman was sentenced to twenty years to life. In 1990, he was interviewed at Attica State Prison by the *Rochester Democrat and Chronicle*. Chapman claimed that his life of disappointment had boiled over when he saw a picture of Lennon in a Beatles photo book. "I saw him on the roof of the gabled, luxurious Dakota apartment. And I became hurt. Enraged at what I perceived to be his phoniness." Chapman hung out in front of the Dakota Hotel with an album for Lennon to autograph and a pistol to kill him. In a quote that revealed more probable motives than battling hypocrisy—envy, a thirst for notoriety, and the obsessive fan's urge to touch the life of the beloved celebrity—Chapman said, "When his limousine pulled up, he got out and he looked at me. I'm sure he remembered me."

Lennon once said, "Life is what happens while you are making other plans."

1991   Fort Pierce, Florida. Kimberly Bergalis, 23, died of AIDS acquired during dental work from a dentist who continued his practice knowing he had the disease. Four other patients also contracted the disease from him. Bergalis suspected the dentist of being the source of her illness, but she was attacked by doubters who insisted that it was impossible to contract the disease through dental work and that she must have gotten the disease through drug use or unsafe sex. It was only after Bergalis proved she didn't use drugs and that she was a virgin that her charges were considered. Testing proved she had contracted the disease from the dentist.

Bergalis campaigned for legislation requiring mandatory testing of health care workers and patients. AIDS activists, the American Medical Association, and the American Dental Association oppose such testing. Bergalis was scheduled to appear before a congressional committee, but when her appearance was repeatedly delayed, it was suggested that she was being stalled so that her illness would kill her before she could testify. Bergalis held on to life and testified, but the legislation wasn't enacted.

At the time of her death, Bergalis couldn't eat or speak and could barely breathe. Her mother said, as she and her husband put Bergalis to bed, "We want you to go to sleep, get a peaceful rest and think about whether you want to face all this suffering and torment again tomorrow." Bergalis died in her sleep.

– December 9 –

1792   Near Charleston, South Carolina. The first formal human cremation in America occurred. Diplomat Henry Laurens, who died in his 68th year, had a fear of being buried alive, so he instructed his son to wrap his body in twelve yards of tow cloth and burn it on the family estate in Mepkin. Apparently, Laurens had no fear of being burned alive.

1972   Santa Monica, California. Gossip columnist Louella Oettinger Parsons died of generalized arteriosclerosis. She was 91—or at least that was the gossip.

– December 10 –

1946   New York City. Writer Damon Runyon, 62, died of cancer. Runyon, whose work dealt with urban characters, was born in

Manhattan—Kansas. He once said, "All life is six to five against." And on another occasion he said, "The race may not be to the swift nor the victory to the strong, but that's how you bet."

1989 Los Angeles. Lindsay Crosby, 51, was one of Bing Crosby's sons. Like his brothers, he had a trust fund that supplied him with an income of over $100,000 a year. Also like his brothers, Lindsay suffered from alcoholism and marital problems. Unlike his brothers, Lindsay was a manic-depressive, and his trust fund, based upon oil income, was about to be halved. To worsen matters, Crosby, who bought cars and houses for his drinking buddies while in his manic state, was nearly $200,000 in debt. On this date, Crosby visited his third ex-wife, Susan Marlin Crosby. He was concerned for his four children, repeatedly saying "I don't want to be a burden." He returned to his suburban condo, where he killed himself by firing a .22-caliber rifle into his head.

– December 11 –

1964 Los Angeles. Singer Sam Cooke, 33, brought a girl to a motel room, but she changed her mind, took her clothing and his pants, and ran. Cooke ran after her, wearing only his overcoat. The girl hid in a phone booth. Cooke confronted the motel clerk, Bertha Lee Franklin, 55, accusing her of concealing the girl. Franklin said he hit her twice. She grabbed a gun that she kept under the counter and fired three times, killing Cooke. Cooke's most popular song was "Darling, You Send Me."

– December 12 –

1968 New York City. Actress Tallulah Bankhead, 65, died of double pneumonia. She was famous for her loquaciousness. Fred Allen said of her, "A parrot around Tallulah must feel as frustrated as a kleptomaniac in a piano store." She said of herself that she was "as pure as the driven slush," "I've tried several varieties of sex. The conventional position makes me claustrophobic and the others give me a stiff neck or lockjaw," and "If I had to live my life again, I'd make the same mistakes, only sooner." Tennessee Williams observed, "I suppose you could say Tallulah was a tramp, in the elegant sense." Toward the end of her lively life, Bankhead was approached by a fan who asked her if she was the famous movie star Tallulah Bankhead. She answered, "What's left of her."

– December 13 –

1784   Off Fleet Street, London. Lexicographer and poet Dr. Samuel Johnson, 74, died of high blood pressure and renal disease following a life of ill health and an obsessive fear of death. At birth, he was thought still-born, but vigorous slapping elicited a cry. He was then accidentally nursed on cow's milk infected with tuberculosis, which produced the gland infection scrofula, then called the "king's evil" because it was thought that the touch of the king or queen could cure it. The three-year-old Johnson was presented to Queen Anne, but her touch proved ineffectual, so surgery removed the diseased glands. In the meantime, the illness blinded his left eye and deafened his left ear. Johnson went on to endure facial tics, gout, asthma, bronchitis, temporary aphasia, dropsy, emphysema, gallstones, a scrotum swelled by fluid, manic-depression, and persistent flatulence. In his last days, he was bed-bound and incontinent and could barely breathe. His last words were to the daughter of a visiting friend, "God bless you, my dear...I am dying now." At seven in the evening on this date, he stopped breathing. He was buried at Westminster Abbey.

James Boswell, Johnson's biographer, wrote that when he asked Johnson whether we should strengthen ourselves to face death, Johnson said, "No, Sir, let it alone. It matters not how a man dies, but how he lives. The act of dying is not of importance, it lasts so short a time." Unfortunately, this was not true for Johnson.

– December 14 –

1799   Mount Vernon, Virginia. George Washington, 67, first U.S. president, died following bleeding for a severe case of laryngitis, which he contracted after going riding in a snowstorm. Washington said to his doctors, "I die hard, but I am not afraid to go...I feel myself going. I thank you for your attention; but I pray you to take no more trouble for me. Let me go quietly, as I cannot last long." His last words were, "'Tis well."

His doctors' treatment included a molasses, vinegar, and butter drink, sal volatile applied to the throat, a foot bath, Spanish fly applied to the throat to raise blisters (thought curative), steam from vinegar and water, sage tea laced with vinegar, calomel (a poison), tartar emetic (which caused extreme dehydration due to diarrhea), a mustard plaster applied to his legs, a wheat bran poultice applied to the throat, and lots of bleeding.

Washington requested that his body be buried two days after his death, probably to avoid premature burial. Napoleon ordered ten days of mourning in France. The British Navy fired salutes in the English Channel to its respected foe. Washington's brother had served in the British Navy, and Washington himself enlisted at 15, but his clinging mother pleaded with him to stay at home where he was needed, and he did so.

Washington said of becoming president, "My movements to the chair of Government will be accompanied by feelings not unlike those of a culprit who is going to the place of his execution."

1920   South Bend, Indiana. Notre Dame football star George "the Gipper" Gip, 25, died unexpectedly of pneumonia and a throat infection. His last words were to his coach Knute Rockne, "One day when the going is tough and a big game is hanging in the balance, ask the team to win one for the Gipper. I don't know where I'll be, Rock, but I'll know about it, and I'll be happy." Years later, Rockne did just that, and his team won the day.

1934   Bremen. Fourteen touring actors were killed when their bus driver drove around a crossing guard and into the path of a speeding train. The train was Chancellor Adolf Hitler's special express train. It remained on the rails. Had it slipped off, Hitler might have been killed. He climbed down from the train, walked back to the wreck, gave the corpses the Nazi salute, and helped pick them up.

1944   Beverly Hills. Mexican-born actress Lupe Velez, 34, was a genuine "spitfire." Her numerous lovers included John

Gilbert and Gary Cooper. In 1933, she married Johnny Weissmuller, but she was soon divorced and back hunting cowboys, stuntmen, and bit players.

Lupe's career soured. Deep in debt and pregnant (the man didn't want to marry her), she decided to kill herself. She ordered lots of flowers, had a last meal of her favorite Mexican foods with friends, and then, in a silver evening gown, surrounded by candles and flowers, she lay down upon a couch and swallowed most of a bottle of Seconal. She planned for the authorities to find the elaborate scene and be awed by her stilled beauty.

Unfortunately, the spicy food and the pills didn't sit well in her stomach. She ran for the bathroom to vomit, slipped on the smooth tiles, jammed her head into the toilet, and drowned. It was in this less-than-awesome position that her dead body was found.

– December 15 –

1944   Director of the U.S. Air Force Band Major Glenn Miller, 39, was lost flying from England to Paris. His pilot, Major Norman Baesell, said just before takeoff when Miller expressed some reluctance, "What's the matter, Miller, do you want to live forever?"

It was assumed that bad weather had caused his plane to crash, but in 1984, a British RAF veteran said that British bombers were responsible. The bombers had aborted their mission because of the weather and were flying back to their base. To prevent landing accidents, the bombers jettisoned their bombs over the Channel. The veteran said the concussion of the bombs exploding knocked a plane matching Miller's out of the sky. As there had been no action against the enemy, the bomber crews weren't debriefed, and no one associated the incident with Miller, as officials didn't announce his disappearance till much later. The veteran didn't make the connection till he saw a film about Miller on television in the 1980s.

1966   Los Angeles. Cartoonist Walt Disney, 65, died of circulatory collapse following treatment for a cancerous lung lesion probably caused by smoking. Rumors that he was frozen and stored beneath Disneyland's Tomorrow Land have circulated, but quite the opposite procedure was used. Disney was cremated. He was buried in Forest Lawn Cemetery in Glendale, California, following a private service.

Disney's first cartoon character wasn't a mouse. It was a rabbit called Oswald. Many of Disney's enterprises brought him to the verge of bankruptcy, so to save money, Disney was the voice of Mickey for years. Alfred Hitchcock said, "Disney, of course, has the best casting. If he doesn't like an actor, he just tears him up." Disney said of his rodent creation, "I love Mickey Mouse more than any woman I've ever known." Disney originally called his rodent "Mortimer Mouse," but his wife said it was a horrible name.

– December 16 –

1965   Nice. British author W. Somerset Maugham, 91, best known for *Of Human Bondage* and *The Moon and Sixpence*, died of lung congestion. Shortly before, Maugham told his nephew, Robin Maugham, "Dying is a very dull, dreary affair. And my advice to you is to have nothing whatever to do with it."

Maugham once said, "American women expect to find in their husbands the perfection that English women only hope to find in their butlers."

– December 17 –

A.D.   According to Biblical scholars, for the second time Lazarus
63   died.
1943   Williamsport, Pennsylvania. Annie Knight Gregory, 100, died of natural causes. She was the last real daughter of the American Revolution. Her father, Richard Knight, had enlisted with his father in a Pennsylvania regiment. Knight was just 11 years old, but served as a drummer boy and wintered at Valley Forge. He went on to fight again as a captain of infantry in the War of 1812, and then fathered Annie when he was 77. Annie lived to see two of her own great-grandsons enlist in the U.S. Army for World War II.
1957   Witham, Essex, England. English mystery writer Dorothy

Leigh Sayers, 64, died of coronary thrombosis. She had been Christmas shopping and collapsed, amid her parcels, as she entered her home. Her gardener found her there. Her most famous creation was the aristocratic detective Lord Peter Whimsey. Sayers was said to have had a crush on her own fictional hero. She abandoned mystery fiction for religious writing in the 1940s. She said, "One of the reasons I no longer write detective stories is the income tax. Anything that is liable to sell well may be ruinous."

– December 18 –

1989   Tamarac, Florida. Jerry Olson, 46, was unemployed, depressed, and, after being thrown out by his sister, living in his van. His brother, Bob, 56, suffered from cardiomyopathy and had been on a waiting list for a transplant heart for three years. Olson decided to kill himself so that his brother could have his heart. An Elvis fan, he left his daughter, whom he had named Lisa Marie, a tape recording. In part, he said, "Uncle Bob's got everything to live for. And if they find out he can use it and Uncle Bob wants it, I'm going to be his donor, Lisa. I figure I could do more good for him than myself." The tape contained a rendition of "I'll Be Home for Christmas" sung by Olson, which he wished played at his funeral. A note on his person said he had had "too many downs and no ups for me on this roller coaster ride of life."

On this date, Olson parked his van by the door of Tamarac's University Community Hospital, then placed a gun in his mouth and pulled the trigger. Unfortunately, it was at least ten minutes before a nurse leaving for home discovered Olson slumped over his steering wheel. After an hour of heart massage, Olson died. The delay in discovery had rendered his heart useless for transplant purposes.

– December 19 –

1959   Houston. Walter Williams, 117, the last Civil War veteran, died peacefully. He had fought for the Confederacy. John B.

Salling, 113, a fellow Confederate soldier, had died on March 16, 1959, in Kingsport, Tennessee.

1983   Potsdam, New York. Professor A. Steven Giannell de Jannell, 61, was a child psychology expert devoted to the study of violence and was known for his letters to local newspapers decrying the brutality of the police, government, and authority in general. It seemed he was always battling someone for the sake of nonviolence. Despite this, de Jannell's wife was seeking a divorce, charging cruel and inhuman treatment, and de Jannell's 13-year-old son, Steven Jr., was notorious for throwing such violent temper tantrums that the police were frequently called to control him. The boy's grandmother, Flora Giannell, 85, had died following a heart attack while swimming in the family pool. Police didn't suspect foul play, but Steven Jr., devoted to her, blamed his father. Father and son had screaming arguments that shocked even the police. Consequently, when the house was quiet for a long period of time, the police were called in to investigate.

On this date, police entered the de Jannell home and discovered the place a wreck. Even the Christmas tree was overturned and torn apart. They also found the corpses of Steven Jr., his 16-year-old sister Robin, and de Jannell. The brutal killer wasn't the boy. The father had shot the boy, stabbed the girl, and then stabbed himself. Police speculated that the boy had thrown another tantrum, causing the professor to go berserk.

A fellow member of de Jannell's psychology department said, "If Steve had a fault, it was that the kids could do no wrong. Steve never disciplined them."

Professor de Jannell had once written, "You don't correct teenagers by throwing the book at them, but by reaching them and motivating them appropriately."

– December 20 –

1930   Poona, India. James Brandon, formerly of Nashville, Tennessee, had lived in a cave as a holy man in India for 15 years. He treated the sick with the help of a pair of "God-given spectacles." He made a good income until a band of young vandals looted his cave of everything—including the spectacles. He offered a reward, but they weren't returned and on this date, Brandon died. The coroner ruled the cause was "a broken heart, superinduced by a belief that God had deprived him of the divine power of healing." Brandon was cremated upon a pile of sacred sandalwood in the Hindu fashion.

1987   Philippine Sea. The 2,215-ton ferry *Dona Paz* and the 629-ton oil tanker *Victor* collided. The tanker exploded, and both vessels sank in flames. Passengers were forced to jump into the sea, which was covered with burning oil and infested with sharks. Fifteen hundred to 3,000 died. The number is uncertain, as the ferry was heavily overloaded. Only twenty-six survived. The ferry's captain had turned over the bridge to an inexperienced seaman so he could drink beer and watch a videotape with his officers.

– December 21 –

1940   Los Angeles. Writer F. Scott Fitzgerald (the "F" stood for Francis, after Francis Scott Key, a distant relative) died of a heart attack at 44. He was visiting with Sheilah Graham, who was going out to purchase some chocolate for him. His last words were to her when she asked him if he'd like some Hershey bars: "Good enough. They'll be fine."

Scott's works included *The Great Gatsby* and *Tender Is the Night*. He gave the name "The Jazz Age" to the 1920s and enjoyed great success then; however, by 1940 none of his books were in print. Fitzgerald's finances were in a precarious state, his wife, Zelda, had sunk into incurable mental illness, and Fitzgerald had become an alcoholic. In 1934, he wrote, "It grows harder to write because there's much less weather than when I was a boy and practically no men and women." In 1936, he compared himself to a cracked plate that "one wonders whether it is worth preserving." He wound up working as a scriptwriter in Hollywood and was beginning to reassemble his life when he died.

According to Ernest Hemingway, Fitzgerald was convinced that his male member was too small. Hemingway assuaged Fitzgerald's doubts by taking him to an art museum and showing him the Greek statues.

Fitzgerald once observed, "Show me a hero and I will write you a tragedy."

1945   Mannheim, Germany. General George S. Patton, 60, who had survived World War I and World War II, died in his sleep from complications following injuries received when his olive drab 1938 Cadillac limousine struck a military truck on December 9. His neck was broken, paralyzing him from the neck down. Patton was buried in a military cemetery in Luxembourg under a standard-issue headstone among thousands of similar graves of men killed in World War II. Patton was noted for his uninhibited remarks. Probably the most famous of these was: "The object of war is not to die for your country but to make the other dumb bastard die for his."

– December 22 –

1989   2:40 A.M. Interstate 390, Greece, New York. James Vandermeer, 25, had been drinking, but this didn't stop him from driving. Gilbert Nettles, Jr., 26, was also driving on Interstate 390 when his car broke down. He was near an exit, so he started walking. Vandermeer drove his car straight into Nettles, killing him. The impact was so severe that Nettles' corpse was embedded in the smashed windshield. This didn't bother the drunken Vandermeer. He continued driving down the highway, traveling nine miles before a Monroe County sheriff's deputy pulled him over. Vandermeer was charged with felony drunken driving.

– December 23 –

1978   Chicago. Robert Piest, 15, had said he was going to see a builder about a summer job. When Piest disappeared, police secured a search warrant for the builder's home. In the crawl space of the ranch-style house, they discovered the first two of thirty-three bodies of young boys. The builder, John Wayne Gacy, 46, had lured the boys to his home, had had sex with many, and had murdered them all by strangulation. Gacy often entertained sick children as a clown and was active in the local Democratic party. A photo of himself with then–

First Lady Rosalyn Carter decorated his wall. Gacy was sentenced to death but has avoided that penalty through legal maneuvers. He occupies his time painting landscapes.

1982   Los Angeles. Actor Jack Webb, 62, died of a heart attack. He is remembered as the flattopped, clipped-speaking Sergeant Joe Friday of *Dragnet*. Webb was also that TV show's producer and director. Webb was popular with police everywhere, but he had especially helped improve the image of the Los Angeles Police Department. As a tribute, the chief of that police force ordered flags flown at half-mast at police buildings throughout the city.

– December 24 –

1954   Houston. Rhythm-and-blues singer Johnny Ace, 22, was waiting backstage before a performance. For some reason, he passed the time playing Russian roulette. He lost. Within weeks, songsters recorded several postgame tributes, including "Johnny Has Gone," "Why, Johnny, Why," "Johnny Ace's Last Letter," "Salute to Johnny Ace," and "Johnny's Still Singing."

1980   Aumuhle, West Germany. Admiral Karl Doenitz, 89, died of a heart attack. Doenitz masterminded the U-boat war, which sank 14 million tons of Allied shipping and nearly won the war for the Nazis. After Hitler shot himself, Doenitz became Hitler's successor and thereby "Der Führer II." This lasted for a week, while the German surrender was completed. Doenitz spent ten years in Spandau prison for war crimes.

– December 25 –

1946   Hollywood. W. C. Fields (born William Claude Dukenfield), 66, when prodded by the begging of his mistress Carlotta Monti to stir in his hospital bed, pressed a finger to his lips, winked, and lost consciousness. At dawn on this date, he died of liver damage and a stomach hemorrhage. During Fields's last days, a visitor to his hospital room found Fields reading a Bible. The amazed visitor asked Fields what he was doing. Fields replied, "Just looking for loopholes."

Fields died on Christmas, of which he said, "I believed in Christmas until I was eight years old. I had saved up some money carrying ice in Philadelphia, and I was going to buy my mother a copper-bottomed clothes boiler for Christmas. I kept the money hidden in a brown crock in the coal bin. My father found the crock. He did exactly what I would have done in his place. He stole the money. And ever since then I've remembered nobody on Christmas, and I want nobody to remember me either."

Fields isn't buried in Philadelphia, as is widely thought. His body was buried in Glendale's Forest Lawn (his wife, a Catholic, refused to have it cremated despite Fields's wishes). Before he died, he suggested as his epitaph, "Here lies W. C. Fields. On the whole, I would rather be here than in Philadelphia." It wasn't used.

Of the drinking that would kill him, Fields said, "A blonde drove me to drink, and my one regret is that I never thanked her," and "I make it a habit to keep a reasonable supply of medicinal stimulants on hand in case I encounter a venomous snake—which I also always keep on hand."

Fields was once a professional "drowner" in Atlantic City. He would fake that he was drowning, another employee would "save" him, and food peddlers would work the crowd that gathered.

1977   Vevey, Switzerland. Comic actor Charlie Chaplin, 88, died of old age a few hours before his family was to begin their holiday celebrations. Chaplin had made his last public appearance at a nearby circus. He watched the performance, then left after shaking hands with a clown. In 1922, when a producer was planning a life of Christ, Chaplin was keenly interested. He said, "I want to play the role of Jesus. I'm the logical choice. I look the part. I'm a Jew. And I'm a comedian." He didn't get the part. James Thurber said of him: "He was one of the great comedians, and one of the worst appreciators of comedy outside himself and his own genius." Chaplin once said, "In the end, everything is a gag."

Chaplin's body was stolen on March 1, 1978. It was recovered eleven weeks later in a cornfield ten miles away. Two refugees, a Pole and a Bulgarian, had held it for a ransom of $250,000. Police traced a ransom call to a phone booth, arresting the Pole before he could hang up. The body was returned to Vevey.

– December 26 –

1913   Mexico. Ambrose Bierce, while traveling with Pancho Villa's army, wrote his last letter, then disappeared in his 72nd year. The letter read: "Goodbye, if you hear of my being stood up against a Mexican stone wall and shot to rags please know that I think it is a pretty good way to depart this life. It beats old age, disease, or falling down the cellar stairs. To be a Gringo in Mexico—ah, that's euthanasia!"

1972   Kansas City, Missouri. Harry Truman, 88, thirty-third U.S. president, died. He had caught a cold that settled in his lungs. As fluid filled his lungs, his heart weakened till it failed on this date. Truman's last words: "I'm a broken machine, but I'm ready." Truman was buried at the Truman Library in Independence, Missouri.

Bess Truman, the First Lady, couldn't find a laundry in Washington that met her standards, so she sent the First Laundry home to Missouri to be washed, with the exception of Harry's underwear, which he washed himself. The First Mother-in-Law lived with the Trumans for twenty-six years but always called Harry "Mr. Truman" and was convinced Bess had married beneath her. She also disparaged Harry's abilities as president and said other men, including "that nice man, Thomas E. Dewey," would be better presidents.

– December 27 –

1969   Zambia. Hippopotamuses in the Namwala River were reported to have killed nine. Each year several hundred Africans are killed by hippos. The hippos knock them out of boats, drag them under water, or chew them up in jaws that open to four feet.

The *Las Vegas Sun* reported an incident wherein the width of a hippo's jaws led to an unfortunate conclusion. Austrian circus dwarf Franz Dasch was performing stunts upon a trampoline in front of a crowd of 7,000 when he misbounced and hurtled off the device. Hilda the Hippo was standing nearby yawning. Dasch fell into her mouth, Hilda gagged, and the dwarf was swallowed to thunderous applause. He suffocated before circus attendants could extract him.

1988   Dallas. Tim Rhea, 19, and Jerry Apodaca, 21, were debating whether it was possible for a man to knock a pistol from an attacker's hand without getting plugged in the process. Apodaca got his .45-caliber automatic and, with Rhea playing the role of the defender, the pair set to testing their theories through experimentation. They proved conclusively that the defender was likely to get shot when Apodaca accidentally pulled the trigger. Apodaca called an ambulance, then, full of remorse, shot and killed himself. Rhea died shortly afterward in the hospital.

– December 28 –

1935   New York City. Clarence Day, known for writing *Life With Father*, died at 61. Day had been stricken with severe arthritis in his mid-twenties and had spent the rest of his life an invalid. He took up writing in his forties. He had little success but was sure his latest work would be a hit when he sent it to his publisher. However, the printer lost the manuscript. The publisher, spurred by the knowledge that this was the only copy and that Day was dying, searched everywhere—the printer's, the warehouse where waste paper was sent and even the paper mill in Connecticut that recycled the waste paper. It was there that the manuscript was found just as it was about to be dumped into a vat of acid.

1983   Marquesas Way Pier, Los Angeles. In the early 1960s, Dennis Wilson, with his two brothers, a cousin, and a friend, formed the Beach Boys. Wilson was the only member who was a surfer, and the hit "Surfin'," which launched their career, was his idea. But with the group's success, Wilson became involved in drugs and alcohol. For a time he was friendly with Charles Manson and his "family." After this association ended, Wilson received death threats from the group.

    To encourage Wilson to get medical care, he was excluded from the Beach Boys till he got his problems with drugs and alcohol under control. He finally sought treatment on December 23, 1983, but the Christmas holiday intervened. Perhaps as a last fling, Wilson partied for days with some friends on a yacht. He had once had a similar boat, which he had anchored on the same spot. Wilson recalled that after an argument with his ex-wife, he had tossed mementos overboard. He began to dive in the twelve-foot-deep water to see what he could retrieve, despite his having drunk a great deal. Wilson found several pieces of junk and a silver-framed photo of himself and his ex-wife. He stopped diving to continue drinking, then decided to make one last dive. He apparently misjudged how long he was under, ran out of breath, and drowned. Wilson, 39, was buried at sea.

Fellow Beach Boy Mike Love said of Wilson, "He was very suicidal about life. It was amazing he lived as long as he did with the things he did to his body."

– December 29 –

1170   Canterbury Cathedral, England. Four knights murdered Thomas à Becket, who was about 52, was archbishop of Canterbury and head of the Church in England. Henry II was angry with Becket because of Becket's loyalty to the church. It is said that in an outburst, Henry rhetorically asked who would rid him of "this troublesome priest." The knights took his remark as an order the obliged, cutting Becket down in front of the altar at Canterbury Cathedral. Henry later did public penance for the death by being whipped. Four hundred years later, during the Reformation, Henry VIII ordered Becket's bones burned. According to legend, Becket's skull was saved and hidden by priests in Canterbury Cathedral.

1975   Sundbury, Pennsylvania. Natural food expert Euell Gibbons, 64, died of a stomach ailment.

– December 30 –

1916   Petrograd, Russia. Grigory Yefimovich Novykh, 44, known as Rasputin, was assassinated by four aristocrats fearful of his influence on the czarina. They lured the sex-obsessed monk to a castle with the wife of one of the killers. They reportedly poisoned him with enough cyanide for ten men, homosexually raped him, castrated him, stabbed him several times, and, as he was still fighting, shot him six times. They bound him in chains and carried him to a frozen river, where they hacked a hole in the ice and shoved him in. When the body was discovered, it became evident that he had still been alive. He had freed himself, swum under the ice to the other side of the river, and smashed through it with his head. There, he finally died of exposure and drowning. Rasputin's escapades hastened the Russian Revolution and, when the czar fell, Rasputin's body was pulled from the chapel the czarina had dedicated to him and burned on a pyre.

– December 31 –

1948 Hollywood. Kay Van Riper, 40, who had helped write the "Andy Hardy" film series, which always ended happily, was found dead of an overdose of sleeping pills.

1985 De Kalb, Texas. Singer Ricky Nelson, 45, was killed in an airplane fire probably caused by a faulty cabin heater. Rumors of drug involvement in the crash were disproved.

Nelson's biographer Joel Selvin says that Ricky's father, Ozzie Nelson, predicted in 1956 that rock and roll was going to be a huge success and coached Ricky into becoming a pseudo-Elvis. It was a lucrative effort. When Ricky reached 30, he had a $4 million trust fund. Five years later, he was broke. Drugs played a large role in this transition. To rebuild his fortune, Ricky toured the country, using an old DC-9. It was in this aircraft that he died.

Nelson was said to live almost completely upon a diet of cheeseburgers and Snickers bars.

Index

Ace, Johnny—12/24/1954
Acord, Art—1/4/1931
Adams, John—7/4/1826
Adams, John Quincy—2/23/1848
Adams, Nick—2/7/1968
Adamson, George—8/20/1989
Addams, Charles—9/29/1988
aged couple's honeymoon death—
    6/12/1831
air crash, first victim—9/17/1908
air crash, worst U.S.—5/25/1979
air-raid panic—3/4/1943
Alamo, The—3/6/1836
Alcott, Louisa May—3/6/1888
Alden, John—9/12/1687
Alexander the Great—6/13/323 B.C.
Alexander VI, Pope—8/18/1503
Alexander, Ross—1/2/1937
Alger, Horatio—7/18/1899
Allen, Ethan—2/12/1789
Andersen, Hans Christian—8/4/1873
Anderson, Sherwood—3/8/1941

"Andy Hardy" writer suicide—
    12/30/1948
Angeli, Pier—9/11/1971
antislavery shootout—9/16/1859
antiwar bomb—8/24/1970
Antoinette, Marie—10/16/1793
Aquinas, St. Thomas—3/9/1274
Arbuckle, Roscoe "Fatty"—6/29/1933
Archduke Ferdinand—6/28/1914
Aristotle—3/7/322 B.C.
Armendariz, Pedro—6/18/1963
Armstrong, Edwin Howard—2/1/1954
Arnold, Benedict—6/14/1801
Arthur, Chester A.—11/18/1886
Astor, John Jacob—3/29/1848
attorney's demonstration death—
    6/16/1871
Austen, Jane—7/18/1817
auto, first fatality—8/17/1896
auto, first U.S. death—9/13/1899
autoerotic deaths—5/5/1968
automatic door death—5/20/1913

Halloween gag deaths—10/26/1990
Hamer, Rusty—1/18/1990
Hamilton, Alexander—7/12/1804
Hamilton, Margaret—5/16/1985
Hamilton, Neil—9/24/1984
Handel, George Frideric—4/20/1759
hanging, last done in public in U.K.—
    5/26/1868
Happy Land club fire—3/25/1990
happy face air crash—5/1/1987
Harding, Warren G.—8/2/1923
Hardy, Oliver—8/7/1957
Hare, William—1/28/1829
Hari, Mata—10/15/1917
Harlow, Jean—6/7/1937
Harrison, Benjamin—3/13/1901
Harrison, William H.—4/4/1841
"Haunted Castle" fire—5/11/1984
Hawthorne, Nathaniel—5/19/1864
Hayes, Rutherford B.—1/17/1893
Hays, Wayne—2/10/1989
Hayworth, Rita—5/14/1987
headache act death—2/15/1949
Hearst, William Randolph—8/14/1951
heart donor suicide—12/18/1989
Hegel, George Wilhelm Friedrich—
    11/14/1831
Heine, Heinrich—2/17/1856
Hemingway, Ernest—7/2/1961
Hendrix, Jimi—9/18/1970
Henry, O.—6/5/1910
Henry, Patrick—6/6/1799
Henson, Jim—5/16/1990
Hess, Rudolf—8/17/1987
Hexum, Jon-Erik—10/18/1984
hiccupper—5/1/1991
Hickok, James "Wild Bill"—8/2/1876
hippo killings—12/27/1969
Hiroshima bombing—8/6/1945
Hitler, Adolf—4/20/1889,—4/30/1945
Hitler, train crash—12/14/1934
Hoffa, Jimmy—7/30/1975
Holden, William—11/16/1981
Holiday, Billie—7/17/1959
Holliday, John "Doc"—11/8/1887
Holly, Buddy—2/3/1959
holy spectacles death—12/20/1930
Hood, Darla—6/13/1979
Hoover, Herbert—10/20/1964
Hoover, John Edgar   5/2/1972

Hopper, Hedda—2/1/1966
Horton, Willie—10/26/1974
Houdini, Harry—10/31/1926
Howard, Moe—5/4/1975
Hudson, Henry—6/23/1611
Hughes, Howard—4/5/1976
Hull, Josephine   3/12/1957
Huntley, Chet   3/20/1974

I TOLD YOU death—6/18/1979
Ibsen, Henrik—5/23/1906
icicle impalement—1/10/1951
Ivan the Terrible—3/18/1584

Jack the Ripper—8/31/1888
Jackson, Andrew—6/8/1845
Jackson, General Thomas
    "Stonewall"—5/10/1863
Jackson, "Shoeless" Joe—12/5/1951
James, Henry—2/28/1916
James, Jesse—4/3/1882
Jarry, Alfred—11/1/1907
Jefferson, Thomas—7/4/1826
Jellison, Melvin—9/10/1947
Joan of Arc—5/30/1431
jockey, wins race while dead   6/4/1923
John "Lackland" of England
    10/19/1216
John Paul I, Pope   9/28/1978
John the Baptist—8/29/29
"Johnny Appleseed" (John
    Chapman)—3/18/1845
Johnson, Andrew—7/30/1875
Johnson, Dr. Samuel—12/13/1784
Johnson, Lyndon B.—1/22/1973
Johnstown Flood—5/31/1889
Jones, John Paul—7/18/1792
Jonestown massacre—11/18/1978
Joyce, James—1/13/1941
Julian the Apostate—6/26/363
Jung, Carl—6/6/1961

Kafka, Franz—6/3/1924
kamikaze, first—10/25/1944
Kant, Immanuel—2/12/1804
Karloff, Boris—2/2/1969
Kath, Terry—1/23/1978
Kaufman, Andy—5/16/1984
Kaufman, George S.—6/2/1961
Keats, John   2/23/1821

Model T, last—5/25/1927
molasses flood—1/15/1919
Molière—2/17/1673
monkey, first U.S. space traveler—
11/29/1984
Monopoly murder—7/19/1991,—
11/2/1991
Monroe, James—7/4/1831
Monroe, Marilyn—8/5/1962
Moore, Henry—8/31/1986
More, Sir Thomas—7/6/1535
Morrison, Jim—7/3/1971
Morton, Jelly Roll—7/10/1941
Moskone, George—10/21/1985
Mozart, Wolfgang Amadeus—12/5/1791
Murray, Arthur—3/3/1991
Mussolini, Benito—4/28/1945
mutiny, only U.S. hanging for—
12/1/1842

Nation, Carry—6/9/1911
Nelson, Ricky—12/30/1985
Nero, Roman emperor—A.D.6/9/68
New York, invaded by pirates—
9/18/1705
Newton, Sir Isaac—3/21/1727
Niagara Falls kayaking death—
6/5/1990
Nicholas II, czar of Russia—7/16/1918
Nietzsche, Friedrich—8/25/1900
Nightingale, Florence—8/13/1910
Nijinsky, Vaslaw—4/8/1950
Nitti, Frank—3/19/1943
Northfield Raid—9/17/1876
Novarro, Ramon—10/31/1968
Nuremberg Laws—9/15/1935
"Nutty Buddy" death—4/9/1991

O'Neill, Eugene—11/27/1953
O.K. Corral shoot-out—10/26/1881
Oakley, Annie—11/3/1926
Obregon, Alvaro—7/17/1928
"Old Abe the Eagle"—3/26/1881
Oswald, Lee Harvey—11/24/1963
Otway, Thomas—4/14/1685
Ouillette, Shaun—11/20/1986

Paine, Thomas—6/8/1809
Panzram, Carl—9/5/1930

parachute forgetting—4/2/1988
Paris, Richard James—1/7/1967
Parker, Bonnie and Barrow, Clyde—
5/23/1934
Parker, Dorothy—6/7/1967
parking ticket corpse—1/27/1989
parrot witness—7/12/1942
Parsons, Louella—12/9/1972
passenger pigeon, last—9/1/1914
Patrick, St.—3/17/461
Patton, George S.—12/21/1945
Pearl Harbor attack—12/7/1941
Pearson, Drew—9/1/1969
Peiper, Jochen—7/14/1976
Pepsi girl—5/26/1984
Pepys, Samuel—5/26/1703
Perry, Matthew—3/4/1859
Peshtigo fire—10/8/1871
Peter Pan's model—4/5/1960
Petrarch, Czartan—1/5/1724
Philby, Harold "Kim"—5/11/1988
Philippine Sea ferry/tanker disaster—
12/20/1987
piano, rising death—11/23/1983
Picasso, Pablo—4/8/1973
Pierce, Franklin—10/8/1869
Pike, Bishop James—9/7/1969
Pisa, Leaning Tower of, suicide—
6/4/1982
Place, Martha M.—3/20/1899
Plath, Sylvia—2/11/1963
Platt, Ed—3/20/1974
playing-cards suicide—10/9/1930
Pocahontas—3/21/1617
Poe, Edgar Allan—10/7/1849
Polk, James—6/15/1849
Pompeii—A.D. 8/23/79
Powell, William—3/5/1984
Powers, Francis Gary—8/1/1977
Presley, Elvis—8/16/1977
Prince Imperial of France—6/1/1879
Prinze, Freddie—1/29/1977
Purvis, Melvin—2/29/1960
Pushkin, Aleksandr—2/10/1837

Radner, Gilda—5/20/1989
rain prayer flood—4/26/1989
Raleigh, Sir Walter—10/29/1618
Rasputin—12/30/1916